D1083522

UPTON SINCLAIR
AND THE OTHER
AMERICAN CENTURY

UPTON SINCLAIR

AND THE OTHER AMERICAN CENTURY

KEVIN MATTSON

WILEY

John Wiley & Sons, Inc.

5/3/07
WW
$25.95

Published by John Wiley & Sons, Inc., Hoboken, New Jersey
Published simultaneously in Canada

Design and composition by Navta Associates. Inc.

Photo credits: All photos reprinted by permission of the Lilly Library, Indiana University, Bloomington, Indiana.

For general information about our other products and services, please contact our Customer Care Department within the United States at (800) 762-2974, outside the United States at (317) 572-3993 or fax (317) 572-4002.

Wiley also publishes its books in a variety of electronic formats. Some content that appears in print may not be available in electronic books. For more information about Wiley products, visit our web site at www.wiley.com.

Library of Congress Cataloging-in-Publication Data:

Mattson, Kevin, date.
    Upton Sinclair and the other American century / Kevin Mattson.
       p. cm.
    Includes bibliographical references and index.
    ISBN-13 978-0-471-72511-4 (cloth : alk. paper)
    ISBN-10 0-471-72511-0 (cloth : alk. paper)
    1. Sinclair, Upton, 1878–1968. 2. Novelists, American—20th century—Biography.
3. Social reformers—United States—Biography. 4. Social problems—United States—
History—20th century. 5. Journalism—Social aspects. I. Title.
    PS3537.I85Z97 2006
    813'.52—dc22
                                              2005030450

Printed in the United States of America

10 9 8 7 6 5 4 3 2 1

For Jeff Boxer and the socialism of friendship

CONTENTS

ACKNOWLEDGMENTS

Some things in American intellectual life never change. Upton Sinclair always groveled for money to support his writing habit. In 1909 he wrote a very sad letter to Gaylord Wilshire, "millionaire socialist," in which he desperately asked for money now that his royalties from *The Jungle* had been sunk into his communal living experiment, Helicon Hall. The place had burned to cinders. Reading the desperate tones in that letter made me wince.

I've been luckier than Sinclair. The money has been found, and that is where my first set of thanks must go: First, to Patricia Connor Study, whose gracious support to my home institution of Ohio University helped me research this book. Second, to the Lilly Library and its Everett Helm fellowship. And also to Jim Rutman, my agent, who helped me deal with contracts and all that other capitalist stuff that I'd rather not have to deal with.

Then there are those who helped out with the research and writing of this book: Jeff Bloodworth read through newspapers and other documents to help me push this project along. Shae Davidson was a master researcher who always turned up amazing things in ways that I truly appreciate. He fixed notes and did other things for which I cannot thank him enough. Everyone at the Lilly Library was very helpful, and I especially thank Saundra Taylor, who provided last-minute corrections. My editor, Eric

Nelson, hung in there and gave me the support I needed, even when the race was on (he knows what that means). Believe it or not, besides making acquisitions, Eric actually *edits* books, and he does a superb job of it. My thanks also go to production editor Hope Breeman and to freelance copy editor Alexa Selph.

To those who came before me, I am indebted. Floyd Dell's biography of Sinclair, written in 1927, should still be read. There are some damn funny comments about ministers and Sinclair's quirks there, and a lot more. So too the biographies by Leon Harris and William Bloodworth. And, of course, Sinclair's own autobiography.

As Sinclair knew, money and the writing heroes who came before us are not everything in a writer's life. I have to thank those who helped out in other ways: my family first and foremost. My wife, Vicky, has been everything to me. Her commitment to social justice and a smart form of activism has inspired me. My son, Joseph, has made me prouder than I could ever have imagined, and it's been fun to take him on backpacking and fly-fishing trips that kept my sanity throughout this process. My mom gave me the sort of support that only a mom can offer. She even read this book. Finally, I dedicate the book to my friend Jeff, who is a labor lawyer and an intellectual. There are other friends, of course, and they know who they are. But Jeff came through some dark times with me, and I appreciate his trust in what I have become today.

THE PROBLEM OF BEING UPPIE

In the first place you must understand
that I myself am a "cause."

—UPTON SINCLAIR, 1926

UPTON SINCLAIR WAS FAMOUS. PHOTOGRAPHERS WERE TAKING his picture every day. The newspapers hounded him and asked him questions about what it was like to meet the president of the United States and what he would do now that his novel *The Jungle* had sold out in nearly every bookstore across the country. His response seemed bizarre. He said he would write a book explaining the doctrine of socialism to a wary audience. In it he would declare himself a "scientist and prophet." The statement was telling. He could speak like a Moses, showing his people the promised land and performing miracles to get there, and also like a Darwin, explaining laws that were cold and clinical and lacking religion's certainty. The statement was a contradiction; no surprise, since *he* was a contradiction.[1]

One of Sinclair's heroes was Walt Whitman, the great poet who extolled the virtues of ordinary people in a style befitting a democrat. Whitman wrote toward the end of his most famous poem, "Song of Myself": "Do I contradict myself? Very well then I contradict myself, (I am large, I contain multitudes)." Sinclair loved Whitman because this nineteenth-century poet believed in a "programme of culture, drawn out, not for a single class alone, or for the parlors or lecture rooms, but with an eye to practical life, the working men." But Whitman's willingness to contradict himself must also have pleased Sinclair.[2]

Sinclair lived Whitman's ethic, a life of contradiction, and sometimes even multitudes. He was like the country he inhabited, a country of contradictions and abundances. Sinclair was truly an American. As *Time* magazine pointed out, some would claim Sinclair an "agent of Moscow," because of his radicalism. Even though the editors didn't like his politics, they had to admit that "Upton Sinclair is as American as pumpkin pie." But his Americanism drew from his desire to call attention to the darker side of American life. He condemned the way the United States treated its immigrants, shoving them into crappy jobs and making them use their communal resources just to get by, while trumpeting the greatness of individualism, the glories of making money, and the virtue of pulling one-self up by the bootstraps. Sinclair could dissect the viciousness found in Chicago's meatpacking industry while clinging to his heroes like Abraham Lincoln and Thomas Jefferson—deeply American heroes who espoused deeply American ideals like equality and democracy.[3]

BORN IN 1878, a year after Reconstruction put a close to the Civil War, Sinclair died at the age of ninety in 1968, the year Richard Nixon was elected president. Those dates meant that Sinclair witnessed America's rise to industrial and global power. Henry Luce, the owner of *Life* magazine, a publication that Sinclair abhorred, declared midway through the twentieth century that sometime in 1940, or thereabouts, marked the beginning of the "American century." It was a time when the nation would lead the free world because its greatness, established throughout the course of the twentieth century, was self-evident. Sinclair's life plays a key role in this American century. But it's a distinct role. He spoke not just to Luce's American century, but to the *other* American century, which began at the time of Sinclair's birth. It was evident in the mistreatment of immigrants that Sinclair saw when he visited "Packingtown" to gather details for *The Jungle*. Sinclair could hear the other American century when he spoke to the widows of miners who had been shot dead during the Ludlow Massacre of 1914. He witnessed it when legitimate critics of the United States' entry into World War I were censored. He felt its power when the big money of Hollywood did all it could to destroy his run for governor of California in 1934. He worried about the other American century when he openly expressed his concerns that the United States might not win the cold war since its consumer culture nurtured flabbiness as much as it did prosperity. Sinclair lived in the shadow of the towering majesty of the American century, and he lived to publicize what he found in its darker corners.[4]

In speaking to the other American century, Sinclair built his argument on the class inequalities that festered beneath the rhetoric of a society that cherished equality, the mob tendency that cold-blooded patriotism could whip up during World War I, the stench in the abattoirs, and the cheapness of American culture marketed to young people at home and to people living in poverty around the world. While documenting the underside of the nation, Sinclair ensured that his activism would speak to those in power; he took responsibility for his ideas being turned into action, thus influencing the course of American history.

Sinclair was anything but a marginal figure in American history. Consider the list of leading figures that Sinclair interacted with and influenced in some way: He met Teddy Roosevelt in the White House to discuss the merits of *The Jungle* and what should be done to confront the horrors depicted in the novel, and then later, he met with President Franklin Delano Roosevelt (FDR) to discuss Sinclair's run for governor of California, aiming to pull FDR in a more radical direction (which most people believe happened a year after Sinclair's defeat). Sinclair corresponded with Harry Truman about Sinclair's Lanny Budd novels, and then he made it to the White House again, to meet Lyndon Baines Johnson and Lady Bird Johnson as the "Great Society" took off. Sinclair expressed pride in having his ideas "stolen" and "robbed" by presidents and leaders. He loved the impact his work had on the course of American history, and that story deserves telling today, even more so now that it is in danger of being forgotten.[5]

There was also his involvement with leaders who didn't inhabit the highest rungs of power. The list of organizations that Sinclair influenced remains impressive: the American Civil Liberties Union (ACLU), the Democratic Party, the United Auto Workers (UAW), and the United Mine Workers (UMW). He knew the leading reformers of his day, including Mother Jones, Jane Addams, Lincoln Steffens, and Clarence Darrow—all activists who shaped the social conscience of the United States during the early twentieth century. Then too consider the literary and cultural figures Sinclair knew as friends: the popular literary hero Jack London, the great writer Theodore Dreiser, the German expatriate and father of modern physics Albert Einstein, the comedic genius Charlie Chaplin, the movie celebrity Douglas Fairbanks, and the great opinion leader Walter Lippmann. In many ways, the figure of Lanny Budd—one of Sinclair's greatest literary accomplishments—who flew around the world and seemed to meet, unrealistic as it might seem, with almost every world historical figure, was not unlike Sinclair himself. Uppie, as his friends called him, was at the center of American life, even while being in touch with the other America. He had an ability to make the other American century speak to the leaders of the American century, and in the end, the country is better for that.

AT THE SAME TIME, there was something cosmopolitan, or dare we say universal, about this American author. After all, his novels often sold better overseas than in the United States. More than that, his life of ideas mixed with political combat seemed better suited for Europe, where writers were always more respected than in the United States. As Floyd Dell pointed out, Sinclair belonged to the "Voltairean tradition of the literary man as a fighter against wrong," that is, a distinctly European tradition. Sinclair lived in an era gone by, one in which intellectuals could be heroes. The intellectual had replaced the priest as a person who spoke to the public about issues of morality and gained the respect of readers. The twentieth century was a time of intellectual heroes—of Arthur Koestler, André Malraux, and George Orwell—the intellectual as a fighter for truth against power, for justice in the name of those whose voices were not being heard. These thinkers wrote novels, but they were also expected to have something to say about politics, about what needed to be done to make the world a better place.[6]

The three intellectuals I mention here put their lives on the line to make the ideal of truth speak to power. Before the United States and England pledged to fight against fascism's demonic plot to take over the world, for instance, these three risked their lives to battle fascism. Koestler spent time in one of Franco's prisons, Orwell was shot in the throat while fighting in Spain on the side of the republic, and Malraux flew fighter planes against the forces of Spanish fascism. They continued to plunge further into the cause, with Malraux risking his life in the French resistance. After World War II, when communist totalitarianism appeared to threaten freedom just as Hitler once had, they engaged again. Orwell, unable to do anything more, wrote courageous works attacking communism, before the West had pledged itself to fighting the cold war. Koestler traveled the world organizing the support of Western intellectuals to speak out against the "God that failed" at conferences in West Germany during a time when Soviet tanks could have rolled in and crushed them. Malraux threw his weight behind de Gaulle and against the communists in France, "his antifascism turned into anti-Sovietism," in the words of a recent biographer.[7]

Today, we rarely think of intellectuals as heroes, and our biographies of these characters show it. Instead of brave defenders of the truth, intellectuals are portrayed as ordinary humans, or even villains. Fat biographies of Koestler, Orwell, and Malraux grace bookstore shelves. Koestler has been deemed an opportunist and a serial rapist, Orwell an informant who turned over names to the authorities, and Malraux more a "mythmaker" than a hero. These thinkers talked up their heroism beyond what they deserved. Throats might have been shot, but the raspy talk of sacrifice wasn't merited. The big books about these big thinkers today read more like obituaries for a way of intellectual life that has vanished.[8]

Now that these grand intellectuals appear as humans, as fallen angels, we are in danger of forgetting the promise their lives once offered. And this ties in with the subject of this book. There was a good side and a bad side to speaking about big ideas, about the romance of intellectuals as the carriers of truth and the guardians of noble action, the way Sinclair lived his own life. Big ideas always carried big scary consequences, such as when some intellectuals believed communism would save the world (or in Sinclair's case, believed the ideology deserved to be defended because it was the only existing alternative to capitalism). But we are now left with a world that grows cold in the face of intellectual excitement and a culture that can't take ideas and debates seriously, seeing in every public pronouncement some sort of spin or lie. The death of the grand thinker portends the death of thinking itself, perhaps. Today we inhabit a world where big ideas are being replaced with fast-paced information tossed at us on the information superhighway—a superhighway that prevents thinking beyond the impact of each immediate event that whizzes by.

My writing on Sinclair reflects my ambivalence about the role of ideas in changing our world for the better. When it comes to Sinclair's life as a thinker who spoke to grand themes and tried to live a life in accord with truth, I'll discuss both his successes and his failures. I haven't decided whether the growing sense that we're witnessing the death of the "universal intellectual"—the grand thinker—is entirely good or entirely bad. In many ways, it just is. The big ideas could be so wrong so many of the times—consider communism—but our thinking shrivels as we shed big ideas. Remembering Sinclair allows us to see both the good and the bad aspects of a time when intellectuals still mattered.

This book focuses on the intellectual as engaged in political combat. I see Upton Sinclair as more a political than a literary figure. A biography focusing on Sinclair the writer would be flat, since Sinclair's literary style became set at an early age and remained the same throughout his life (although it certainly became more sophisticated and less centered on propaganda in later years). He wrote mostly to convince others of his views. Thus, I read Sinclair's novels as political tracts, not as exercises in literary expression. His writing rarely reaches the level of literature, like the work of Hemingway or Faulkner. His plays were almost always tossed off quickly and easily condensed into the political arguments they were intended to make. Most of his novels read as if Sinclair is cruising through them, wishing he didn't have to spend time developing plot or dialogue. The characters often seem devised to make points better made in non-fiction.

In his most honest moments, Sinclair acknowledged his failings as a novelist. He once explained to his daughter-in-law that "my mind is absorbed in politics" and that he had "a tendency to be indifferent to personal individual affairs. It is a bad handicap in a novelist." He also knew that "as a rule, I write rapidly, perhaps too rapidly." He was more a recorder of historical events as they occurred than a novelist who took time to develop characters or draw out long narratives for readers to enjoy. But that could be a strength as much as a weakness. When writing a historical novel about Sacco and Vanzetti, the Italian immigrants put to death in 1927 by the Boston justice system, Sinclair noted, "Let no fiction writer imagine that his powers of invention can rival those of the Great Novelist who makes up history." The point is well taken. Sinclair's life matters more for his role as a political and historical activist, as a writer and recorder of contemporary history, than for his role as a literary figure. He was never in the league of a Henry James or Mark Twain. But this does not diminish the importance of his life; if anything, it makes it that much more interesting. Sinclair's most significant work emerged when he refused to lock the world out and live for the realm of the imagination. In his greatest life accomplishments—the writing of *The Jungle*, the run for governor of California, and the Lanny Budd books—it was real people and the events of history that tugged at him and that helped prod him toward his highest accomplishments. As is often the case, he was best when he rushed into the complications that only history provides.[9]

SO TO TELL A STORY about the American century and the other American century, I write this biography of Sinclair. Biography, as so many have pointed out, runs the risk of becoming hagiography in telling the story of a great man who has directed the course of our past. To distill history into a life threatens to become too focused, too narrow, simply describing the tiny world of the "I." It's easy to be pulled this way, to discuss the smaller details of a life. But biography can also be about sorting through the ashes of the past by showing how a person's life intersects with a bigger story. No life is perfect, nor is any life completely devoid of lessons for the present. Sinclair's life is full of lessons, not only about the other American century, but also about the possibilities and limitations of radical protest. His life offers lessons about the power of imagination and the limitations of utopian ideas, about the challenge of reaching a large audience without falling prey to the world of entertainment and celebrity, and about how to align our democratic faith with the military action the United States takes abroad. To get a better sense of these themes I wrote this biography, not just to give a sense of a life but to give a sense of what that life means for those who dream of a better society, one more just and egalitarian for those at the bottom.

Biography can help to focus on historical questions that sometimes seem too broad, and it's interesting to examine events through Sinclair's eyes—especially World War I, the New Deal, the early stages of the cold war, and the beginning of the 1960s. There are distinct questions that Sinclair's life helps us answer: How does idealism live into adulthood? How do people ensure that their core values don't fade as they approach maturity? Sinclair's life illuminates this theme nicely, and that's one reason his life still matters. If he were still alive, he might not be happy with all of the lessons that I've drawn from his life, but I think he would agree that his life—one of public record, as he constantly pointed out to biographers who approached him while he was still alive—is fair game for those asking questions about the American past. Our lives seem devoid of Sinclair's idealism today, and he can teach us why that may be bad but also why it is sometimes necessary.

As a biographer, I have been troubled by the question of what it means to "render a life." James Agee pondered how to do this, suggesting that another person's "meaning through me" is "limited" and that the "true meaning" of a person's life is always "much huger" than what appears on the page. As I wrote this biography, I became aware that I could never do justice to a life that spanned ninety years, and that was complex and full of twists and turns. Aspects of Sinclair's life will remain mysterious and shrouded, as things in the past inevitably are. What I had to say here is as much about my own concerns about how the past interrelates with the present as it is a record of Sinclair's life (although it's also that). So consider this a work of history and political interpretation as much as biography.[10]

The writing of history has always been a political act, not simply the recording of what happened in the past but also making sense of it for the present. Recently, history has become more politically charged and polarized. Howard Zinn's radical *A People's History of the United States* plays itself against *The Politically Incorrect Guide to American History* from the right. This is a sad reflection of our times. Sinclair's life would seem to suggest that I write from the perspective of radical history; after all, Sinclair was a hero to Zinn. But nothing could be further from my intention. Yes, Sinclair exposed the uglier side of American life and politics. But he also believed that this tale had to be placed squarely at the center of the American story, a reminder of how acknowledging our limitations realistically makes us a better country. Sinclair's goal was not simply to document all the sins of our country but to use them as a means of understanding our society's possibilities in spite of our reluctance to confront problems of our own making. Though the complexities of his life can never be entirely captured within the pages of a book, the retelling of his life serves as a way to get to a better understanding of the American century.

ONE

"A VERY DEVOUT AND EARNEST LITTLE BOY"

1878–1892

The old universe was thrown into the ash-heap
and a new one created.

—HENRY ADAMS, THE EDUCATION OF HENRY ADAMS

He tends to live his private emotions in public.

—HAROLD LASKI ON UPTON SINCLAIR

U PTON SINCLAIR MADE PLENTY OF ENEMIES OVER THE COURSE
of his long life. It was simply the way he lived. Some hated his
writing, believing his books were hastily assembled, overly contrived, and
overtly political. Some thought him naive and moralistic. Some thought
him puritanical. Some considered him an opportunist, obsessed with self-
promotion rather than telling the truth. Some tired of his proselytizing the
gospel of socialist politics (especially, as Lincoln Steffens once grumbled,
before they could have their morning coffee—one of many drinking habits
Sinclair abhorred). Sinclair recounted once, "I never could give up the
effort to make everybody into a Socialist; naturally I annoyed a great many
people." One of his numerous critics was the famous journalist and opinion leader Walter Lippmann, whom Sinclair called an "old friend" since
they had known each other when both were socialists. But before World
War I, Lippmann decided socialism was unrealistic, and in 1927 he wrote
an essay that skewered Sinclair's utopian flair. Having dumped his youthful socialism, Lippmann couldn't understand why others hadn't as well.
Writing for the *Saturday Review of Literature*, he lobbed some of the complaints mentioned above and then argued that Sinclair was fast becoming
irrelevant to national public discussion.[1]

No matter what one thinks of Lippmann's charges, one claim goes to
the heart of Sinclair's biography. "The child," Lippmann explained about

his old friend, "has been father to the man." Much of Sinclair's adult life can be understood from a brief examination of his childhood and the world he grew into. There is an inherent danger in a biographer's playing the role of psychologist, putting the subject under a microscope and examining a detail of family or a parent and then reading too much into those things, rushing to a conclusion that only a biographer's hindsight can provide. But in Sinclair's case, the benefits far outweigh the risks.[2]

Examine any photograph of Sinclair from his childhood. There's one of him at age eight where all the criticisms of Sinclair the man are already apparent on the face of the child. He is outfitted in the swankest duds, which, undoubtedly, his mother had dressed him in, probably hand-me-downs from the wealthier members of her family. As usual, Upton's lips are pursed and stiff, like a clenched fist. He stands with his elbow perched on a chair, his posture more like that of an adult, suggesting his precocious nature. He wears the self-assuredness that many an only child possesses, especially those whose mothers are convinced of their future greatness. There's a smugness that would not be expected from an eight-year-old. He is a boy with all the answers, an orientation he retained until the end of his life. Still, his photograph is similar to photographs taken of other children at the time. Appearing against a backdrop of gentility, the child appears to have a sense of dignity and purpose that being born into the upper ranks of society brought with it. Sinclair's eyes seem to stare ahead at some point beyond the photographer's studio. There's a sense of a world where certain expectations are a given: a nice sweet world or at least the appearance of a nice sweet world. But if Sinclair had looked out, he would have seen a world in the process of changing, a world that would shake the foundations of his perceived security.

EIGHTEEN SEVENTY-EIGHT, the year Sinclair entered the world, was a time when the United States was still overcoming the most cataclysmic event in its history. The Civil War was thirteen years past, but in its wake the country had gone through the painful process of figuring out how to put itself back together. By the time Sinclair was born, Americans were hoping that a period of reconstruction was over. They hoped that the South could redeem itself by escaping the scrutinizing eyes of the "Radical Republicans" who wanted to use their military dominance over the region to ensure that African Americans would become the equals of white southerners. Some, both northerners and southerners alike, hoped that the country could leave behind the world of plantations and slavery and national strife and unify around a new system that could ensure America's economic growth—a new age in which every worker labored for his own wages in factories that pumped out products for bustling national markets.

The new forces unleashed during Sinclair's childhood were just as tumultuous as the gunfire of the Civil War. The railroad roaring to life—with its speed and its ability to unify disparate communities throughout the country—symbolized this most of all. Transcontinental lines were being established, connecting the old frontier of the West with the already developed East. The trains traveled more quickly than anything people had seen before. Wealth accumulated at a faster and faster pace, with Sinclair's own grandfather a living testimony to this fact, having grown rich from managing rail lines just outside of Baltimore. The transcontinental railroads helped a city like Chicago, a city that made Sinclair famous later in his life, grow at breakneck speed. The United States was experiencing the power of what Henry Adams called the "dynamo"—new machinery, speed, and power that tore apart older ways of life.

The railroads not only produced new markets and rapid change, they also consolidated levels of wealth never before seen. Suddenly in the midst of the American social scene appeared robber barons, men who sat at the top of great industrial empires possessing vast sums of money and power. Cornelius Vanderbilt, for instance, built his wealth "step by step, from the manipulation of small railroad stocks, wresting profits many times the millions he originally possessed in short order, until his system of iron rails was fixed in the industrial heart of the country, all entrenched at its key positions." The big bankers of the time, especially J. Pierpont Morgan, stood ready to lend money; his credit allowed even further expansion of wealth. America's iron and oil production—so central to an industrializing country—thrived, and so grew the wealth of Andrew Carnegie and John D. Rockefeller. Both of these robber barons wanted strong control over the way they produced their goods. They exerted power from the top down, demanding faster output from the workers they employed, ultimately generating labor conflicts that were as much a mark of the Gilded Age as was the consolidation of wealth.[3]

One year before Sinclair was born, the Great Railroad Strike of 1877 erupted, one of the most violent and shocking strikes in history. It was a great spontaneous outpouring of anger, coming as it did before the formation of national labor unions that could coordinate labor protest. Workers simply walked off their jobs, no longer willing to work long hours for meager wages. Word spread throughout the nation and started a whole wave of strikes. The world of "free labor" that the United States hoped to rally around after the Civil War began to seem less and less promising. As the historian Alan Trachtenberg notes, "The 1880's witnessed almost ten thousand strikes and lockouts; close to 700,000 workers went out in 1886 alone." The country seemed on the verge of chaos and breakdown.[4]

At the same time, southern and western farmers were becoming discontented with the conditions they faced after returning from the Civil War. In the South, they returned to burned-over farms and to bankers who charged them more and more to pull themselves out of this situation. They returned to find railroads increasingly important for shipping their wares, and they found these railroads charging more and more to ship their goods, cutting into their profits and killing the notion that the small farmer was the backbone of the nation's economy. When these farmers grew fed up like the workers on the railroad lines, they declared themselves Populists—believers in the ordinary worker fighting against odds determined by pernicious wealth. Their anger seethed during Sinclair's early years and then erupted into political organizing by the time Sinclair's picture was taken at the age of eight. The Populists bellowed their disgust at the world that surrounded them, complaining in 1892 of a "nation brought to the verge of moral, political, and material ruin." The anger of the farmers, and of the railroad workers before them, would shatter the stability that many Americans longed for after the bloody Civil War was over. Sinclair was too young to know of these things, but they would come to shape his life in profound ways. The secure world of an upright boy in knickers could no longer hold.[5]

The Fighting Sinclairs

Sinclair's family tried, but ultimately failed, to keep these changes at bay. As with all good Victorian families of the time, there was a desire to ensure that the outside world would never invade their haven. They had reason to believe the barriers might hold. The big city, the steam machine, the speed of railroads—these were things associated with the American North, while Sinclair was born and bred a southerner. In 1904 he would write, "I am a Southerner and dearly love the South." Though Sinclair never really knew the Deep South, his family extended from a lineage of well-to-do Virginians, the sort of family that would prefer to ignore the plight of small, poor southern farmers or urban workers.[6]

If Sinclair was not born into wealth, he was born into at least the pretension of wealth. "I was born in what is called the upper middle class; my parents were members of the ruined aristocracy of the South," he explained. Here you get a sense of how the outside world invaded Sinclair's life from an early stage. Sinclair explained in his autobiography: "The family had lived in Virginia, and there had been slaves and estates. But the slaves had been set free, and the homestead burned." As a child, Sinclair poked around his family's houses and once pried open an old trunk to discover "reams of Confederate paper money, now useless." The time of the South's greatness and, to a certain extent, its distinctiveness had passed—that was the lesson of his family's fall from grace in the wake of the Civil War. The "New South" of Sinclair's boyhood was a time not of plantations but of industrialization, when the South tried to fill in the holes of northern development by extracting its crude resources and then sending them north, where factories would finish them. Cotton growing, coal mining, logging forests, and crude textile mills—these were the harsh industries of the New South that ensured that it would remain poorer than the North, even as it watched the plantations and the world of slavery burn away. The arm to the forehead as the big house burned down, and people wondering what they would do next in life—this was the world of young Upton Sinclair.[7]

The change might have been easier for the Sinclairs if the family had not been so bound to the southern tradition of honor and military virtue. Sinclair's family was noted for its naval officers—one after another of the elder male Sinclairs got on boats and fought it out, all the way up to the Civil War itself. This military prowess found itself unmoored in the new world of industrialism. In celebrating factories, railroads, and markets, the British sociologist Herbert Spencer and his American disciple William Graham Sumner pointed out, the captains of industry now rightfully displaced the captains of the military. Gun-fueled heroism now paled in comparison to the world of pursuing one's own self-interest by piling up wealth and reinvesting it in the making of more wealth. A world was dying, and though people like Spencer and Sumner celebrated it, others hated it. Critics of northern industrial capitalism—not just socialists—worried about what would happen to the virtues that only war and its sacrifice could teach young men. Sinclair, as a boy, first dreamed of becoming the "driver of a hook-and-ladder truck" but then soon decided he wanted to go to Annapolis, to follow in the footsteps of his male predecessors and fight wars on battleships. When he took up a pen instead, many of his earliest stories dealt with naval cadets training to become officers or with navy officers escaping enemy enslavement. Stories about fighting heroes conquering enemies came naturally to Sinclair. As he matured, he became a swashbuckling captain himself, fighting evildoers in the realm of wealth and of finance, the perfect revenge for a boy who watched capitalism displace military prowess.[8]

Sinclair's father was one of the first men in the family to pursue a career outside of the military (he had himself done his fair share of fighting). His career could not symbolize the new forces of capitalism better. He became a traveling salesman, hawking liquor on the road. It was a manly profession in its own right—the bartering, cajoling, and talking over cigars and, of course, drinks. His father looked and acted the part well. He was sociable and jolly, a short man who had the appearance of the "southern gentleman" and who, in Sinclair's own words, was a "swell dresser." Even though a charmer, Sinclair's father had slipped from the world of hearty military heroes into the ranks of drunken salesmen—next to the southern gentleman, one of America's most classic character types. Hawking wares, drinking away one's disappointment in life, slapping a client on the back, and returning to drink. It was especially hard because the men on Sinclair's maternal side of the family—Upton's uncle Bland especially—were doing extremely well in the new world of competitive markets and acquisitive individualism. As Upton's father watched his own fortunes sag and the rest of the family's rise, there was plenty of reason to despair.[9]

Because his father was an alcoholic, young Upton developed a strong sense of responsibility early on. After all, he had to pick his father up out of the gutters of the Bowery and off the tables of saloons. Sinclair remembered mustering the courage to walk into a smoke-filled saloon and past drunken, sometimes violent, imbibers—the "Highway of Lost Men," he would later call it—and then try his best to carry his father home, if he was lucky enough to locate him. In later life Sinclair still remembered the name of one saloon owner to whom his father was indebted and whose establishment was "just around the corner from the place where we lived at that time." This was fifty years after the time it happened, and still it haunted Sinclair. These ghosts lived on well past Sinclair's childhood. As much as he believed that his commitments in later life drew from the southern tradition of honor, they also drew from having a father who was unreliable and the hope that he could create a world of security that his father had never provided.[10]

No doubt, Sinclair got much of his courage to go into those saloons from his mother. She was moralistic and stern, upright and proud. In the simplest of terms, Sinclair was what we would today call a mama's boy, often sleeping alone with her in a single-room boardinghouse, when his father was falling down drunk into gutters. His mother wanted Upton to be an Episcopal bishop, and she took him to church every Sunday, scrubbing behind his ears and getting him into his pretty clothes—outfitting him as a Little Lord Fauntleroy. This would cause problems later and no doubt do some psychological damage, and as an adult, Sinclair resented his mother, seeing her as pushy and demanding, the sort of mother who ate her young. But it's also true that, in Sinclair's case as in that of many others from his generation, the "memories of maternal love," to quote the historian Casey Blake, helped nurture his belief that there could be a better world than the one his father offered the family.[11]

When Sinclair's father became a drunk and his mother tried her best to compensate, the family played out a larger change in American history—the crippling of what some call late-Victorian America. During the late nineteenth century, upper-middle-class families struggled with the changes wrought by industrialization. Henry Adams would write one of the most memorable books in history, his autobiography, in which he recounted how his own aristocratic lineage was devastated in the face of the "dynamo," the small world of Boston torn asunder by railroads and factories. Adams came from one of the most famous political families in American history, and he knew that the world of railroads accelerated the ascent of business over those, like his grandfathers in the past, who managed America's public affairs. Adams told a story of decline. It was a story that Sinclair knew, though his world had the added dimension of the fallen South. His childhood witnessed a father unable to cope with the changes of the new world, while his mother tried to uphold an illusion of stability.

The wider breakdown of genteel culture invaded Sinclair's boyhood and nurtured the pretend world that his mother tried to create. It was as if a social and historical virus became a virus inhabiting his little body. He explained to an interviewer that "when I was an infant I was given up for dying, I think of scarlet fever." From an early age he was "subject to colds and sore throat." He also complained of suffering from pneumonia, typhoid, and headaches. This sickly child tried his best to live in a dream world, one that was bookish, much of it lived under a couch at his grandfather's house, where Sinclair would steal away to read. He had learned to read on his own by using blocks with letters on them that he had found in the family home. He claimed to have written his first story at age five, about a family that lost a pin that had fallen into a garbage pile; the pin was then eaten by a pig, which was made into sausage, and then the pin reappeared as the family sat down to eat its sausage (strangely presaging both the impurities documented in *The Jungle* specifically and his complex relationship to food generally). His mother nurtured this imaginative side of the young Sinclair, seeing it as a promising sign of genius and brilliance that might allow him to escape his father's fate. She probably especially liked how he seemed drawn to the Bible and a children's book entitled *The Story of the Bible*. Sinclair, as some later critics were probably not surprised to learn, was a good Christian boy.[12]

He may have been a mama's boy prone to sickness, bookishness, and Christianity, but a little of his father could be seen in the young boy's desire to get out of the stuffy confines of gentility. Like Teddy Roosevelt, who grew up around the same time, and likewise in a world of gentility, Sinclair overcame his sickliness by playing up his toughness. He didn't find it in the saloons his father frequented but in "the streets," a term of derision when used in the circles that Sinclair's mother hoped to inhabit. Upton loved city life. He remembered the games he played with the toughs in his urban neighborhoods, both in Baltimore and later in New York City. He would go skating and bike riding and pick on girls his own age, pulling their pigtails. He described himself later as a "regular boy" who played football, tennis, and baseball.[13]

Sinclair, like most children, inherited very different traits from his father and his mother. From his mother, he learned to be upstanding, proper, moralistic, and self-controlled. From his father, he learned to be more impulsive and to look beyond the confines of the family to the urban culture that hustled and bustled around him. This dichotomy between the streets and upright morals, between impulse and control became a central feature of Sinclair's life. When he started writing in later life, he would consistently come up with new ideas that burned inside him and then be able to sit for sixteen hours a day and write them down. He distilled his mother's self-control and his father's passion.

Beginnings in Ballamaw*

As Sinclair explained, he was "born in a boardinghouse on Biddle Street" in Baltimore, Maryland. Sinclair's earliest memory was of a small room with a "bed, a sewing machine, a stove, and a trunk." There were bedbugs

---

*The way natives pronounced *Baltimore*, according to Upton Sinclair.

there, and once the family was able to afford a lamp—a luxury then for the
Sinclair family—he thrilled at waking in the middle of the night to watch
the bugs scurry into the cracks of the walls and into his mattress. He
would try to squash them, listening to them snap under his feet. Life was
full of challenges like that for Sinclair, heightened by the fact that they
contrasted with the wealth of his mother's side of the family, who still
lived in the city. Not only had his grandfather gotten rich off railroads, his
uncle "became one of the richest men in Baltimore," serving as president
of the United States Fidelity and Guaranty Company. Very often the
young Sinclair would live with his uncle Bland, especially when things
became difficult with his father.[14]

Baltimore was a small port city, certainly not the Deep South by any
means, but with a long history of being established by "old families from
Virginia." Sinclair's family thus fit in as members of the local elite. Located
not far from the Mason-Dixon Line, Baltimore was a city that knew both
the North and South (it's where Frederick Douglass escaped from slavery
to freedom). But being southern, this was a city that was gentle and quiet
in its feel. It was not the sort of city that bustled or rocked with the forces
of industrialization. Sinclair remembered, "The red brick houses were built
in solid blocks, wall to wall, each house with snow-white marble steps
which the colored maid washed off every morning, and on which the family sat on warm summer evenings." Sinclair also remembered having fun
on Baltimore's streets, out of the watchful eye of his mother, where, on the
occasion of a rare snowfall, he could sled down Mount Vernon hill, nar-
rowly making it through the wheels of the horse-drawn carriages that
were still the primary mode of transportation. Sinclair remembered friends
and the children of his uncle Bland going to ten-cent museums where
they would stare at a man in tights who was supposed to be half man and
half woman, thus drinking in the new world of entertainment in this
young city. In Baltimore Sinclair knew both the world of comfortable
homes that refined wealth promised, and the world of the streets.[15]

Within a few miles of his grandfather's home lived another boy whose
life would eventually intertwine with Sinclair's and whose boyhood symbolized the realities of class in Baltimore. H. L. Mencken did not know
Sinclair when they were both boys in Baltimore; in many ways, they
couldn't have known each other, since they inhabited different worlds. In
the words of Mencken's biographer, "Virginians and Marylanders of
English descent" controlled "the city's political and social institutions," creating a world of struggle for German Americans like himself. Later in life,

Mencken would come to celebrate the saloon, which contrasted nicely with Sinclair's later prohibitionism. While Mencken loved the he-man culture of drinking and carousing, the world of Sinclair's father, Sinclair would stick with his mother's moralistic world, becoming a teetotaler who drew upon the self-control that his Virginia lineage taught him. The debates Sinclair and Mencken would have in later life grew out of their distinctly different backgrounds within the provincial confines of Baltimore.[16]

Mencken would never have been allowed into the home of Sinclair's maternal grandfather. The fact that Sinclair was able to spend time there helped save his life. Sinclair's Grandfather Harden was a key influence on the young boy—if only for his library and the stability of his wealth. When things got bad with his father, Sinclair would go to Grandfather Harden's house on ritzy Maryland Avenue and pick up a copy of Shakespeare and then go to Druid Hill Park and sprawl out under a tree and read. When he couldn't get to his grandfather's library, Sinclair would steal away to the Pratt Library on Mulberry Street. Baltimore had a burgeoning civic culture that could nurture the needs of a small, bookish boy like Sinclair. Through the escape of books, Sinclair became what he was later in life. He also possessed the virtue of self-education, the sort practiced more in the self-directed reading in libraries than in formal lessons found in schools. This thirst for learning provided Sinclair with skills that he honed in his adult years.[17]

The bizarre and fantastic side of southern culture was also part of his experience—the extravagance of wealth that would come to alienate Sinclair with its ostentation, its pretense, its seclusion, its decadence. Sinclair recalled seeing terrapins brought into his grandfather's backyard and how he enjoyed watching them lumber along. He remembered his uncle Pow—another drinking man—relishing deviled crabs, oyster crabs, broiled shad, and other foods of the Chesapeake Bay. This was the gluttony of the South, the gluttony traditionally associated with the aristocratic element of any society. Sinclair remembered his childhood diet consisting of "fried chicken and hot biscuits and chocolate cake." This stuck with Sinclair, making him aware of what wealth could buy, at the same time exemplifying a value system that he would rebel against later in his life, through his love of dieting and embrace of asceticism. Again, the genteel expectations of his mother would win out over the extravagances of the wealthier members of the Sinclair family. But so too would his father's desire for escape from this world.[18]

God, Gotham, and Going into the World

At age ten, Sinclair received the news that the family was going to move to New York City. Though only a few hundred miles away, New York was a different world from Baltimore. Skyscrapers were going up fast in the downtown area that we now know as a commercial and financial center for the country. The city was, in the words of Henry James, showing off its "perpetual passionate pecuniary purpose which plays with all its forms." The city was quickly modernizing through new electrical lighting systems and telephones, making rapid communication possible. It was already getting "frantic" and hard to get "used to," as one of William Dean Howells's characters observed in *A Hazard of New Fortunes*, a novel about a man moving from Boston to New York City around the same time that Sinclair's family moved there. Sinclair himself would later decry the "jostling" and "fighting" feel of New York City. The overwhelming nature of the city was symbolized by a massive blizzard that hit the year his family moved there. Sinclair remembers enormous snowdrifts, into one of which his father playfully threw his son headfirst only to watch him disappear for a brief moment and then grow scared. Sinclair's memory of this experience was pronounced, because it was probably one of the better memories of his father in the city. Sinclair also remembered that there were places to drink throughout the city, everywhere he looked. His father got to know these places very well indeed.[19]

For Sinclair, the hustle and bustle of the city was accentuated by the mobility of his own family. In his autobiography, Sinclair remembered the motto that it was "cheaper to move than to pay rent," along with the long list of places that they moved to and from. There was "a dingy lodginghouse on Irving Place, a derelict hotel on East Twelfth Street, housekeeping lodgings over on Second Avenue, a small 'flat' on West Sixty-fifth Street, one on West Ninety-second Street, one on West 126th Street." Today this sort of moving would seem insane, and it did back then as well. There were even times when the family was going back and forth from New York City to Baltimore, when Sinclair's father really hit the skids.[20]

The move to New York could not have been more overwhelming for the Sinclair family, because they could see laid out before them a level of wealth that they could only dream about. New York City was, and still is, a city that loves to display economic disparity. There was the Waldorf Astoria, where wealthy family members sometimes took young Sinclair for lunch, not far from the poverty of Hell's Kitchen. There were also the immigrant poor of the Lower East Side living close to the wealth amassing on Wall Street. Sinclair remembered going to Central Park, where he would come face to face with horse-drawn carriages transporting the city's elite. He only had to poke his head out around the edge of the park to see the new palaces on Fifth Avenue where families like the Vanderbilts lived. He could also see the Metropolitan Museum of Art, erected at the time young Sinclair arrived in the city, a cultural institution where the collections of the wealthy were displayed, safely cloistered away from the bustling downtown. Indeed, it was the wealth of New York City's elite, as historian Michael McGerr points out, that inspired so many of the reforms that would come during the first few years of the twentieth century—reforms that Sinclair helped push forward.[21]

Sinclair's family highlighted the contrast between wealth and poverty by pretending that they too were wealthy like the Vanderbilts and the Astors. Their choice of church was the most obvious element of this pretend world. They were Episcopalians—a "religion very much part of old families of English descent" and "comfortable old wealth," as two historians put it. J. P. Morgan, America's richest banker, was famously an Episcopalian. On top of this, the Sinclairs insisted on attending one of the wealthiest churches in New York City. On Easter Day 1892, Sinclair was confirmed at the Church of Holy Communion, located at Sixth Avenue and West Twentieth Street. Sinclair found the Reverend William Moir there to be a nice man who offered some of the fatherly stability he sought, but he also saw pews filled with an elite group of city rulers he could never be part of.[22]

His experience in school and on New York City's streets contrasted sharply with this life of wealth and worship. It was not until he was ten that Sinclair went to school, his mother hoping to secure a measure of acceptance for the young Sinclair, knowing that he was far ahead of other students in his reading and writing skills. The experience of entering grammar school must have jarred Sinclair's consciousness in ways more profound than most young boys experience. Sinclair was precocious, and his impressions of school focused less on the academics and more on the social life found there. He described hearing the language of the kids at his school almost as if he were an anthropologist. His school was "populated almost exclusively by the so-called 'tough' element," Sinclair explained. "I remember quite well my puzzlement over their ways of speech, many queer words that I had never heard before, and I was particularly impressed by this word 'youse,' because they seemed to use it with such elaborate care."

He also remembered fellow students laughing at his slight southern accent, especially when he said "street cyar." He followed students from school out onto the streets, where he learned games like jumping into the air and flipping over, only to land on the sidewalk and come down on one's backside. Or he would drop garbage off the roof of a building onto construction workers below, running through the streets to avoid being caught. He learned how to skate and ride his bike through the streets, one time making it all the way to Coney Island and back in a day. He saw the old gangs of the city on the Lower East Side and marveled at their toughness and brutality. Everywhere he went, he noticed a culture very different from the one he was being brought up in. He seemed able to hide these adventures from his mother, who would have abhorred the word "youse" or stories about Coney Island.[23]

As much as Sinclair absorbed the culture of New York City and learned about a new world of immigrants from its streets, he never left behind the South or the genteel world of his mother. In the first place, the family would often go back to Baltimore. And for a time, Sinclair lived in the Weisiger House on Nineteenth Street, where other natives of the Old South whiled away the hours. Sinclair explained to Floyd Dell, "It was kept by Southerners, inhabited by a hundred or so of broken down Southern Aristocrats, generals, colonels, majors, judges, frequently drunk, and always prating of the Old South." There was Major Waterman, a "venerable warrior," who shared stories of the Old South. Little Sinclair once embarrassed him by suggesting that he could never refuse a drink, and this old southern man went into hysterics. It seemed a fantasy world the way Sinclair described it: "We killed flies on the bald heads of the colonels and majors, we wheedled teacakes in the kitchen, we pulled the pigtails of the little girls playing dolls in the parlor." All the while, this little island of southern gentility—with its overwhelming sense of its day passing—contrasted with the bustle and boom of the streets outside. This provided Sinclair with a sense that his old world, the world of his family, was dying, being replaced by a world that was more vibrant but not necessarily one he felt entirely comfortable in.[24]

There was another place that could pull Sinclair out of the bustling world of New York City—Central Park, where he would see the new wealth set out before his eyes, but where he would also learn the joys of being outside. He learned how to play tennis, his favorite pastime from boyhood on, and he learned to start becoming what he would ultimately become: a writer. Central Park, as its designer Frederick Law Olmsted intended, offered an escape from the tougher life of the streets, a small bit of nature amidst a city quickly growing into a crowded and bustling place made of cement and iron. Here Sinclair could dream, and that's what he did. He walked the park and dreamed up stories. He remembered having inspiring visions during "winter nights in Central Park," where he gazed upon "tree branches white with snow, magical in the moonlight." The natural world of Central Park, albeit refined, kindled a sense of romantic genius in Sinclair's earliest years.[25]

The importance of nature in his life grew as Sinclair became older. He remembered his mother bringing him to summer resorts, sometimes in Virginia, but just as often in the Adirondacks, a place becoming known for its "haute rustic" of wealthy hotels and less expensive camps where city residents could escape the stress of urban life. The desire to be outdoors—the romantic vision of the freedom of nature as freedom of inspiration—stuck with Sinclair his whole life. When things went bad or when he needed new inspiration for a book, he often took a canoe trip or simply staked out a tent in the woods. When he lived in California, he would insist on hauling his typewriter out of his study and writing outdoors, where he could hear birds and smell flowers. He would counsel others to "sleep outdoors, if you possibly can." His exposure to the world of Central Park and summer resorts allowed Sinclair as a boy to pull away from the life of the city and dream.[26]

In church Sinclair found the real inspiration to write. And this brings us back to the growing sense in Sinclair's life that his parents' world and the wider world of gentility were crumbling. By all appearances, Sinclair did what most boys his age did: he followed his mother into church (more rarely would his father be there, dreading, as many men did at the time, the experience of the sermon). Sinclair learned a great deal from the minister there and made such an impression that he was allowed to teach Sunday school himself at the age of fifteen. This outside appearance of Sinclair as a dutiful churchgoer belies his growing doubt, at a very young age, about what he was learning. He could sense that his father dreaded church, and he was smart enough to wonder about the stories of the Bible, especially stories about men living inside of whales or Christ walking on water. This sentiment, this doubt about religion and boredom with its rituals, pervaded American culture during the late nineteenth century; there was a broad crisis of faith then among many middle- and upper-class Americans. Henry Adams once explained his own experience in church: "The boy went to church twice every Sunday; he was taught to read his

Bible; he prayed; he went through all the forms; but neither to him nor to his brothers or sisters was religion real."[27]

Sinclair's experience was similar to that of Adams. His early experience in the church was not that of fearing a strict God or fearing the wrath of ministers. The ministers were nice to him; they taught him things and rejoiced in his intelligence. Sinclair's memory of churchgoing was, like Adams's, of being distracted as his active mind raced away from sermons and the singing of psalms. His was a gradual falling away from the church, not a cataclysmic break with religion. As he explained to Frank Harris, he "gave up calling myself a Christian" when he was seventeen years old, after a period of increased doubt.[28]

When in church as a boy, Sinclair sought out explanations to alleviate his declining faith. Eventually he would emphasize the importance of Christianity's moral teachings over the practices of the church, as many American reformers would. But before this happened, the boy would simply pull away from the church's demands. He would go to the Episcopal church with his mother and think up stories about his fellow churchgoers. He especially liked to "make up jokes on the phrases in the prayer book and hymn book." Instead of turning off his mind and absorbing the lessons being preached, Sinclair kept his mind tuned in and started to write the jokes that would become his first published work. In a scrapbook that his mother kept of his early writings, there's one of Sinclair's earliest: A Parson asks an invalid, "Is you, is you prepahed t' die?" And the Invalid answers, "Ah—ah guess so, pahson! I ain't nevah died befor', so ah ain't quite suah." The joke captures Sinclair's southernness, his poking fun at religion, and his desire to put words down on paper and quickly dash things off. By thinking about language as a game to be played in his head while sitting in his pew, Sinclair began to drift from religion to the world of imagination and writing at a very early age.[29]

Sinclair knew as he sat in that church with his mother that he had to figure out what he would become in his life. Sinclair's mother had wanted him to become a bishop in the Episcopal church. His father hoped he would become either a naval officer or a lawyer. This was where the family influence ended, and his young adulthood began. Sinclair was to be neither of the things his parents hoped for. In the end, though, he found what might be considered the best of both worlds. He could be a moralist, as the Episcopalian bishops were to him as a boy. He could also become a rationalist and someone who argued without the help of the Bible. In other words, he could become what he became—a writer. Neither of his parents would be proud of this choice, but they could at least believe that their influence lived on within their precocious son. He finished grammar school, hoping to enter the City College of New York (he had to wait for that). Still, he had already started on the path of life. "The child has been father to the man," as Lippmann pointed out. Sinclair walked into the world of young adulthood with memories of the South, dreams of the military, the genteel moralism of his mother, and the romanticism of the urban parks he had inhabited as a child and that represented the natural world for him. He also walked into his adolescence with a growing knowledge of the streets—of a new, modern, urban culture that was quickly challenging the world his parents wanted to create for him. It was time to write his way out of this contradiction, or better yet, to articulate the contradiction in his writing. But first he had to learn more.

"WOULD-BE SINGER AND PENNILESS RAT"

1892–1904

Perhaps the chief obstacle to the youth's education,
now that he had come of age, was his honesty;
his simple-minded faith in his intentions.

—HENRY ADAMS, THE EDUCATION OF HENRY ADAMS

My religion is my Art.

—UPTON SINCLAIR, THE JOURNAL OF ARTHUR STIRLING

A chemistry professor walks into a college classroom. He's clearly a hard-ass towards his students. He tells them that it's always important to verify whatever finding you discover in the laboratory. Then he turns his back to the classroom and retrieves a test tube from a cabinet. He turns to the class and tells the students that he believes that what he holds in his hand is a poison. A student raises his hand and says, "Say, Doctor, you verify that one first, will you?" The class breaks into laughter.

That was a joke Sinclair wrote during the 1890s. Such was the humor of a young man who was making his living by hack writing while attending college. And such was Sinclair's life at the time—the life of a budding writer and an impoverished student.[1]

In 1892 Sinclair had completed his grammar school lessons and passed his entrance exams for college. He was ready for college at the ripe age of thirteen. So this precocious boy entered a building located at Twenty-third Street and Lexington Avenue in Manhattan and began his formal college education. It wasn't quite college, as Sinclair explained in one of many memoirs. The City College of New York (CCNY) was "actually a combination of high school and college, which gave a bachelor's degree after five years." It was the right choice for Sinclair, because of his young age and eagerness to fly through college quickly. It was also the right choice because the American college was rapidly changing at this time; more and more higher-education institutions were becoming training grounds for the new professional activities of America's middle class. Graduate schools started to grow in popularity and, with them, specialized departments and decreasing attention paid to undergraduate education. CCNY was not such an institution. There was still a generalist feel to an education at CCNY, where professors knew a field but didn't necessarily become specialized scholars, and this provided Sinclair with a well-rounded learning experience. As well, since the school didn't have many extracurricular activities (it was, after all, predominantly what we would call today a "commuter" college), Sinclair could easily avoid the "rah rah" culture present at other institutions and keep up his own reading on the side. One of his rare extracurricular activities was to write for the school newspaper, which nurtured his career choice.[2]

Though CCNY allowed for a certain amount of freedom for the young Sinclair, there was still a lot of rote memorization. He remembered boring lesson plans and homework that he passed over. Obedience from students was expected as well, and Sinclair chafed at it. "Mr. Sinclair, it is so because I say it is so," one teacher would often bellow at him, much to Sinclair's chagrin. Another called him an "insolent young puppy." A dogmatic Catholic taught his literature class, making Sinclair recoil from the field (ironic as that might be in retrospect). It also compelled him to rush through his studies. Sinclair was a quick learner, and his childhood had already taught him the importance of being self-directed, a skill that paid off at CCNY. Sinclair would later say that it took him little time to learn foreign languages, since he would memorize words while getting dressed in the morning and then practice constructing sentences while walking the streets of New York City. His intellectual independence often created gaps in his field of study; for instance, he was never exposed to modern literature or economics while at CCNY. It also meant that he was not a stellar student, for when he found that a course didn't interest him, he simply slacked off. His individuality is best illustrated by his decision to skip the graduation ceremony, choosing to receive his degree in the mail.[3]

Sinclair graduated from CCNY in 1897, in the middle of his class. For graduate school, Sinclair simply moved uptown to a rooming house on West 126th Street in Harlem (then a Jewish community) and enrolled in Columbia University. Columbia was making a transition from the more democratic leadership of Seth Low to the more autocratic Nicholas

Murray Butler—a man whom Sinclair hated from the time he took a course with him on Kant's ethical system while attending Columbia to the time when Butler fired professors for their opposition to World War I. Sinclair had moved from a public-funded institution to a private one, and he noticed that the professors there seemed cowed by academic politics and the power of the trustees; the professors were frightened of being controversial and therefore became "deadly dull." This dullness only encouraged Sinclair to continue to pursue his own informal education at a formal institution. "Most of my experiences at Columbia consisted of beginning courses, and dropping them after a few weeks." Among the professors there were a few who stood out for Sinclair, including James Harvey Robinson, who was then pioneering a "new history," which tried to make the past speak to the interests of those living in the present, rather than providing an itinerary of dates to be memorized by students. There was also Edward MacDowell, a professor of music, who would play compositions in his classes to try to convey the raw emotional power of music. Sinclair loved this, and MacDowell, not surprisingly, was one of the few professors who encouraged young Sinclair to pursue his writing career.[4]

His love of music and its capacity to transcend the intellect conveys a theme that Sinclair shared with other intellectuals and activists of his generation. Many had found that their family and religious upbringing failed to explain the world around them, as did their education. For an increasing number of young people during the 1890s, education appeared meaningless, the teaching of lessons that seemed unreal and useless, frilly literature and empty morals that didn't relate to the torrent of real life. The glaring contrast between the ideals of education and the forces of the real world is a theme that appears again and again among writers coming of age during Sinclair's young adult years.

Take the examples of two people Sinclair would befriend as he grew older. Jane Addams moved to the city of Chicago in order to found Hull House, a place where young people lived, and in order to help out the immigrant poor of Chicago. She would play a big role in bringing the other American century to the fore, by showing the tough realities of life in America's ghettos. The literature she had studied while in a female seminary, plus the prevalent moralistic worldview, seemed useless to her as she proceeded in life. "What we were all doing," Addams explained in describing her education, was "lumbering our minds with literature that only served to cloud the really vital situation spread before our eyes." Frederic Howe, who would help out Tom Johnson, a progressive and controversial mayor who ran the city of Cleveland, Ohio, during the early years of the twentieth century and who would then go on to serve in President Woodrow Wilson's administration, would always contrast his schooling at Johns Hopkins University with the real lessons learned by doing hard-boiled politics. Howe argued that he had to undergo a process of "unlearning" what he learned in school in order to grasp the real world. Howe and Addams were not alone in seeing real-world experience as a better education than the abstract lessons offered in the ivory tower.[5]

The world of academe appeared increasingly vacuous to Sinclair as well. Though he didn't pledge himself to the sort of activism that Addams would endorse, he had his own contrast to face between the lessons at Columbia and the realities of the world he was living in. This contrast stemmed from the hard reality that his family wasn't rich. Sinclair had to use his writing skills honed in childhood to make a living for himself and acquire his college education. The fact that he had done poorly in his CCNY literature class must have made Sinclair chuckle, since he was already pumping out stories for publication by this time. That publication record would heat up when he came to Columbia. He might not be able to learn literature, Sinclair probably thought to himself, but he sure as hell could *write* literature, or at least something close to it. Writing for money put food on the table and paid for his lodging and some support for his mother. Strange as it might sound, it also made clear to him what it meant to be a member of the working class: in deciding to write serialized stories for commercial magazines and dime novels about adventures for a company called Street and Smith, the young man became a working man. He would drift into school to hear professors prattling on about art and then go back home to grind out words that brought him a paycheck.

Hack

Sinclair won independence from his family at an early age. He had turned down an appointment at the Naval Academy in Annapolis, as well as an offer to work for his uncle Bland's business in Paris. His childhood had given him a glimmer of another route to independence, one that was more of his own making. While attending CCNY, he moved into a rooming house on the top story of a building across the street from the college. It only cost $1.25 a week. He paid for it by writing stories for the urban reading public that lived in places like New York. It was a good time to do this. After all, as more Americans became educated, they were ready for more reading materials, especially short serialized novels that were easy to read on the trains that shuttled them around the city, or better yet the jokes that Sinclair wrote and got artist friends to illustrate for him. These writings reached Americans by the same process of industrialization that was changing the world Sinclair was growing up within. "These were the days," the historian Christopher Wilson points out, "during which an individual press which cranked out hundreds of copies a day gave way to steam and electric-powered presses capable of tens of thousands of (longer) papers per *hour*." The audience was primed, the presses were prepared, and Sinclair delivered.[6]

Sinclair learned to live cheaply and to keep his personal costs down in order to pursue his writing career. He bought his clothes secondhand and learned to barter with salesmen for cheaper goods. He learned how to put up with cramped quarters and live ascetically, a skill easy to acquire in New York City, with its abundance of small apartments and rooming houses, and one that he practiced the rest of his life. He ate poorly and bartered with the friends he made in his rooming house. One friend would play the violin for Sinclair as he wrote. He used the city to his advantage, moving from freelance job to freelance job, personally taking copies of manuscripts to various publishers, having meetings with editors, and all the while keeping up with his coursework as best he could. He even worked a brief stint as a reporter.[7]

Stories poured out of him at a rapid pace, and there were always jokes bouncing around in his head. Some of these jokes drew from his college experiences, while others came from stories he had heard at summer camps and on the streets of the city. When writing a serialized story in 1900, entitled "A Battle with Misfortune," Sinclair had one of his characters explain how strange it was to become a "joke factory" and how it was easier to dream up jokes than to sell them to magazines. This was certainly an autobiographical reference (though it should be pointed out that Sinclair wasn't all that bad at selling jokes to editors, perhaps picking up on his father's knack for salesmanship). Sinclair was definitely a joke factory, from his earliest childhood on, until he became a story factory. He wrote stories about black boys in the South being saved from punishment by befriended birds and stories about mothers in Revolutionary America hiding contraband from British soldiers in their ovens. He tried to have his characters speak a realistic dialect, the way Mark Twain had already done in *Huckleberry Finn* and *Tom Sawyer*, two novels Sinclair tried unsuccessfully to emulate.

Drawing on his family's background, Sinclair developed a knack for writing adventure stories, like the one about two Englishmen who steal a deity from natives and thereby prompt an adventure. Some stories never got published, like the one about cowboys stealing gold from Indians and then getting in a gunfight (Sinclair admitted that the story had a striking resemblance to *Treasure Island*). Nonetheless, enough stories were serialized in magazines in order to allow Sinclair to survive.[8]

Most of his work wound up on the pages of *Argosy*, one of America's earliest pulp fiction magazines. At one point Sinclair decided to look up the publisher of this magazine, Matthew White Jr. White asked Sinclair if he would like to see the "plant." Sinclair walked with him and saw "two or three rooms full of bookkeepers and office girls stamping envelopes." It looked more like a factory than a place of imagination and artistry, and that was an important lesson for Sinclair. It dawned on him that he was now officially a "hack writer." Once he realized that, it wasn't hard for him to accept a job with Street and Smith, one of America's most popular publishers at the time. He had tried unsuccessfully to pitch a story to this publisher in the past, so he was delighted when he was offered a full-time job. Sinclair came here while transferring up to Columbia. The press churned out stories for urban residents who had little money or time and wanted something more sensational than the literature Sinclair was learning about at CCNY or Columbia. They published stories by and for working-class readers, like "Bertha, the Sewing Machine Girl," while also publishing westerns, kid stories, and adventure tales. They published the work of Horatio Alger, whose stories for boys were what comic books would become during the 1950s: quick, easy, and exciting reads for younger people (though often looked down upon by the middle class). They would tell the story of a young boy in the city who, typically by a stroke of luck (a chance meeting, say), would make himself wealthy, providing nice dreams for kids who might be hawking newspapers for dimes. One of the Street and Smith series that Sinclair would write for, "Books for Young People," centered on stories of ranchers, rangers, and sports heroes. The stories, in the words of a Street and Smith publicist, were "bright and sparkling, not overburdened with lengthy descriptions, but brimful of adventure from the first page to the last."[9]

Street and Smith was pleased with its new employee. Sinclair certainly delivered, pumping out eight thousand words a day and keeping two stenographers busy throughout the morning. While there, he took on pen names (which later pleased him, no doubt, since people couldn't attribute this writing to him) and helped develop two heroes who kept little boys goggle-eyed about their adventures. To develop the first, Sinclair visited West Point in order to get some local color. He created a hero named Mark Mallory, a poor kid who got into West Point only because a fellow who was traveling on a train with him to New York injured himself (much like what would happen in a Horatio Alger story). Delivering a story to a newspaper about the train accident, Mallory got enough money to enter West Point. From there, Mallory moved on to new adventures. Sinclair's other hero was named Clif Faraday. This character was also a noble young man who often had to fight the nastier kids recruited into Annapolis, where naval cadets were trained; he was virtuous, whereas the rich kids who slid into Annapolis because of family connections often weren't. When Sinclair wrote about Faraday, he piled on adjectives and wrote in flowery prose. So, for instance, Faraday is contrasted with his enemy Judson, who had "flabby" muscles. Faraday's "breast, arms, and neck were as smooth as marble, and the sinews slipped and moved under satin skin like those of an ancient gladiator." These stories of gladiators might have been drawn from Sinclair's family memories and were certainly chock full of racism. The heroes were always white, while black and Asian characters are seen as contemptuous and stupid. The stories were easy to read, easy to follow, and thus utterly acceptable to Street and Smith.[10]

In April 1898, while Sinclair was toiling away on his heroes, a "splendid little war" broke out, and suddenly the nature of writing about gladiators changed for Sinclair. In Cuba, an insurrection against the Spanish empire had been brewing, getting hotter as the American Civil War ended. Businesses had invested heavily in Cuba, especially in sugar production, and by the 1890s the United States was doing more business in Cuba than was Spain itself. Cuban rebels hoped to get Americans on their side, and when U.S. journalists went down to cover the war, the rebels got exactly what they wanted. There was talk of heroism and cruel Spanish colonialism, and by 1896 the U.S. Congress had recognized the legitimacy of the insurgents. Then a U.S. ship, the *Maine*, was blown up, and 260 Americans were killed. President McKinley promptly declared war against Spain and decided to extend the battle in Cuba to the Philippines and Guam, pushing a newly founded American empire eastward and opening trade routes to Asia.

For some, the war against Spain was a chance for heroism. Most famously, Teddy Roosevelt led his Rough Riders up San Juan Hill. The "strenuous life" grew flush in the midst of battle. But others saw the war as a travesty, threatening to turn the United States into what it should never become—a colonial power. By establishing rule over Cuba and the Philippines, the United States was becoming too much like Britain when that country had squashed an uprising in the thirteen colonies. William James, one of America's most prominent and popular philosophers at the time, believed that the country was losing sight of its "ancient soul," its anticolonial beginnings, and should oppose all such forms of imperial ambition. At the same time, writers like Stephen Crane saw the war as a chance to report on the realities of bloodshed. Crane had become famous for his novel *The Red Badge of Courage*, which had appeared in papers five years before the Spanish-American War broke out, and in that story, Crane told of a young man who had dreamed "of battles all his life—of vague and bloody conflicts that had thrilled him with their sweep." The young idealistic warrior (not too different from Mark Mallory perhaps) then saw the realities of war, its carnage and mayhem, and learned that reality made the ideals seem dubious. Crane went to Cuba in hopes of reporting the war realistically, and he wound up literally sick from the experience.[11]

Of all these responses, Sinclair's was most like Roosevelt's. He too saw the war as an opportunity for heroism, if only for his own imagination and for the readers of Street and Smith products. Sinclair thrilled at news of war and remembered that "a young man who had been a fellow student at Columbia was killed in battle." But for Sinclair, this loss only bolstered his desire to see romance in Cuba's battles and to use the war to the advantage of his make-believe heroes who fought the "dark and dirty and ugly Spaniards." His pulp novel gladiators "killed enough Spaniards to people a nation," as he would recall later, and his stories became "absurdly crude" in the process. But they sold, and Sinclair just kept cranking them out as America's youth looked for entertainment that could match the adventurous escapades of real heroes like Teddy Roosevelt that were being captured in the daily press.[12]

While the more disturbing events of the war—its carnage and then the suppression by the United States of an independence movement in the Philippines—never penetrated Sinclair's consciousness (at least not in his writings), the writing became exhausting. As U.S. soldiers charged hills, Cuban insurgents whooped it up, and the Spanish lost their colony, Sinclair kept cranking out story after story. Eventually he needed a break and decided to take a fishing trip to Ontario, where he stayed in a "pioneer cabin near a tiny jewel of a lake." He then set off on a whitewater canoe trip through Canada. Nature reminded him once again of his romantic side, the side that wanted to express itself in new and bolder ways than Mark Mallory and Clif Faraday would allow. He was tired of spilling words onto the page about imaginary heroes. He was ready for something new to arise from his imagination.[13]

Singer and Poet

Like the hero in "Battle with Misfortune" (1900), Sinclair still had something like an epic poem he wanted to write. During his last year in college, he took time off occasionally to read romantic writers, some of whom he had read as a child. He pored through Percy Bysshe Shelley, Ralph Waldo Emerson, and Thomas Carlyle. Shelley, a poet inspired by the power of nature, was especially appealing for his criticisms of the ugly budding factories in England and for pledging himself to the egalitarian principles of the French Revolution. Sinclair liked Emerson, who he thought "had a Puritan conscience." And Carlyle's embrace of hero worship must have appealed to a young man constructing his own heroes in the guise of Mallory and Faraday. Sinclair also loved Shakespeare's *Hamlet*. Here was a young man struggling with inner demons, wanting to do right in a complex world. Sinclair, like many young adults, struggled with wanting to find meaningful work, while he also started to feel love for a young woman named Laura Stedman, whom he had known at Weisiger House. It was Sinclair's first love, and he fell for her at the same time that he took up the violin. Both served as sources of romantic inspiration for Sinclair. He would write Stedman long letters about how he was playing the violin until his fingers went numb. He then explained that he went to hear an orchestra play a concert, hoping that it would fill his soul with hope. As Sinclair would write later, "Music was time made beautiful, the means whereby many people" playing together "could organize and make harmonious the process of their souls."[14]

In April 1900, he took a more radical step than attending a concert. He decided to realize his dreams of becoming an artist. And so he stole away to the country to write his own book. Despite his love of nature, he was not a particularly good outdoorsman, and his attempts to live the simple life were nothing short of comical. He traveled to Quebec and planned to move into a log cabin on Lake Massawippi. That plan fell apart due to a flood, so Sinclair secured a cabin in the surrounding forest. It was named Fairy Glen, perfectly capturing Sinclair's romantic mood. He could do no more hack writing; it was killing his spirit. There were problems, of course, like the time he set a trap for a skunk, who ruined his pants. When he washed his odorous pants in a nearby stream, he found that he had ruined his source of drinking water. At least he had become a master at canoeing and could trap animals and hunt squirrels and deer. In his "little cabin in the wilds of Quebec" he would toil for sixteen hours a day in order to produce his first novel. He was in romantic thrall to the work, living his "life upon his knees before his vision." In the end, he would be left with a manuscript he believed to be inspired but that would have a hard time finding a publisher. Romantic overindulgence often brought hangovers.[15]

To add to his romantic hope and misery, Sinclair met his second love, Meta Fuller, during the summer of 1900. Meta was young and naive, and she too wanted to be an artist, though her ambitions were more wide-ranging than Sinclair's narrow focus on writing. She was, in his own words, "a quiet, undeveloped, and unhappy girl, while I was a self-confident and aggressive youth, completely wrapped up in my own affairs." When Meta declared that she wanted to learn about the things that Sinclair knew, he told her he would plan a "course of study for" her, and she worked hard to please him. Meta looked to Sinclair as someone who could teach her things about life, something she desperately wanted. Sinclair explained to her, "Perhaps I am mad to say this, I do not love you, but I love the woman you are to be—the woman I will make you." Neither family was entirely comfortable with the affair, so Meta and Upton did what most young couples do in that situation—they ran off and got married out of the sight of their parents. On October 18, 1900, M. J. Savage, a Unitarian minister with whom Sinclair had developed a friendship, pronounced Upton and Meta man and wife.[16]

As is the case with many young couples, the marriage was a mistake. Particularly horrifying was the sex. Sinclair didn't know what he was doing, nor did Meta. She would describe their honeymoon night this way: "He removed her dress with hard and clumsy fingers. It seemed to be like the ruthless infraction of a natural law, this mute disregard of her physical identity." Things didn't get much better from here. Not surprisingly, Meta got pregnant quickly. They tried to abort the baby—Sinclair was convinced that artists should not have to deal with children—but this failed, and on December 1, 1901, David Sinclair was born. He would be their only son and sometime soon after, the couple decided that it was best not to risk physical intimacy.[17]

Sinclair loved Meta, but he loved his work more. He was determined to finish his first novel, and he did. *Springtime and Harvest* appeared in 1901 and was reissued as *King Midas* the same year. It was a story that opened in a beautiful forest but then quickly introduced the central character of Helen, noting that "surely, of all the flowers of the May-time there is none so fair as the maiden." We also meet a young poet, Arthur, who had to teach in order to make money and who promptly falls in love with Helen. But Helen's Aunt Polly counsels her to marry a rich man instead. Not surprisingly, a rich man enters the story at this time and offers his hand in marriage to Helen, who refuses him and chooses another man instead. The couple lives simply, only to find out that Arthur is actually the son of the man she married, all because of an earlier affair that her new husband had. Arthur returns and finally claims the love of Helen, two souls uniting as one.[18]

The book, with its neatly tied-up story line, was rejected by publishers left and right, and eventually Sinclair would borrow money from Uncle Bland to get it into print. The young author remembered with utter disgust the meetings with publishers who told him there was no chance his book would see print. The experience was etched permanently on Sinclair, turning "all his soul on fire against the commercial judgments he received." The artist had met mammon—a theme tirelessly rehearsed throughout the history of romantic expression. The book made Sinclair a "would-be singer and penniless rat," a "young man just out of his teens, earning four hundred dollars by ghostly 'pot-boilers,' spending it in publishing his pathetic edition, and then waiting on the verge of starvation." *Springtime and Harvest* sold only two hundred copies (many to relatives of Sinclair), and when it was reissued the same year as *King Midas* by the publisher Funk and Wagnalls, it raked in a mere $325. Sinclair had little money left over after paying back his uncle Bland.[19]

It was a struggle to get published and have his voice heard. During these early years of adulthood, Sinclair would describe his life as learning how to "live in tents and shanties, and wash the dishes, and tend the baby, and nurse an invalid wife, and write literature." Meta's father took Meta and David in for a while, then the Sinclairs lived for a bit in a cramped room that Meta's parents rented. Then it was on to the Thousand Islands, with the small bit of money made from *King Midas*. Here they lived next to the St. Lawrence River, setting up on a "remote" island a "wooden platform" and a "small tent" in order to live a "back-to-nature life." They played with the birds and gloried in scooping their drinking water directly out of the river. When storms came, Sinclair would hold up their tent against the winds, as if he wanted to symbolize the great romantic artist struggling against the battering elements within and without. Like the figures in *Springtime and Harvest*, Sinclair believed love and genius were synonymous, that he could build a family out of the love he had for his art. Meta was starting to have doubts.[20]

He turned his attention to a new work, *Prince Hagen*. The novel took place in a forest where the narrator lived. This time Sinclair tried to cram in not only his love of nature but his romantic fascination with music. Much of the story centered around themes developed by the classical German composer Richard Wagner. Prince Hagen has been sent from the underworld up to Earth in order to learn about progress. The narrator worries that Hagen will be corrupted by the force of material progress, and he couldn't be more right. Hagen succeeds, even going into urban machine politics and embracing the new ideology of social Darwinism. At one point, Hagen professes his belief in the "survival of the strong" and embraces the ambitions of the new world, so different from the world of romantic beings below. Once again, we have a tale of corruption at the hands of mammon. Sinclair seemed to want to write a timeless tale about this theme, but chose to set it in the contemporary world of urban existence.[21]

Once again, the novel struggled to find a publisher. One publisher kept the manuscript for close to six months before rendering a negative verdict on its prospects. When it was eventually published, the novel fell flat, like *Springtime and Harvest*, attracting a minuscule audience. So Sinclair went back to surviving and scrounging. From 1902 to 1903, he lived again with his mother and father, separated from Meta and his son. This would become a pattern for the young couple, living together, then apart. During the time away from his family, Sinclair's frustration grew more pronounced. He read the German philosopher Friedrich Nietzsche, whose polemic against the ignorance of the masses and whose embrace of the great delight of genius inspired Sinclair, as it would many young writers who thought themselves superior to the masses who rejected their art. Sinclair learned from Nietzsche to speak of the "tyranny of the populace over the literary men." But he grew weary of Nietzsche since the philosopher was too harsh and cynical, too elitist and rugged for the young poet's liking. "There are two words that are absent from his writings," Sinclair would explain: "love and humanity." Like Nietzsche's hero Zarathustra, Sinclair knew he had to go live in the woods by himself. So he moved from his parents' home. One time during his sojourn, it got cold. Sinclair built a fire, and wound up setting fire to his tent. He learned to live on fried apples and soda biscuits, and when those ran out, he hunted and "lived on fried crow." Things weren't looking good.[22]

He would use his next book as an outlet for the anger welling up within—to show the world just how pissed off he was. The result was *The Journal of Arthur Stirling*, not necessarily a great novel, but certainly a great hoax. His growing cynicism manifested itself in a desire for publicity, the need to generate a buzz in literary circles. He promised himself that this book would cause a sensation. From within his tent, Sinclair wrote a story that took him "six weeks." The story itself wasn't what mattered, since his "desire was to raise a sensation, first to sell the book, of course, and, second, to give me a standing ground from which to begin the agitation of My Cause." Mixing up, as he would throughout his life, self-promotion and idealism, Sinclair was delighted that his publisher announced in New York City's newspapers the death of a young poet. He would write a real-life journal of a young artist who had committed suicide, while the obituaries went out. Reporters scurried around to report on the dead poet, and *The Journal of Arthur Stirling* "made a great stir among the reviews, and was the talk of the literary world for a week or two." Then a reporter figured out that the book was remarkably similar to *Springtime and Harvest*, both in its language and its theme of the destroyed artistic soul. Still, the lesson was learned: publicity mattered as much as quality in building a literary career.[23]

The lesson was also embodied in the product itself. The *Journal* told the story of a young man who had written an epic poem. Overwhelmed by the number of books already in existence, he still felt compelled by his vision—his desire to express himself. He had a belief in his own "genius." Arthur Stirling hawked his wares to publishers, and every time he was turned down. Some publishers lied about the progress his manuscript was making through the evaluation process (something Sinclair himself had experienced); some tried to hide from this persistent little artist. "Oh, what a horrible thing is 'business,'" Stirling concludes after one such rejection. One publisher encourages Stirling to write a novel, rather than an epic poem, suggesting that the novel would be more accessible to the American reading public. At one point Stirling admitted that he admired newspaper journalists since "at least they learn to keep in touch with their audiences, and to write in a way that takes hold of the people." Perhaps Stirling, like Sinclair himself, was toying with the idea of writing in a less romantic and more realistic fashion. Still, for the sake of telling a tragic story, Stirling remains an artist struggling for existence, and he seemed to grow even more alienated from the reading public. To add to Stirling's misery, Sinclair pointed out how he had to live in the city to be close to the publishers who consistently rejected him. The city was loud, noisy, and chaotic—a bad place for a romantic artist. Stirling pledged himself to Nietzsche, and the novel, if it can be called that, built toward its inevitable climax. At one point, Stirling, without a shred of humility, blurts out, "I was a man of Genius. And you have trodden me down." He was forced to subsist in a world whose only rule was to grant "what the reading public likes." The end result was inevitable: Stirling would commit suicide.[24]

After the buzz of this book and its publicity quickly wore off, Sinclair traveled once more to the Adirondacks and hunted on the Raquette River. His wife and child were once again left behind. Then Sinclair returned to the city, where he stayed in a lodging house during the winter. Meta's parents refused to allow him into their home. He arranged to see his baby covertly but even that didn't work out. More frustrating for him was that he wrote a novel that couldn't find a home. It was called *The Captain of Industry*, and it was quickly followed by another unpublished manuscript, *The Overman*. Sinclair began to doubt his capacity as a writer (or at least a writer who published things). The commerce of culture—the beast of mammon—seemed to have won.

The Religion of Socialism

In 1902 Sinclair had started to find a solution to his life's frustrations. He began his conversion to socialism. The word *conversion* makes sense in the case of Sinclair. It was much like a religious experience, in that it seemed to come in a flash, although it had been building for some time. The buildup came in his anger toward the publishing business. He expressed a "savage hatred of wealth" that had less to do with the scientific socialism of Karl Marx and more to do with the feeling of being snubbed as a writer. Call it the socialism of hack writers, and it was probably shared by a number of young writers and artists at the time, including those who had their writings turned down, those who were unable to afford paint to make their paintings, and those who had to set aside their musical ambitions in order to work in their fathers' businesses.[25]

Socialism became religion for Sinclair. He described it as "a wonderful discovery" that gave "me the key to all my problems." Others who discovered socialism out of their own despair over publishing shared this perception of Sinclair's. Harry Kemp, a young tramp poet who would eventually seduce Meta and cause a scandal in New York's tabloids, referred to socialism as "the vision of the glory of the years to be." Though Sinclair would come to that romantic and apocalyptic vision too, his conversion was surprisingly genteel, even tame in its origins. It came when he met Leonard D. Abbott, who worked at Funk and Wagnalls, the publisher that reissued *Springtime and Harvest* as *King Midas*. Abbott handed Sinclair a copy of *Wilshire's Magazine*. Its publisher was a socialist millionaire (for whom Wilshire Boulevard in Los Angeles is named). This colored Sinclair's conversion. It was not carried out by tough proletarians telling him of the misery of factories. Instead, he got the pitch for socialism when he went to dinner with Gaylord Wilshire and George Herron, who became a lifelong friend. It was a fancy affair that made Sinclair uncomfortable, as he had to tuck his frayed cuffs inside his jacket. Herron was a defrocked minister who had divorced his first wife but still believed the ethics of the New Testament were best expressed in socialism. Wilshire believed that the transition to socialism would be gradual and peaceful. It was, in many ways, simply the logical extension of the growth of trusts, turning private businesses to perform for the public good, the way cities were starting to treat electricity and water suppliers. This genteel dinner with its clinking glasses and talk of high-minded socialism was Sinclair's entry into a new world.[26]

Understanding this romance with socialism can be puzzling to readers a century after the fact. This requires stating the obvious: This was prior to the Bolshevik Revolution in Russia, prior to the time when socialism could be cruel and scary, as when V. I. Lenin endorsed revolutionary violence, secrecy, and vanguardism. Socialism was but a dream when Sinclair had his conversion, a dream of a better time over the horizon. Leaders like Eugene Debs spoke of creating a "cooperative commonwealth" where small producers would own their own land or workshops and create goods in harmony with one another, this idea emanating not from the brain of Karl Marx but from the Populist farmers of Sinclair's childhood. The leading socialist publication that Sinclair started to write for in 1904 was *The Appeal to Reason*, founded in 1897 by J. A. Wayland, who was fresh out of the cornfields of Kansas and a believer in Populism. Socialism could then take root in the Midwest and in places like Girard, Kansas, and not just big cities like Chicago or New York, where immigrants were pouring in and where socialism could appear a foreign ideology.[27]

It was also a dream of many well-educated, middle-class people, like the ones who converted Sinclair. The Socialist Party that Sinclair would join was composed largely of lawyers, journalists, and teachers. Many ministers, in addition to Herron, could find in Christ's Sermon on the Mount a socialist message. And the writers who discussed socialism for a wide audience often sounded Christian and American rather than European and Marxist. Edward Bellamy, whose novel *Looking Backward* probably converted more Americans to socialism than any other book, outlined a socialism that came out of a peaceful transition, a logical transition from corporations growing larger and larger to the point when they simply merged with government and started to produce not for profit but for public benefit. Technological advances ensured economic abundance, which allowed for competition to be tossed into the dustbin of bad ideas. Bellamy's socialism, as the historian Daniel Borus points out, was more about millennial Christianity than it was about the scientific socialism of Marx. It was its notion of an orderly transition and its grounding in Christianity that made Bellamy's ideal so appealing to a middle class growing upset with the chaos of capitalist competition. Those who got their socialism from thinkers like Thorstein Veblen, a popular economic and social theorist at the time, got it out of moral disdain for the waste and pomposity of America's robber barons, who strutted down Fifth Avenue, displaying their wealth in walking canes and high heels. Others turned to the social thought of Henry George, who believed that the Jeffersonian tradition of equality between small farmers did not necessarily have to disappear with the new wealth amassed during the Gilded Age.[28]

What these different thinkers and ideas had in common was a faith that socialism would come peacefully, or at least relatively so. Socialists debated among themselves whether large holdings of wealth should be confiscated or compensated, but even those who wanted to confiscate believed that could be done only after socialists had won democratic elections. Socialists were reformers, not revolutionists. Their main body, the Socialist Party of the United States, was very pluralistic and allowed divisions between ideologies and activists within its ranks. Two key leaders, Victor Berger and Eugene Debs, for instance, didn't see eye to eye on many matters. But they did believe in building a socialist power base through gaining votes and elected positions at all levels. Eugene Debs, one of the Socialist Party's more radical activists, didn't pick up a gun; he ran for president. The party had an ability, in the words of the historian Christopher Lasch, "to combine a commitment to thoroughgoing social transformation with 'constructive' political action." Some who were more revolutionary derided it at the time as "slowcialism."[29]

As much as Sinclair pledged his faith to this tradition of socialism, he was also still smarting from publishers' rejections. Anger seethed below the surface of reformist socialism in this young man. He interjected into slow-cialism a romantic edge. One of his first pieces for *The Appeal to Reason* preached to the farmers of America that they should vote for the Social-ist Party. Sinclair would claim that he knew farmers, that he met them on his travels through the wilds and in his surroundings at Princeton, New Jersey, where he moved during his socialist conversion. His memoirs sug-gest that he didn't think highly of farmers; some of them seemed to him terribly ignorant and backward. And this showed in his plea for their vote. After all, many farmers identified with the Democratic Party; it's not hard to imagine that they would have doubts about the Socialist Party, which had been in existence for just a few years.

So too with workers who were losing out in strikes against business owners; they too may have believed that a vote for Debs was a wasted vote. Showing his romantic side, Sinclair bellowed at those who hesitated to vote for the Socialist Party: "You wish to accomplish something. You are a fool!" This was much like Mother Jones, who harangued miners who didn't have the guts to stand up to their bosses, but it was also Sinclair's naiveté speaking. The need to explode the bland politics of compromise for something grander—a revolution in consciousness, a romance and anger that stemmed from his own rejection at the hands of publishers who always spoke of the realities of the market—Sinclair wanted to make a grand gesture and to find overarching solutions to problems that might have seemed more complex to others.[30]

Sinclair didn't become a socialist organizer, although he joined the Socialist Party local in Trenton when the Sinclair family settled in Prince-ton in 1903. After all, Sinclair may have been a socialist, but he still wanted to write novels. George Herron promised to give him a small stipend (thirty dollars a month) so he could write without resorting again to potboilers. Sinclair bought two tents and some land and moved just out-side Princeton with Meta and David. Soon he built a small cabin. His domestic existence made Sinclair want to escape into the romantic imag-ination of writing novels. He lived in a "three room shack—the 'soap box on a marsh'—in the winter time, with Meta desperately ill, and I doctor-ing and nursing her, tending the baby, doing all the housework and even washing the clothes." There were no sexual relations, so Sinclair threw himself into his work, and Meta became depressed as she watched the roof leak and the mud grow deeper around the cabin. At one point, Sinclair discovered her in bed, crying as usual, but this time with a gun in her hand.[31]

It goes to show Sinclair's steely resolve that he could write his novel under those conditions. It was his first as a socialist, but the novel doesn't show that, at least if you go looking for characters that represent Marxist theories of class or the uncomplicated propaganda of his later novels. The reason Sinclair had moved to Princeton was that the university had one of the best collections of writings related to the Civil War, and he had imagined writing a trilogy about that conflict, which had ended just twelve years before he was born. He traveled to Boston to see if he could raise money for himself and to interview surviving members of the abolitionist movement like Frank Sanborn and Julia Ward Howe. The books in Princeton's library and these interviews helped make his first (and last) novel in the planned trilogy, *Manassas*, more realistic than his previous works. Sinclair was finally learning how to temper his romantic effusion with the cold force of historical fact. The *Times Literary Supplement* called *Manassas* his "first really mature novel."[32]

It might seem odd that a young socialist burning with a new religion would think that writing a novel about the Civil War was helping the cause. *Manassas* did not, at first appearance, seem terribly socialist, since socialism seemed a distant theme when dealing with the Civil War. On the other hand, Sinclair, like those forming clubs to promote the ideas of Edward Bellamy and calling themselves "nationalists," believed that Americans must embrace a sense of being unified before socialism could become a reality. Americans needed to see the importance of shared sacrifice that only a national community could teach them. They needed something to transcend their regional self-interests. Sinclair explained, "The Civil War is to me the greatest art-theme." It showed the "sacredness of this Republic." Sinclair's socialism was always a logical extension of his Americanism. In writing historical fiction, Sinclair tried to interweave a novel's narrative with that of American history during the tumultuous decade of the 1850s and the beginnings of the Civil War, and thereby set the stage for socialism.[33]

The central character of *Manassas* was Allan Montague (a name related to Sinclair's own family). A southerner raised on a plantation, Montague read *Uncle Tom's Cabin* and then Frederick Douglass's autobiography, and he started to question slavery. He secretly hoped escaped slaves would make it to freedom. This was no abstract ideal for him, since he himself wound up coming across an escaped slave whom he decided to help, risking his own life. While telling Montague's story, Sinclair documents the vicious beating of Senator Charles Sumner over debates about the fate of Kansas; the Compromise of 1850 that saved the country from civil war for a time, the Fugitive Slave Law that allowed southerners to retrieve slaves who had escaped up north; the Dred Scott Decision, which confirmed the South's wishes in terms of freed slaves' legal status; the Lincoln-Douglas debates; and then finally the actions of John Brown, the radical abolitionist. The novel served as a nice history of the 1850s, a decade of infamy in American history. Allan Montague even tried to persuade Jefferson Davis that the South shouldn't secede, and then realized that this move was foolish. The war had to be fought, as tragic as it might be. And so Montague fought on the side of justice—the North—and preserved the cause of American nationalism.

This was Sinclair's first decent novel. History helped check his tendency to fly off on a tangent. He was bound and tied to describing actual events rather than his internal angst at the world around him. The Civil War brought gore and struggle to the page, leaving behind the social message of a marginalized artist. The realism he was learning from socialists who wanted to reform the system probably helped push Sinclair in this direction at the same time. By writing a historical novel and shedding his emotional baggage, Sinclair made clear that he was ready for bigger literary challenges.

Meeting Jack

In 1904, after *Manassas* was published, Sinclair decided to become politically active. He was a neophyte in this area. His previous political involvement included gathering signatures for a new CCNY building and aiding the anti-Tammany reform candidate William Travers Jerome. Now he would form a national organization dedicated to educating young college students about socialism—something he had missed in his own days of college and graduate school. Sinclair would always be slightly awed by literary celebrities, so he decided to start by writing letters to writers like William Dean Howells and Thorstein Veblen to see if they thought it a good idea to create such an organization (Veblen, as would be his nature, thought the idea to be bunk). Though many responses were negative, Sinclair, true to form, persevered, and by September 1905, the Intercollegiate Socialist Society (ISS) was formally recognized at a dinner held at Peck's Restaurant in New York City. Sinclair soon turned over the reins to Harry Laidler, who would see the organization through a long history. The ISS was a source of pride for Sinclair for years to come.

Sinclair didn't want the ISS to be a political organization; that sort of activism was better left to the Socialist Party. Instead the ISS would dedicate itself to educating youthful idealists about socialism. As with most things at this time, the organization was partly a response to Sinclair's humiliation in the publishing world. He believed that many young people with ideals who were trying to figure out what to do with their lives would be frustrated: the profession of law was corrupt, and newspapers were slaves to advertising, for instance. Still, there was reason to hope, as witnessed by the large number of young people flocking to the settlement houses that began to dot America's urban landscape at this time—the sort pioneered by Jane Addams and others who wanted to give concrete expression to their youthful ideals of equality and Christian brotherhood. Sinclair saw these as fertile recruiting grounds for socialists. Indeed, William English Walling, an early member of the ISS, wrote to Sinclair in support of the idea from a settlement house, and Walling and others were successfully recruited due in part to Sinclair's hard work. He recalled how he and Meta would "sit up until two or three o'clock in the morning wrapping up bundles of literature to send to collegians."[34]

The organization wasn't necessarily big on accomplishments, in part because its desire to educate was so open-ended. There was also the problem that local chapters of ISS determined their own policies, making it difficult to establish an organization that had a clear-cut national reputation. Nonetheless, the number of chapters on college campuses grew between 1905 and the beginning of World War I (as did the membership of the Socialist Party). The organization held essay contests for the best writing in favor of socialism and put together bibliographies of socialist works. It tried to get speakers to visit campuses where they could talk up the socialist tradition. By attracting big names—especially writers—to its ranks, it tried to make socialism more respectable and less scary to young Americans.

On this last count, Sinclair had his greatest moment with the ISS. He successfully recruited Jack London to give a big talk in favor of socialism in New York City, under the sponsorship of the ISS (London would then become the group's president). London was a celebrity at this point, having published *The Call of the Wild* and *The Sea-Wolf* to critical acclaim. Drawing on his own adventures in the Klondike and on oyster pirate boats at sea, the novels told tales of the wild, the ferocious lives of wolves, and the tough world of grizzled seamen. So Sinclair rented Carnegie Hall and publicized the event, talking it up to the press. He was nervous that London had a long route to take to get to the event, traveling from California to Florida by boat and then taking a train to New York. When Sinclair got to Carnegie Hall, the place was packed, and there was no sign of London. His heart started pounding as he considered mounting the podium himself. Then he heard cheers and shouts from the back. London had arrived.

London gave a rousing stump speech. He portrayed socialism not as a science—the way Marx would in his classic works like *Das Kapital*—but as a "great passion." It was a movement that was growing; more people were joining the Socialist Party as the years went by, he pointed out. In contrast to the child labor of factories and the injuries American workers suffered on the job, injuries that London himself had sustained, socialism promised a beautiful dream. Standing above his audience, London argued that socialism offers what is "clean, noble, and alive." It offered a life of "service" grounded in "unselfishness, sacrifice, and martyrdom." The crowd roared, and Sinclair's heart raced. Not only would he not have to make the speech himself, but London's own was a grand success. And he looked forward to the next day, when he would have a chance to sit down and have lunch with the person he later referred to as a "young God, a blonde Nordic god," and a man he would forever remember bringing an audience to its feet.[35]

There was reason to believe that when London and Sinclair sat down together, they would get along splendidly. They were, in fact, brothers under the skin. Indeed, at the time of London's death in 1916, Sinclair would refer to him as "a genial, delightful companion." Both loved the outdoors and the health that came from spending time in the wilds. They had both experienced the humiliation of struggling writers. One of London's best (and Sinclair's favorite) novels, *Martin Eden* (1908), documented the plight of a working-class young man struggling to make it as a writer (it was largely autobiographical). "The editorial machine," London wrote about his character's experience, would shoot out "rejection slips" with "horrible machine-likeness." Authors, London complained, learned to leave behind "masterpieces" and instead did "hackwork—jokes, paragraphs, feature articles, humorous verse, and society verse." London himself had pumped out thousands of words a day while facing rejection slips piling up on his desk. Both he and Sinclair were self-punishing in their production—they both overproduced. London would grind away and grow tired from this work (but at least he had the release of alcohol). Sinclair would grind away for hours on end, only to suffer from headaches or exhaustion. Both writers loved Nietzsche, and Sinclair rightfully believed there was a war going on inside London "between individualism, the philosophy of selfishness and personal domination, and Socialism, the philosophy of brotherhood and service." Of course, it was this burgeoning faith in socialism that had brought these authors together more than anything else.[36]

But as much as they shared, they were worlds apart. The meeting the day after London's speech made this painfully evident to Sinclair. "The occasion was completely spoiled for me," Sinclair recounted, "because Jack was drinking and I wasn't, and he amused himself by teasing me with his exploits." Sinclair recalled how London tore into his "puritanical friend" with "wild tales." Sitting across from him, London perceived something about Sinclair—that the teachings of the Episcopal church and his mother had never really left him. "He was the red-blood, and I was the mollycoddle," Sinclair admitted. London spoke of things that highlighted just how sheltered a life Sinclair had lived. London recounted his adventures on the sea, a life of trapping on the frontier of Alaska, sexual stories about women, and, of course, adventures with drugs and alcohol (London had taken his first drink at age five from his father's beer pail). Jack was notoriously boyish in his qualities, willing to tease, lie, and embellish his past. When Sinclair recounted this meeting to Jack's second and last wife, Charmian, she wrote back to Sinclair in typical fawning exuberance over her dead husband, "He may have been acting a particular part, in order to shock you. He could do that too/Oh believe—he was a wonder!"[37]

Sinclair was depressed by the meeting, but it taught him an important lesson that went beyond London's teasing. Sinclair was learning about a new movement in the arts and literature from London, a movement known as realism. While the workers had their trade unions and the politicians their campaigning, intellectuals in the socialist movement had embarked on the task of expressing realism in their writing. Realism became a revolt against the bourgeois classes just as trade unions were.

After all, realism intended to shock the middle class and make it face the sort of subject matter that was traditionally suppressed. Realist authors took note of Mathew Brady's famous photographs showing dead bodies lying on the battlefields of the Civil War, exposing not heroic gladiators but just dead boys. Artists and writers started in the first few years of the twentieth century to capture what it was really like to live, much the way London had captured life in the Klondike and on boats floating out to sea. Just before he met London, Sinclair had read *The Octopus*, Frank Norris's novel about a conflict between ranchers and railroads (making the novel appear to be about populism). A central character in the novel searches for an epic theme to write upon, missing the theme right in front of his face. The character pines for "realism, grim, unlovely, unyielding. To be true—and it was the first article of his creed to be unflinchingly true—he could not ignore it." Norris himself championed the idea that the great artist wrote for the sake of truth over money, giving voice to the wishes of other realist authors. By the time he read *The Octopus*, Sinclair had already met the realist author Theodore Dreiser, who described Sinclair as "wide-eyed, poetic, overflowing with Napoleonic vanity." Dreiser's novel *Sister Carrie* told how a city transformed an innocent rural girl into a woman who could ruin the life of a respected gentleman. And if Sinclair could get beyond the ribbing that Jack London gave him at their lunch date, he would have recognized that one of London's major goals in life was to write realistically. As a character of London's, Martin Eden, explained, his "work was realism" and "life as it was."[38]

Realist writers gave expression to the lives of Americans that the middle class would prefer to hide from—the working class, that other set of Americans that activists like Jane Addams worked with. Eventually artists like John Sloan and William Glackens would paint smudgy-faced boys on the streets of New York City. They didn't want to paint what they were expected to—family portraits of the middle class sitting in their safe homes. They wanted to paint the streets. By dealing with working-class themes, artists and writers could identify themselves as workers—a step that Sinclair had already taken. William Dean Howells, an early realist who was not as worldly as London, recalled that the author "is merely a working man" who relies upon markets to sell wares. "It ought to be our glory that we produced something and we ought to feel the tie that binds us to all the toilers of the shop and field." The artist, for the realists, was not a genius but a worker. Sinclair's meeting with Jack London taught him that he was not alone, that other writers were struggling to put reality into fiction and were identifying their own work with that of the working class as a whole.[39]

In 1904 Sinclair himself would denounce "bourgeois" literature as "sugar coated romance." The wealthy members of society whom Thorstein Veblen had dissected in *The Theory of the Leisure Class* (1899) only wanted sweet literature that allowed them to live a life of dreams. Sinclair knew that he could not write "bourgeois literature," since his life circumstances put him squarely in the ranks of the working class. "Today competition means that you, the farmer, and I, the writer, and every other man who works in competition is simply the bond-slave of the predatory power of organized and banded capitalism." We are all "wage workers," Sinclair explained, because we face the same plight "whether we be magazine writers or bootblacks." Now it was necessary for Sinclair to take the realist spirit and ally it with his socialist politics. That was easy. As London's character Martin Eden would explain, "Realism is imperative to my nature. The bourgeois spirit hates realism. The bourgeoisie is cowardly. It is afraid of life."[40]

Sinclair had already made the realities of the American past his subject in *Manassas*, and he had started to pay closer attention to events in the world around him rather than the eternal echo in his head that rang about artistic purity. He read with great distress about a strike in the stockyards of Chicago, where workers had gone down to defeat as they had so many times before. The editor at *The Appeal to Reason* suggested that he write a book about that strike and the struggles of workers who slaughtered cows for a living. Jack London had already shown the way when he released *The People of the Abyss* (1903), a book that documented the wretched poverty of Britain's slums. A writer could live among, and write about, the lowest ranks of society, the way painters like Sloan and Glackens would. And most shocking of all to Sinclair, London had become famous even while publishing such a book. Sinclair hungered for the fame that made London able to get onto that speaking platform and be heard; he had tasted just a bit of it in the Arthur Stirling controversy and had enjoyed the experience.

Now that Sinclair's cause was the cause of the working class and his tool the realism of his fellow authors, he was ready to embark on a new journey in life. He recognized his own flaws (something that didn't happen too often with him). Between 1900 and 1903, he became a romantic artist, and in so doing, he made a mistake. "My error," he explained in 1906, "lay in supposing that it is literature that makes life, instead of life that makes literature." His early writing was admittedly poor because he "lacked a knowledge of life" and lived in a "Tower of Clouds," Sinclair would later recount. Jack London told him this over lunch and pointed to another direction in life. And Sinclair was ready to see what it would bring.[41]

THREE

⟨⟩

SOCIALIST "CELEBRITY"
1905–1914

One could not stand and watch very long without becoming
philosophical, without beginning to deal in symbols and
similes, and to hear the hog-squeal of the universe.

—UPTON SINCLAIR, THE JUNGLE

It is true that I am what the world calls famous, and shall
also perhaps be rich; I might go over to England if I chose,
and meet with duchesses and lords, and be a "personality."

—UPTON SINCLAIR, 1906

F ROM 1904 TO 1905, SOCIALISM OVERTOOK UPTON SINCLAIR'S
consciousness. He could think of little else; this dream of a better
world allowed him to escape the domestic hell of his marriage and the
poverty of his Princeton cabin. Socialism allowed him to direct his
crusading spirit in another direction. Sinclair no longer wanted to be a
romantic poet decrying the philistine book publishing world, nor did he
want to be an underread author. He wanted to reach large numbers of
Americans in order to grow the ranks of the Socialist Party and use his gift
of publicity and writing for a cause. In 1905 he found his moment.

There were important changes underway in America at the time. On
September 16, 1901, President William McKinley, the man who led the
United States into the Spanish-American War, was shot by an anarchist.
Suddenly, Theodore Roosevelt was propelled into the presidency. Roosevelt
turned out to be a bold president who never forgot his predecessor's assas-
sination. He wanted to prevent future chaos in the country, not by jailing
every radical out there but by eliminating the causes of their most strident
and politically poignant complaints. He passed social and political legislation that confronted the problems generated by industrialization, problems he believed allowed radical assassins to justify their actions against a
recalcitrant system. He described his presidency as "a corrective to Socialism and an antidote to anarchy" and pledged himself to "conservative

radicalism." He stood up to the businessmen who wanted to use their economic power for selfish political aims. When Roosevelt attacked the interests of J. P. Morgan, America's most powerful banker, Morgan messaged the White House to inquire. "If we have done something wrong," Morgan said, "send your man to my man and they can fix it up." Roosevelt's response was a resounding: "That can't be done." In a stance that, in many ways, epitomized the times, he drew a line in the sand between the White House and corporate influence, pursuing what he considered to be the public good. When coal-mining companies refused to negotiate with striking miners, Roosevelt threatened to nationalize the mines. When he learned that private loggers were devastating America's forests, he pledged himself to conservation. His was an activist and reformist presidency.[1]

Roosevelt's action from on high reflected growing concerns coming from below. He knew about the activism of settlement houses, where studies of child labor and other forms of exploitation were being conducted. In the case of the coal strike, Roosevelt noted labor unions organizing to provide an outlet for the anger of overworked and underpaid employees. He had also read work by a group of writers he called "muckrakers," who kept bringing up "the filth of the floor" so that everyone could see it. These journalists wrote stories about corruption, about how companies like Standard Oil, owned by John D. Rockefeller, destroyed competition in underhanded ways—by bribing railroads so that they would refuse to carry the goods of competitors or by threatening competitors directly with physical violence. These stories reached large numbers of middle-class readers in magazines like *McClure's*. Middle-class readers voted and expressed concern about the fate of the country, further energizing the work of politicians like Roosevelt to do something. Reform movements were gaining steam at this time, and it was in that atmosphere that Sinclair's *The Jungle* appeared.[2]

Accidental Muckraker

The Jungle was a novel very unlike his first, *Springtime and Harvest*. Most obviously, it wasn't set in a forest but rather on the killing floors of Chicago's slaughterhouses. Less obviously, the novel didn't come like a flash into the mind of Sinclair. Instead, an editor at *The Appeal to Reason* suggested the idea to him, which hinted that this young author did better under tutelage than on his own. The book would require research, much in the way that *Manassas* required research, except this time it was socio-logical, not historical, in nature. "I spent seven weeks in the stockyards dis-trict alone, living with the people, meeting with them in their homes, in the places where they worked, in their saloons and clubs." While compil-ing facts, Sinclair never dropped his prejudices. He followed in the foot-steps of southern social critics who decried the industrializing society of the North. Southern writers during the antebellum period, like George Fitzhugh, for instance, delighted in telling northerners that they were no better than the South—"cannibals all!"—since wage work was more degrading than slavery. Sinclair himself believed that southern slaves had it better than wage earners. But he had taken the time to do research to justify his regional prejudices.[3]

Chicago was the perfect city for Sinclair to set his novel, a place where all of America's new problems and progress were fiercely converging. To celebrate the four-hundredth anniversary of Columbus's voyage in 1893, the city erected a set of buildings named the White City and held an enormous exposition to celebrate industrial and moral progress in the country. It's now known that the work done to erect the White City was incredibly exploitative for its immigrant workers. Chicago had already had its fair share of strikes and labor conflicts, most famously the Haymarket Affair of 1886 and the Pullman strike a year after the White City went up. In 1904 meatpacking workers walked off the job, and this was the incident that prompted Sinclair's visit. Chicago had become a place of violence and strife—a perfect setting for a dramatic novel like *The Jungle*. Besides, Chicago had already provided background for realist novels, like Theodore Dreiser's *Sister Carrie* (1900), a shocking story about a young woman mov-ing from a small Wisconsin farm to the industrial underbelly of Chicago and embarking on an affair with a married man.[4]

Chicago also provided a progressive infrastructure for Sinclair's research. Numerous social workers helped him get in contact with work-ers and explore the underside of the city. Sinclair met Jane Addams, the founder of Hull House, the most prominent settlement house in Chicago. He argued with her that settlements should convert members to socialism. Addams was a good judge of character and told someone after Sinclair left, "That young man has a great deal to learn." He at least learned a great deal from other social workers who showed him around the area. As Sinclair explained, when he arrived in Chicago, he got a "small room" at the Stock-yards Hotel and went to the University Settlement for his meals, where he relied upon Mary MacDowell, head of the settlement, to expose him to the world of meatpacking. One social worker told him of a child drowning in the pools of water that formed in unpaved streets, and Sinclair made sure to incorporate the story into his novel. Others took him to Bubbly Creek, where meat refuse was tossed, quickly becoming an "open sewer" that was "thickly coated with grease and filth." Settlement house activists brought him to the dump where children picked with sticks for food scraps. As he saw these things, Sinclair grew increasingly convinced that he had the setting for a novel that could help him reveal the previously hidden story of America's underside.[5]

If Chicago was the perfect city, the meatpacking industry was the perfect line of business for Sinclair to investigate. It was a quintessential trust that had centralized its economic power. Meatpacking demanded the sort of management systems central to modern business. As one economic historian explained, a beef trust robber baron like Gustavus Franklin Swift had to coordinate the "purchases of live animals, the activities of its large slaughtering and butchering plans in the Midwest, and the transport of its dressed beef" in order to "to match the fluctuating demand in the cities where the meat was consumed." Swift and J. Ogden Armour could afford to invest in refrigerated train cars; those companies that couldn't simply died off. By 1899, according to Algie Simons, a socialist who helped Sinclair gather information for *The Jungle*, competition was officially dead in the meat industry. And with centralized economic power came centralization of the way work was managed. Henry Ford's famous assembly line was foreshadowed in the meat factories. One historian points out that already by 1870, "it took 157 men engaged in seventy-eight separate processes to take apart a steer" that would move down the line. Simons believed that workers could "perform the work equally well with eyes open or closed." The "disassembly line," as one historian later called it, captured a pattern of work that was spreading throughout the country at the time.[6]

Not only was the meatpacking industry modern, it was perfectly set against the public interest. It was an equal opportunity exploiter. It paid the farmer and rancher less and less money for cattle, it mistreated the workers in the slaughterhouses by depressing their wages, and it covered up the quality of its products to the consumer. Anyone who paid attention to markets and prices would have noticed that, just as Sinclair was poised to investigate the stockyards, the price for cattle was going down, while the price of meat for consumers was going up. Sinclair couldn't have picked a more perfect target.[7]

After collecting his data, Sinclair returned to his "board cabin, eight feet by ten" in Princeton, to write. Sometimes he'd break down in crying fits, because the material was so troubling and because his own family's poverty was so abject. He began the novel on Christmas Day 1904 and finished it during the summer of 1905. David was sick much of this time, as was Meta, and the cabin was cold and wet. These conditions may have contributed to a sense of desperation in the novel. Sinclair wrote with vehemence, hoping to put his own suffering and those of the workers of Packingtown squarely within the pages of the novel. When it came time to conclude the novel, Sinclair grew tired and confused. He admitted that the novel's end was poorly constructed, explaining later to a friend that "I had to finish the book when I was ill and busted."[8]

The novel was not entirely a realist novel, because it was so infused with Sinclair's earlier romantic impulse. He called *The Jungle* the "result of an attempt to combine the best of two widely different schools; to put the content of Shelley into the form of Zola." It was also tinged by moralism, since Sinclair had wanted it to be "identical" with *Uncle Tom's Cabin*, the famous antislavery novel that tugged at the sentimentalism of the American middle class to show how inhumane the peculiar institution of slavery really was. Like Harriet Beecher Stowe, Sinclair yanked at his readers' heartstrings, piling one episode of tragedy on top of the other and turning his characters into the passive victims of lascivious exploiters.[9]

The Jungle tells the story of Jurgis, a Lithuanian immigrant to America who believes in pulling himself up by his own bootstraps.* He believes that he will prevail, and the story that unravels shows how everything is stacked against him. Jurgis desperately struggles throughout the novel to keep his family together and uses any available contacts—a deli owner who got the family housing and jobs, for instance—to get by. When Jurgis finds a job, he is thrilled. But instead of achieving self-sufficiency, Jurgis discovers men who are treated like animals. Sinclair compared the animals being shipped in for slaughter to the men doing the killing, men separated from one another based on their individual tasks in a vast division of labor. Workers lacked a sense of the overall slaughtering process, and managers turned this to their advantage by speeding up each stage of

---

*All quotes from the novel come from Upton Sinclair, *The Jungle* (New York: New American Library, 1960); page numbers are provided in parentheses throughout the following passages.

the process. They could require "the same work in a shorter time, and paying the same wages, and then, after the workers had accustomed themselves to this new speed, they would reduce the rate of payment to correspond with the reduction in time" (112). Workers also learned how to turn their eyes from the awful things they were doing, like watching sickly cattle labeled unfit for consumption pass through the slaughterhouse anyway. They also noticed rats and how poison was set out to kill the rats, and then how the whole mess was ground up and shipped out to the consumer in the form of different meat products.

Jurgis's salvation from all this was found in his family, and the book documents his marriage and the birth of his first son and the purchase of something he thought he could only dream of, his own home (55). But then Sinclair documents how these sources of pride for Jurgis become sources of pain. Ravenous real estate dealers trick Jurgis into signing bad agreements. He's stuck with a punitive mortgage. He then drinks away his grief in saloons whose owners feed on his limited supplies of cash. And then the rapacious forces of industrial capitalism destroy the family. His wife is forced into prostitution (109). In telling these stories, Sinclair hammers home his message: for immigrants like Jurgis, exploitation doesn't occur only at work, but in all areas of life. This was Horatio Alger in reverse, going from down to lower down.

When Jurgis is injured, Sinclair brilliantly shows how something that might seem to be a small event can turn big quickly. Jurgis has no net to capture him when he falls through the cracks of the industry, and so after missing work and growing weak, Jurgis becomes unemployed and desperate. He sinks to the rank of fertilizer man, the lowest rung in the workplace hierarchy, and at the same time, his wife gets sick. She lies about her forced prostitution, and when Jurgis finds out, he assaults the factory boss who preyed upon his wife. With no legal defense, Jurgis lands in jail. While he is incarcerated, his house is repossessed, leaving Jurgis to feel like "the victim of ravenous vultures that had torn into his vitals and devoured him" (177). His wife, growing sicker by the day and now nine months pregnant, dies in childbirth, along with the infant she was carrying. The dark details start piling on faster and faster, with Jurgis blacklisted from work and then his son drowning in the unpaved streets of a neighborhood with no sewers.

Jurgis travels to the country in order to escape, becoming a "tramp" (214). Pulling away from the society he was once trapped in, Jurgis starts to gain perspective, and so too does the reader, who begins to see what

Sinclair meant by the term "the jungle." "He saw the world of civilization then more plainly than ever he had seen it before; a world in which nothing counted but brutal might" (229). He returns to the city when the weather turns cold, and he witnesses the hierarchy of class when taken to the home of a wealthy drunk. Though the wealthy man gives him some money, a well-connected barkeeper steals it. After fighting the barkeeper, Jurgis lands in jail again, where he learns how to live a life of crime (249–253), only to return to the "hog killing room" of his past (258). He joins a union and then takes part in the strike that had originally propelled Sinclair's interest—the strike of 1904. But Jurgis switches to become a scab (264–266). Seeing Connor, the man who led his wife to prostitution, he lashes out again, only to become an "outcast and a tramp once more." (276) And soon thereafter, Jurgis is destitute again.

Sinclair drew his characters into a pit, creating an almost over-the-top description of human destruction. The novel became trapped in its own internal logic of desperation. But Sinclair could not end here, so he has Jurgis wander into a meeting where he hears the words of a socialist speaker. Sinclair projects the religious quality of his own conversion to socialism onto Jurgis. "There was a falling in all of the pillars of his soul," Sinclair explained, "the sky seemed to split above him." Jurgis is left to whisper, "By God! By God!" (304) He is "converted to Socialism" (308) in a way that's described as "supernatural" (311). He starts to read *The Appeal to Reason*, full of "ginger and spice, of Western slang and hustle," and of course the paper where *The Jungle* was originally serialized. Jurgis now believes in the "cooperative commonwealth" made up of "self-governing communities" (331). The book ends with hopefulness about socialism's growth and then climaxes in a rabble-rousing speech that was likely lifted from one of Eugene Debs's.

Once he had completed the novel, Sinclair had to do what he most dreaded—find a publisher. Not all publishers would have the guts and tenacity of *The Appeal to Reason*. There was the obvious fear of legal reprisal with a novel such as this, and when he sensed cold feet on the part of the first publisher he approached, Sinclair prepared for self-publication. Then Doubleday said they'd entertain publication so long as a lawyer could confirm Sinclair's assertions. The lawyer traveled to Chicago and met with a friend at the *Chicago Tribune*, who told him Sinclair was a liar. The lawyer's next stop was the publicity department of a meatpacker who said, "Oh, *The Jungle*! Yes, I know that book. I read it and prepared a 32-page report on it for a friend on the *Chicago Tribune*." Doubleday then rushed the book into print, while Sinclair had his own copies to circulate (his had the emblem of the Socialist Party on their cover). The publisher had made a smart choice. The book became a literary event never before seen.[10]

Reading the book, it's hard to miss its romantic passion to convert readers to socialism, but its intentions were muddied by the realities of history. The book entered a world not of its author's own making or under his control. Sinclair would famously state that he aimed for America's heart but hit its stomach. Yet at the time, he knew full well that the descriptions of the meatpacking industry's lack of cleanliness would make an impact. How could he imagine differently when he had written about "piles of meat" with "dried dung of rats" on top of them, and about how there was "no place for the men to wash their hands before they ate their dinner," so workers would wash "them in the water that was to be ladled into the sausage"? How could passages like these not turn the stomachs of Americans and make them demand something be done?[11]

That's exactly what happened. Teddy Roosevelt read the book and quickly summoned Sinclair to the White House. Roosevelt knew the slop that passed for meat, having eaten military rations during the Spanish-American War that made him retch. But he needed his own investigators to check out the situation. Fearing delay, Sinclair quickly dispatched his investigator, Ella Reeve Bloor, to ensure that Roosevelt's boys wouldn't be misled by the meat industry. They weren't. The only thing they could not confirm was Sinclair's report that men fell into vats and wound up on the tables of beef-eating Americans. Sinclair knew that the families who had experienced this had been paid off, so he was not surprised that the rumors couldn't be proven.[12]

As he watched the president, Sinclair came to believe that Teddy Roosevelt was "an aggressive and fearless servant of the general welfare" who had a "genius for publicity." But he still trusted his own sense of these things more. When he learned that Roosevelt's investigators had confirmed his novel's details, Sinclair rushed to the *New York Times*, where the editor supposedly screamed out "Stop the presses!" to include Sinclair's news in the next day's paper. Whether this story was true or not, the report went all over the place. Meat sales plummeted. People were talking about the book throughout the country. The public had awakened, and now it started demanding that something be done. So too did Sinclair, who kept writing Roosevelt to do more. Roosevelt had to tell Sinclair that it was he who ran the country, not a lowly muckraker.[13]

The result of all this was the Meat Inspection Act of 1906—a major piece of legislation that helped empower the federal government. It's too easy to think that once *The Jungle* hit bookshelves, legislation was drafted. In fact, a bill to regulate the meat industry had been before Congress as early as 1884. There had also been the research of Harvey Washington Wiley, M.D., chief chemist of the Department of Agriculture, who had been testing foods by the late nineteenth century, painstakingly providing scientific evidence that impure alteration of food products was taking place. Also important was the profession of nutritional science that was well advanced by 1900 and was suggesting that something was wrong with almost all aspects of America's food supply. Sinclair's novel certainly contributed to this general momentum by making legislation seem unquestionable. It still required legislative corralling, and Roosevelt was not the only one who pushed on this front. So did Senator Albert Beveridge. He helped draft the Meat Inspection Act, which passed on June 30, 1906. It imposed new codes of sanitation and more rigorous enforcement. Beveridge himself called the act "the most pronounced extension of federal power in every direction ever enacted." He was right.[14]

It should come as no surprise to find that Sinclair was disappointed with the way things worked out. He believed that the solution to the problems outlined in *The Jungle* had to be total. Investigations were not enough; socialism was the only cure. Sinclair espoused the "municipal slaughterhouse" that was popular in some European countries. He believed government inspectors would be pushed around by the meat industry, as he himself showed them to be in *The Jungle*. Thus, the slaughterhouses should be operated for the public interest by the government itself. Sinclair called the Beveridge Bill "admirable" but said it wasn't stringent enough toward those who violated it. This was typical of Sinclair, this all-or-nothing attitude. And it represented his desire to embrace utopia over the practical reforms that Roosevelt believed in.[15]

Becoming a Celebrity in a Personal Utopia

The Jungle created not just sweeping legislation but a star that the American public could lustily feast upon. Soon after the book became a sensation, Sinclair set up his own press room in Manhattan. His publisher helped him out. Isaac Marcosson explained, "Sinclair was the centre of an

almost continuous interview. We kept a photographer making new photographs of him." Sinclair knew something had changed in his life. "I was
a sensation," he would explain a few years later, "almost as much as if I had
won the heavy-weight championship of the world." He was no Arthur
Stirling any longer. When the famous socialist and novelist H. G. Wells
came to the United States in 1906, he demanded to meet Sinclair. Sinclair
grew excited about all of this. But one newspaper gave a dire warning that
Sinclair should have taken to heart. Though it believed *The Jungle* had
accomplished a great deal in changing the course of American history for
the better, the editors stated, "we are not sure that" Sinclair "may not spoil
it all by a lack of discretion and of reticence. He is making rather too
much capital out of the whole affair."[16]

The warning was legitimate. After *The Jungle* appeared, Sinclair's life
followed the path of many celebrities throughout American history—his
life and reputation nose-dived. The most damaging thing he did was to
seek revenge against the publishing world. Now with a name that rang
bells in the heads of America's readership, he could rummage through his
files and publish the stuff he couldn't get published before. And he did this
in spades. There was *The Overman*, originally written in 1901–1902, which
told a story of a young man who discovers his brother on an isolated island
living for music and cherishing isolation, becoming in the process Nietzsche's new heroic man who lived for his own ideals. It was Arthur Stirling
redux, simplistic and sloppy, but nonetheless, it hit the bookstores in the
wake of *The Jungle*. There was another story Sinclair had written in the
dark years before fame, *A Captain of Industry*, which recounted the make-
believe life of a wealthy steel mill owner's son. Characters had metaphor-
ical names like "Dyemondust" and "Minergold." The son was, as would be
the case in all of Sinclair's novels about the leisure class, amoral, having an
affair with his own illegitimate daughter. The daughter kills herself, and
the son of the mill owner proceeds to drown himself in alcohol first and
then, more literally, in the sea. A reader at Macmillan, where Sinclair had
originally sent in the manuscript four years before *The Jungle*, asked,
"What is the matter with this young author?" But Sinclair did not care
about this judgment enough to amend the product. His name was well
known, and in getting revenge on the publishing world for his prior destitute state, he diminished his own stature. To add insult to injury, Sinclair
tried to make *The Jungle* into a play, only to find the project untenable.[17]

Sinclair also wrote *The Industrial Republic*. Unlike *The Overman* and *A
Captain of Industry*, this was not a work of fiction, nor was it a bad book.

It explained socialism to an audience that still thought of it as an idea brought to these shores by wild-eyed revolutionaries. Sinclair made socialism sound American, arguing that "the essence of Socialism is democracy." He elucidated how socialism would not enslave people to the state but would free them from the obligations of producing to survive. Sinclair's future society would be one of artistic expression, civic participation, and equality between the sexes. But the book also fell into the celebrity tendency of talking big—making sweeping generalizations that were ill-conceived. Like Hollywood stars today, Sinclair spoke of things he knew little about. One of his prophecies was that William Randolph Hearst would win the presidential election in 1912 as a progressive candidate and would likely bring socialism to America. Sinclair also predicted that a big-profile person like Teddy Roosevelt would "likely" be assassinated and that this would lead to chaos and thus more pressure for socialist reform. Explaining his newfound status as society's fortune-teller, Sinclair called himself a "scientist and prophet." Only two years later, he admitted that "the Hearst movement is dead." And Theodore Roosevelt died of natural causes seven years after 1912. Sinclair would write Louis Filler in 1938 that "there is nothing I am more ashamed of in my whole life than my having believed in Hearst." But it would take longer than that for him to give up on making prophecies altogether or for the allure of fame to leave his thinking entirely.[18]

While ill-conceived books were being transformed from musty file folders into finished products and Sinclair was making the change from reporter of social conditions to prophet of a better society, he was also trying to figure out what kind of life he wanted for himself. He knew that David needed more attention than he and Meta could provide. In 1909, with striking candor and in print, Sinclair admitted that "many demands make it impossible for [Meta and me] to come up to our ideal of parenthood." He was also growing more aggravated by Meta, though he didn't broadcast this frustration in print (yet). Meta was becoming testy and unwilling to put up with Sinclair's desire to live for his writing alone. She needed other people (and increasingly this would include lovers). A nicer farmhouse that Sinclair bought near his Princeton property might have temporarily solved these problems, but not for long. Sinclair needed something else, a place where David could be cared for and where he and Meta might find a richer social life. In 1906 he decided to found a community called Helicon Hall.[19]

That year Sinclair made a bold statement that began with the obvious but ended with the curious: "I am a Socialist, and consider that the private affairs of most individuals constitute the most important public affair now existing." This was a man who had just been saying that only if America undertook a revolution by voting in a slate of socialist politicians who had the courage to turn privately owned slaughterhouses over to the government could America solve the problems outlined in *The Jungle*. Now he was talking about the private affairs of individuals. The statement reflected Sinclair's frustration. After all, *The Jungle* had created only partial reform, which Sinclair expected would be quickly overturned by the beef trust. It seemed easier and more satisfying to get his own personal house in order. Besides, *The Jungle* made Sinclair relatively rich, and it seemed time to do something with the wealth.[20]

Helicon Hall started as a set of conversations in the summer of 1906. Sinclair had gathered numerous writers, artists, and social reformers who wanted to start a community by pooling resources and child care responsibilities so that its members would be free to pursue their own creative endeavors (the original members included, among others, a professor at Columbia University, a novelist, an editor and journalist, a suffragette, and a playwright). They decided to have a communal kitchen but to respect individual members' privacy at the same time. Before they knew it, they had acquired a juvenile education institution outside Manhattan near Englewood, New Jersey, with Sinclair contributing the money made from *The Jungle*. It was a beautiful place from most accounts, with "goodly porticos, rows of white pillars, and ivy covered walls." It had over fifty rooms and included "a huge swimming tank, a bowling alley, a theatre, a glass covered court" with "tropical plants." Jo Davidson, an artist who would visit Helicon Hall and cause a public scandal by getting in a fight with Sinclair that was reported in the *New York Times*, remembered its "large sized palm trees in buckets in front of an enormous fireplace." That fireplace served as a gathering point for conversations that would go until three in the morning at times, and the community members started using it as early as October 1906. The community's founding had been rushed, and it showed early on. "We had no furniture, and no food, and no cook; we lived on crackers and milk." But after four months or so, the community became a bit more established, reaching almost forty adults and about fourteen children. Members governed themselves democratically and set minimal rules. For instance, they hoped members would dress themselves in "comfortable things" and expressed "dislike" only of "unsightly objects, such as suspenders."[21]

Helicon Hall was not entirely original. It drew upon a long tradition in American history of intellectuals and artists joining together in alternative communities. Most famously, some of Ralph Waldo Emerson's disciples created Brook Farm during the decade of the 1840s. Brook Farm's members, living near Boston when the earliest signs of industrialization were becoming evident, came to hate markets and materialism. They aspired to a life that expressed Emerson's romantic values of poetic self-expression and not the act of moneymaking. They wanted to combine physical and intellectual labor in a way that would keep people honest and humble. They produced and sold farm products to sustain the community but gained fame for establishing a very good school for children and held poetry readings and dances that became the talk of the town. Then the communards converted to Fourierism, an elaborate theory of how to structure communities around a theory of "passions." This change prompted enormous problems of reorganization and soon after the Fourierist turn, Brook Farm burned down. The community had failed to live long, and in retrospect, it seemed to suggest that intellectuals are not always the best community organizers. The blazing end of Brook Farm also eerily foreshadowed the fate of Sinclair's own communal experimentation.[22]

During Sinclair's lifetime, the dream of Brook Farm continued among those on the left. Many members of the Socialist Party believed that all that was necessary to create a better society was to elect the right people to office. Others believed that labor unions could negotiate better contracts for workers and thereby set the course for a gradual transition to socialism. But there were others in the "lyrical left" who believed that such political change wasn't enough. They believed individuals had to transform their personal lives in order to create revolutionary change. This belief was especially popular among early feminists. While some feminists simply wanted the right to vote, others demanded that the personal lives of men and women be scrutinized and changed. For instance, Charlotte Perkins Gilman, a leading feminist intellectual and friend of Upton Sinclair's, argued that if women were to gain equality with men, domestic life had to be transformed. Society should place child rearing in the hands of experts—those with knowledge in modern psychology and nutrition—so women could be freed from subservience to men. Gilman designed feminist apartment houses where there would be community kitchens that could help free women from domestic chores and provide them with the opportunity to express themselves in ways they saw fit. Gilman's writings had a direct influence on Sinclair and his hopes for Helicon Hall. When

he looked back on Helicon Hall, he believed that its "most obvious success was with the children" who were provided with a social life that private homes could never provide. In turn, this allowed the adults, especially
women, to have freedom to follow their own creative ambitions and
engage in free and open discussion within Helicon.[23]

But the issue of children also highlights the problems and limitations
of Helicon Hall. When Sinclair embraced Gilman's idea that experts
could rear children better than biological parents, there was both a legitimate and a more troubling element to his reasoning. Of course, biological parents may not always be the best child rearers, but at the same time,
Sinclair sounded slightly creepy when endorsing the idea of experts raising children. He worried that "future generations" might suffer if raised
by "the ignorant and the callous." In endorsing collective child rearing,
Sinclair betrayed his feelings of inadequacy as a parent, and he seemed to
be grasping for high-minded reasons to justify his own failure. Sinclair
admitted that Helicon was created, in part, because he needed "someone
to take care of" David. He also admitted, in public again, that David
drove him insane. "I have had him two weeks in a New York flat and
seen him turn four able bodied adults into fit subjects for sanitarium
treatment." There was something endearing about this honesty, but also
something troubling.[24]

The real problem with all of this—including his growing tendency to
publicize his family problems to a wider audience—was how it allowed
Sinclair to mistake the remaking of his private life for social transformation. With his frustration at how *The Jungle* had created change but not
the right sort, Sinclair developed a more purist strain in his political
thinking. In his own words, Helicon Hall was not meant to "persuade
anyone" the way *The Jungle* was meant to persuade people to become
socialists. It simply provided those already committed to social justice a
better place to live. Sadly, even if he was seceding from broader political
change, he wasn't doing an especially good job at it. People looked to
Sinclair for leadership at Helicon, and he failed them. He often thought
one meeting could solve a problem, hoping to rush through it in order to
get back to his own writing. He would later admit that he found Helicon
"required the entire time of one man to run it; and that man ought not
to be a person who is chafing inwardly, because of novels" he wants to
write. Finally, as much as Sinclair wanted to avoid public life, he could
never escape the fact that he had become a celebrity. Journalists would

hide out and spy on Helicon Hall, ready to report on its quirkiest episodes, such as when Jo Davidson and Sadakichi Hartmann, two Bohemian artists from Greenwich Village, came to Helicon drunk and caused a ruckus. Sinclair later described Helicon Hall as "a public spectacle, a free-farce comedy for the great Metropolis of Mammon." One reporter, he recalled, labeled Helicon Hall "Sinclair's love nest." These comments symbolized the impossibility of Sinclair's original dreams for Helicon Hall—both to escape the limelight and to allow the remaking of private life as part of a wider social transformation.[25]

All of this paled in comparison to the physical dimensions of Helicon Hall's problems. Once again, Sinclair was a dreamer of big ideas who couldn't deal with the reality of the nitty-gritty details. Helicon Hall's founders had paid too much money for the property, which resulted in high prices for room and board. Members fought over what sort of food they should prepare in their communal kitchens. These fights often took place around the fireplace, which might not seem that important, except that it was becoming clear that its heat was the only heat available for community members. As well, the plumbing was awful, and Sinclair, never known for mechanical ingenuity, worked on this problem himself. Sometimes he hired young writers like Sinclair Lewis—the future author of *Babbitt*, a novel that took the country by storm fifteen years later—to tend the furnace, which should have raised further questions about Upton Sinclair's management skills and the community's safety. On March 7, 1907, the questions of safety and management were answered once and for all. The whole place went up like a torch. Every member escaped without serious injury, but the place was gone for good. The lawyers came in and settled matters, and the members scurried off to their separate existences. In the end, the fire symbolized a bigger problem for Upton Sinclair. Big ideas would never rescue him from the difficult details of managing his everyday life. This lesson was painfully learned in the years following the fire.

Drift, Depression, and Divorce

It is often the case that celebrities are miserable human beings. Smiles captured in the flash of cameras too often cloak feelings of despair. So it was with Sinclair. Life after Helicon Hall became one of drift. It was a drift that pained Sinclair. He was back to a life of trying to write quickly, hoping for another splash like *The Jungle*. At Helicon Hall he started to write *The Metropolis* and, after the fire, finished it in a shack at Point Pleasant, New Jersey. It was essentially a novelized version of Thorstein Veblen's classic, *The Theory of the Leisure Class*, which had examined the myriad ways in which the rich displayed their wealth to the rest of society. Allan Montague, a character cribbed from *Manassas*, is a southerner gone to New York City. He witnesses the decadence of the upper classes there, as they indulge in foxhunting, pheasant poaching, and talk of "crepe de chine lingerie." There are parties, and the wealthy members of society maintain "do as you please" ethics, having casual sex and fawning over their pets. Montague witnesses wealthy men buying stock on the margin and grows shocked at the lack of morals of the bourgeoisie. Eventually Allan strikes it rich but then drops out of society in disgust. The novel was both meandering and didactic, not an especially good combination. As if the story itself didn't make the message clear, Sinclair blurted out, "In the Metropolis the sole test of excellence was money, and the possession of money was the proof of power; and every natural desire of men and women had been tainted by its influence." Sinclair seemed to be worried that his stories weren't enough, so he got in the habit of piling on gory details and then hitting the reader over the head with a clear statement of his message. His characters weren't characters—they existed to prove a point. In *The Jungle*, this problem was apparent, and so too in *The Metropolis*, but there it grew more tiresome since the characters prompted little sympathy, only annoyance. His audience was expecting more from him, as were numerous editors who turned down the book.[26]

The Metropolis, once published, didn't do well, but Sinclair was too busy working on his next novel to pay much attention. It was as if he was back to potboiler writing, though this time with a sense of conscience. The next product was *The Moneychangers*, in which Allan Montague is again deployed. He saves a woman from being raped by a wealthy man, and as a lawyer, he witnesses, once again, shady business deals, this time the attempt to take over a company in order to turn it into a monopoly. Montague grows nervous, as his ethics come into conflict with the cold realities of capitalism. He helps a reporter get the scoop on the inside deal, but not quickly enough to spare the country the Wall Street Panic of 1907 (an event that wasn't fictional). One of the businessmen kills himself, and Montague despairs, deciding to enter politics instead of business. Ironically, this was one of Sinclair's novels that would become a movie (something he always dreamed of), but when it came out, it was a story of Chinatown and the opium trade that he had to disown.

Critics argued that Sinclair didn't know the wealthy society he tried to document in these works. But this wasn't the real problem. He had spoken with wealthy women who gossiped about their social lives with him while he took notes. Sinclair was closer to the truth when later in life he admitted that *The Metropolis* was a "poor book" because he "wrote it in a hurry." It was a combination of all these things that worked against him. The problem was that the material gathered for these two novels about the leisure class didn't sustain readers' interest; it was hard to care about these characters, and Allan Montague came across like a prig walking amongst heathens. The innocence and passivity of Jurgis made *The Jungle* a difficult read in places, and now the snobbish elements of upper-crust decadents parading themselves about generated the same reaction.[27]

As Sinclair's novels seemed to get worse and worse, his private life was also deteriorating. At Helicon Hall, Sinclair had an affair with Anna Noyes, a married woman, or at least Meta believed he did. Like many marriages that involve a celebrity, Meta and Sinclair's was fast coming apart. Sinclair had already flirted with Margaret Mayo, the woman he worked with to try to turn *The Jungle* into a play. They had to follow the performance around to rewrite it, and they stayed in hotels late at night, and at one point, Sinclair looked down her dress and was tempted. Meta too was having affairs and getting stronger and more independent. The marriage had begun as a tutelage, with Upton educating Meta, but now Meta was chafing. Her earlier depression and suicidal moments suggest that this newfound assertiveness was a positive development.

By 1908, *The Moneychangers*, *The Metropolis*, *The Overman*, and *A Captain of Industry* were in the eyes of the American public, and publishers were starting to wonder about Sinclair's ability to write not necessarily the great American novel but at least something that rang true. So he traveled to vacation spots like Lake Placid and Bermuda to get away from the literary world. Now desperate for money, Sinclair wrote to Gaylord Wilshire pleading for support. "I am a worthwhile investment," he blurted out. Wilshire could not help him, and Sinclair watched his book sales plummet even more before he decided it was time to head out west for the winter of 1908. It was significant that he didn't bring Meta or David along with him. He admitted less than a year later that he "went away to California" because "the strain of" his marriage "had nearly killed" him.[28]

His first stop was Carmel, California. Sinclair was still searching for a community where he could live a life of communal existence mixed with artistic independence. Carmel was a good choice, since it was home to an artists' colony. He spent most of his time with George Sterling, a poet he would later call his best friend (Sinclair's definition of friendship was rather broad). He swam by the shore close to Point Lobos, a beautiful spot where cypress trees gripped rocky outcrops. Sinclair enjoyed the company of men and remembered Sterling as "an athlete and beautiful to look at," especially when he was in "bathing trunks" and on the "rocks of Point Lobos." Sinclair was drinking in the outdoor life of California (and thinking of ways to get out there permanently). The only problem was that George was a binge drinker, and a sloppy drunk by all accounts. But at least he promised Sinclair not to drink around him, and on this count he was at least better than Jack London, who was then traveling around on his new sailing ship, though about ready to return to his pretend ranch where he would constantly invite Sinclair to visit (when he had the chance, Sinclair still didn't visit London in California, frightened as he was by the drinking and cavorting that went on there). Carmel was also close to San Francisco, and Sinclair hoped to found "the Sinclair Players," which would be sponsored by the Socialist Party and perform his plays. He was partially successful, putting on three short plays in San Francisco. But the idea was half-baked and required that the Socialist Party pony up money—not something that Sinclair should have expected to be easy.[29]

While in California, Sinclair felt the urge to start writing another novel. He also began to miss Meta and David, and he pleaded with them to meet him in Florida. So he returned east. In Florida he found another small bohemian community in Coconut Grove, where he stayed after recovering from stomach ailments in a local hospital. He swam, fished, and enjoyed the outdoors again while knocking out *Samuel the Seeker*. It was a brutal novel about a boy who leaves a farm for the city and is then mugged on a train and arrested for vagrancy. After he is released, a professor gives Samuel a job, and then he has to search out other work. He decides on a life of crime, seeing no other way out of his poverty (the plot, at points, seemed remarkably similar to *The Jungle*). Samuel then gets a job in a church and is disgusted by a minister who kowtows to the wealthy, at which point Samuel decides to expose the corruption of the church. Finally, and not surprisingly, Samuel converts to socialism. The novel, like most of Sinclair's books after *The Jungle*, didn't do terribly well.

Sinclair's illness in Florida reflected a general obsession with his physical condition, especially his diet. From Carmel, Sinclair wrote pleading letters to Meta about David's eating habits, explaining the virtues of what one reporter called his "squirrel diet" made up of nuts and fruits. To Meta, he wrote, "I tell you there is no excuse for anything but nuts." Meta listened to Upton's advice and then fed David all the cake and candy he wanted. Meta was starting to annoy Upton intentionally (which wasn't difficult). She realized that diet was one place where she could aggravate him most. Ironically, she also aided his obsession with diet. In the summer of 1909, suffering from nervousness and exhaustion herself, she decided to go to the Kellogg Sanitarium in Battle Creek, Michigan, which was promoting vegetarianism and relaxation as a means to overcome stress. Sinclair decided to follow her. During that summer, Meta would have an affair with a young man; Sinclair would meet his future wife, Mary Craig Kimbrough; and Harry Kemp, a tramp poet who would eventually instigate the final stage of Sinclair's increasingly miserable marriage, would visit. The stage was set for the end.[30]

Before it all collapsed, Sinclair continued his frantic search for the right diet. Seeing it in hindsight is a lot like watching a child furrow through boxes, searching for the right toy to play with, all the while throwing trash in every direction. Later in his life, Sinclair would claim that "everything I wrote on diet was in the nature of a report of experiments." Nothing could have been further from the truth; he was a zealot when each new discovery was made. He was first a disciple of Horace Fletcher, who believed in thoroughly chewing food. He then adopted the vegetarian and cooked-food diet promoted at Kellogg's Sanitarium. But after leaving the sanitarium with its overall regimen, he got sick. He worried about roughage in his diet, so he started to "chew out the skins of young green peas, and set them to one side on my plate." Not surprisingly, this led to recurrent constipation. So, though it made little sense, he tried a diet of buttermilk and yogurt (a diet that George Sterling had suggested). He also tried "good lean beefsteak," following the advice of Dr. Salisbury, who also counseled drinking "at least a pint of very hot water" two hours before each meal.[31]

Sinclair ditched this diet because it got too expensive. So he went back to a "raw food" diet he had picked up in California This included "nuts, ripe olives, salad, vegetables, and a variety of 'the kindly fruits of the earth,' both fresh and dried." His typical day's allotment in 1910 was as follows: "For breakfast, half a shredded wheat biscuit, three peaches and three dates; for dinner, a tablespoonful of almond meal (one half ounce), one shredded wheat biscuit, three peaches, and a dozen dates; and for supper, the same as dinner." This wasn't exactly a great advertisement for his cause, nor was pointing out that the diet was justified because of humans' "monkey ancestors," who ate a diet similar to his. But at least it was cheap, as Sinclair showed by giving precise numbers to his readers on how much certain nuts cost.[32]

When Sinclair broke with J. H. Kellogg, he broke big. The bone of contention involved fasting—one of Sinclair's discoveries that he championed as a new form of dietary salvation. He wrote Kellogg an open letter that lacked subtlety, as was usually the case, and declared that the "cooked vegetable diet is the worst diet that human beings can possibly follow" since it provided too much "starch" and not enough "organic salts." Kellogg's Sanitarium, Sinclair hinted, was selling canned foods to its clientele and promoting its plan out of self-interest and profit. It was also ignoring the teachings of another sanitarium right across the street from it—Bernarr Macfadden's, where Sinclair learned the new art of fasting, which he now combined with his diet of "nuts, fruits, green vegetables," and wheat.[33]

Once again, Sinclair was on the warpath and sounded like a sectarian socialist screaming at someone who was deaf to the rightness of his cause. Though he might complain that Kellogg had questionable financial motives, his next teacher, Bernarr Macfadden, made Kellogg seem tame. This was a man who knew the world of publicity even better than Sinclair himself. He catered to Americans' growing obsession with fitness and health. He was about the same age as Sinclair and, like him, had had the nasty combination of a sickly childhood and an alcoholic father. He decided to build himself up through physical exercise and fasting. To demonstrate the success of his body's transformation, Macfadden would have public shows where his wife would jump up and down on his stomach. He loved to publish photographs of himself almost naked and flexing his muscles, which got him into trouble with the censors of the time. He hated the prudishness of Americans and promoted his work through publications like *Physical Culture*, where Sinclair published many of his essays about diets and fasting. Sinclair and Macfadden shared very little politically (Macfadden was a libertarian who hated Sinclair's socialism), but they thought of themselves as rebels against the "overcivilization" that marked the country at the time, with its processed foods and lack of physical exertion. The only thing Sinclair and Macfadden disagreed on was

that Sinclair broke his fast with juice rather than the milk that Macfadden counseled and that his sanitarium fed to its clientele in gallons at its
central bar.[34]

There were numerous ironies about Sinclair's obsession with diet. His
celebrity status allowed him to make grand pronouncements that he then
had to go back on in print. He spoke in absolute terms when it came to
dietary matters. In 1911 he wrote a book called *The Fasting Cure*, where
he exclaimed, "I have not only found good health, but perfect health; I
have found a new state of being, a new potentiality of life; a sense of light-
ness and cleanness and joyfulness, such as I did not know could exist in the
human body." Fasting as the cure for everything, including cancer, is essentially what the rest of this book argued. In becoming so obsessed, Sinclair
had ironically crossed over into the world of the leisure class he was
famous for denouncing in his recent novels—a world whose members had
the luxury of escaping civilization for sanitariums where they could drift
around and have others care for them. You never saw workers from
Chicago's stockyards at Kellogg's or Macfadden's Sanitarium.[35]

Sinclair believed that there was a political content to all of this, once
again mixing his personal life with the concerns of the wider world. He
believed that the health of the body related to the health of the body
politic. This comparison between body and civilization was fairly common
during this time, seen in the work of sociologists and social critics who
were often comparing human bodies to social organisms (the French sociologist Emile Durkheim did this most explicitly). Sinclair could warn: "I
believe that today our civilization is rapidly degenerating." He believed it
was the leisure class who overindulged in food, thereby ignoring that many
who entered the sanitariums at the time were wealthy themselves. He
cited the Roman "vomitaria" as a symbol of decadence and portending
civilization's collapse. He made his diet into a cause, much like what socialism had once provided him. "I propose for the rest of my life to do all in
my power to open the eyes of others to the crime which they are committing against their stomachs." Class war seemed to have been dropped, at
least for a moment, for dietary war.[36]

Some of Sinclair's dieting beliefs were no doubt motivated by a search
for better health, but there was also the ongoing desire to make his life
efficient for his writing career (like his need to find child care for David).
He always bragged about how few plates he had to wash and how little
time it took him to make his meals. He would report that with the raw-
food diet, one could do away with plates altogether by just tossing shells

and skins into a newspaper quickly deposited into the trash. He described having wooden plates at his home that he could simply burn at will. He often painstakingly measured his food's weight to ensure he wasn't over-eating. It was this side that suggested he was a modern Puritan, someone who saw what gave many people enjoyment (eating and drinking) as an opportunity to streamline life and get rid of excess. He showed how cheap his raw-food diet was—listing exact dollar figures for each item he bought. And as he wrote about this issue more and more from 1910 to 1911, it was hard not to see some of his own psychological problems creeping into his new personal cause. After all, many of his digestive problems probably stemmed from overwork—from precisely the self-imposed efficiency he openly documented—and had little to do with diet. Later in life, Sinclair would celebrate a rice diet as a successful cure for headaches, without recognizing that he had also turned down the decibel level of his work life by then.[37]

While sifting through diets and championing each one more loudly than the one before it, Sinclair also searched for a way to re-create Helicon Hall. He still wanted to find a way to raise David more communally. In October 1909 he promised publicly to create a boys' school where he would feed students "an ounce or two of nuts, a dish of soaked wheat with a little olive oil, and some dates, and an apple or two to finish off." It was hard to imagine herds of young boys flocking to the school when they heard this regimen, but that didn't dampen Sinclair's hopes. Some might have been excited to learn of his plans for a school where boys could play outdoors most of the time and do physical work. He didn't believe "book-learning" was best for young boys, and here he took a page from the educational theory of John Dewey—a philosopher whom Sinclair knew and admired. At this school would be born the "New Mother," who would be knowledgeable about health and teach children about sex. The real "new mother" behind this all was Adele Munger, a newly divorced woman living near Carmel. She and Sinclair carried out a heavy correspondence in which she tried to map out the details of this new school. Once again, his leadership skills failed him, and the idea collapsed. Munger had sold her house and was frantically trying to figure out how to acquire property and recruit members when Sinclair called it quits.[38]

Sinclair had found another way to create his ideal community. It required him to abdicate what he wasn't good at in the first place, leadership. At the time Sinclair was frantically exploring the possibilities, there were already alternative communities in existence. Two of them had organized around the principle of the "single tax." Henry George had proposed the provocative idea that if government placed a single tax on land, it could remain small and yet at the same time prevent real estate speculation, allowing small farmers to acquire property for little money, thus ensuring a Jeffersonian future of equality for all Americans. This small-government version of socialism appealed to numerous reformers, including some who were forming rural communities. As a brochure for the community of Arden, Delaware, explained, it was "an attempt to develop a village community holding its land in common, in the spirit of medieval times, but under modern conditions, in accordance with the single tax philosophy of Henry George." In addition to Arden, there was the Fairhope community on the eastern shore of Mobile Bay in Alabama. That's where Sinclair went first in the winter of 1909, because he had heard of a good experimental school there. He then decided to be closer to New York City and moved to Arden during the spring of 1910.[39]

When Sinclair moved to Arden, the community was ten years old, and some members resented having a celebrity in their midst. They wanted a quiet existence, where they could live simply and produce arts and crafts furniture. Sinclair fit in with this ideal surprisingly well at first, and was often seen wearing a flannel shirt with an ax in his hand, ready to chop down dead trees around the farm in order to clear the land, provide wood for furniture, and, of course, stay fit. He built his own cabin, the Jungalow, and then sought out friends to play tennis with. But this peaceful stay was interrupted in August 1911, perhaps one of the worst months in Sinclair's life. First, an anarchist shoemaker, angry about being locked out of certain meetings because he preached free love to young girls, got revenge against the community by reporting members who broke local blue laws. Sinclair had been playing tennis on Sunday, and the police arrested him and sent him to jail. Journalists rushed in to get the scoop, as Sinclair refused to pay a fine and served a short sentence (fortunate, since it was hard to imagine what he would eat in jail). He even got in a dig against America's class system when he was released. Walking out of jail to a crowd of reporters, he said that if Arden's residents were harassed again for such a stupid law as this, he would "swear out warrants for the arrest of all the members of the Wilmington Country Club who play golf on Sunday." Needless to say, Sinclair played tennis on Sunday with impunity from then on.[40]

This was a minor incident in comparison with the unraveling of Sinclair's marriage, which happened almost simultaneously with his arrest. A year before coming to Arden, when traveling in California, Sinclair had granted an interview with a San Francisco newspaper. He was still a celebrity, and his remarks about his rocky marriage made great copy. Meta could not have been pleased to read the headline in the *San Francisco Examiner*: "Sinclair Sorry He Is Married to Wife." Never drawing much of a line between his own personal life and his public persona (his dietary writings made this abundantly clear), Sinclair decided to write about his marriage in a new novel, *Love's Pilgrimage*. Everyone who read it knew it was an autobiography. In it, he described how Thyrsis and Corydon (the nicknames Upton and Meta had taken from a poem by Milton), met, married, and had a son together. The birth scene was seen as a true shocker because of its gory detail. Sinclair discussed Meta and his decision to abstain from sex, and then how Corydon drifted toward "melancholia and despair" and attempted suicide. He ended the book by suggesting another one was in the works that would document the final collapse of the marriage; and, for once, Sinclair succeeded as a prophet, not about the book but about the impending collapse of his marriage. Everyone now knew what was happening in Meta and Upton's private lives, and the book caused a sensation when it was banned in England. Jack London called it the "rawest, reddest meat that has been slammed at any American publisher in the last five decades." But many of his friends told him that it didn't rise above autobiography and was therefore not a work of literature. Charlotte Perkins Gilman, who had documented her own dementia and problems in her private life in *The Yellow Wallpaper*, believed Sinclair was doing an injustice to Meta with this book, revealing secrets without her consent. What Gilman didn't understand was how much Sinclair the celebrity could not divorce his private life from the life that the wider public consumed.[41]

While completing *Love's Pilgrimage*, Sinclair was joined by Meta at Arden. It was amazing that the relationship could still be considered a relationship, now that both of them had had affairs and were talking openly about divorce. The couple was living in tents and then the Jungalow, pretending to carry on with their marriage. And then Harry Kemp arrived. Kemp was a tramp poet whom Sinclair had helped, even raising money for him from the wealthy single-tax devotee Joseph Fels, who had also helped finance Arden. Sinclair played the elder to the younger Kemp, giving him advice, even about love, in July 1911. During that time, Kemp told Sinclair he wanted to come visit since his fiancée had left him for another man. After his arrival, Sinclair started to grow suspicious. Kemp and Meta were hanging out together a lot, and Sinclair told Kemp that Meta was a nymphomaniac to be avoided at all costs. Then it happened. Sinclair wandered close to his writing cabin, where he claimed to see Meta and Kemp having sex. It was a last straw for Sinclair, who decided to do what he had planned to do all along—divorce Meta and move on with his life.

Things heated up, and fights broke out, with Sinclair throwing a coffeepot at Harry, or so some newspapers reported (Sinclair hated Meta's coffee-drinking habit). Things got confusing. Kemp claimed that Sinclair called him to tell him that reporters were coming to Arden, now that it had gotten out that Sinclair was pressing for a divorce, and that Harry should flee Arden with Meta. Sinclair claimed that Harry and Meta had bolted in order to pursue their lust. Whatever the case, Harry and Meta took rooms together down the coast of New Jersey. This didn't prevent reporters from tracking them down when they arrived in New York City. Meta retreated to her parents' apartment on West Eighty-seventh Street, where she lay on a divan and gave interviews about the whole affair. It was now Meta's turn to be a celebrity. She declared Upton an "essential monogamist," while Kemp declared that Sinclair was "a radical when it suits his ends to be a radical" but had now turned "conservative" and abdicated the cause of free love. Meta made her case for trial marriage and more tolerance for divorce—ideas that Sinclair also believed in. Both Kemp and Meta declared that they were simply putting into practice Upton Sinclair's ideal that people should be honest about love, no matter their marital state. Reporters took it all down, not because they cared about these ideas but because it all made good copy about free-love advocates turning jealous and shaggy bohemians warring with one another. It was just what the press was looking for, a mess among America's rebels and intellectuals.[42]

Sinclair filed for divorce in August, and he was forced to make the case that Meta had cheated on him with Kemp. He asked women who ran rooming houses on the New Jersey coast to testify on his behalf. He introduced evidence that Meta's own mother thought her irresponsible. Unfortunately, the judge felt Sinclair provided more detail than either Meta or Kemp could contest in court (they weren't present). Sinclair would later claim that the judges were Catholic and therefore refused him a fair hearing. Others cynically claimed that he was just trying to increase sales of *Love's Pilgrimage* by getting this story into the press (ironically, it was the opposite that occurred; sales went down because people could pay much less for newspaper reports about Sinclair's divorce than it would cost to pick up a copy of *Love's Pilgrimage*). In the end, Sinclair's case for divorce failed twice in the courts, forcing him to pursue a divorce overseas. In February 1912, Sinclair left the country, having made money from writing for Bernarr Macfadden's magazine, *Physical Culture*. He would go to Holland, and with the help of his friend, Frederik Willem van Eeden, get his divorce. The divorce was declared on September 14, 1912, though Sinclair knew that he would have to travel around Europe and stay close to Holland in order to look as if he was considering residency.

In the end, this episode in Sinclair's life and the philosophy that surrounded it seem less shocking today than it was when it happened. After all, he believed in monogamy, and so did Kemp and Meta at the time. Sinclair didn't counsel divorce at the drop of a hat or "free love," but rather trial marriages that would allow couples to see how compatible they were (routinely practiced today by those who live together before marrying). Sinclair never advocated that people should sleep around as much as they wanted, and he even suggested it might be good to have people fill out an application before getting married, making it more difficult for people to make a permanent commitment to a bad relationship. While counseling birth control, he called abortion a "murderous horror." He wanted marriage to become a "science," by which he meant that people should have the freedom to find the right person to spend the rest of their lives with. Sex was not enough. "Permanent love," he explained, "depends on something higher—a deep common interest." Sinclair still believed essentially in "the tradition of romantic and spiritual love" that transcended physical intimacy. He saw marriage as companionship, not wild, passionate love.[43]

He made this clear by marrying Mary Craig Kimbrough on April 21, 1913, not long after he acquired his divorce. There was a scandal in the making here, since Upton and Mary Craig had been openly traveling together before the divorce was final. Mary Craig had also been corresponding with Meta, pretending that she didn't know what was going on between Meta and Upton. But no matter how messy the situation was, it resolved itself in the best way possible, at least for Sinclair. Upton wrote Dave Howatt right after the wedding that "Dr. Johnson said that a second marriage was a triumph of hope over experience." So it was for Upton and Mary Craig Sinclair. Mary declared herself a "Sinclair fan!" after hearing him speak in Battle Creek, Michigan, the first time they met, in 1909, but she was not certain if she loved him in a romantic way. Their relationship was more like that of student to teacher, much like Sinclair's early relationship with Meta. Mary Craig remembered Sinclair "gave me many books to read" and kept "instructing me." Because she enjoyed this tutelage, Craig was the perfect wife for Sinclair. When she considered at one point early in the marriage taking up a crusade against women's fashion—a crusade Sinclair would have had no problem with her championing—she quickly put the idea behind her. "I knew I couldn't afford any kind of crusade; Upton had a monopoly on this in our family." By recognizing this, she committed to her relationship in a way that made her husband happy.[44]

After marrying, Upton and Mary Craig went back to Europe to retrieve David from a school he attended there and to satisfy the residency requirement that had been a condition of the divorce. Sinclair supported himself by sending back to the United States biting articles about French grafters and poor German eating habits for *Physical Culture*. He also continued to pursue work that examined intimate relationships between men and women. He translated Eugene Brieux's play *Damaged Goods* into English, as a novel, and he also wrote *Sylvia*, a fictional account about Mary Craig in the guise of a southern woman who winds up falling in love with a man who would have upset her aristocratic family. She is pressured to end that relationship and enter into an unhappy marriage for the sake of the family and money. He then took the theme of the play *Damaged Goods* and developed it further in *Sylvia's Marriage*, a novel he wrote while in Bermuda about a man who marries, knowing that he has syphilis, and who passes his illness on to his child. Sylvia leaves her husband, saying, "I know it all now—the things I should have known before I married." The novel's message was clear: sex education should displace sexual ignorance. Sinclair might have been upset by the so-called free-love doctrine when it came to his relationship with Meta, but he never went back on his belief in honesty between the sexes. The message of all these works was that love could and should exist on a rational foundation.[45]

Back to Politics

What's perhaps most remarkable about Sinclair's life from 1910 to 1914 was how apolitical he was. Sinclair's political disengagement—his obsession with creating an alternative utopia and diet as well as his divorce—coincided with one of the most exciting years in U.S. politics.

Nineteen twelve was a year that should have excited Sinclair. That year Eugene Debs received the highest percentage of votes he had ever won, or ever would in the future. Theodore Roosevelt ran as the candidate for the Progressive Party, which had formed a coalition of progressive leaders, including Jane Addams. And the candidate who won was also a progressive, albeit a southern Democrat named Woodrow Wilson. It was the height of a general leftward tilt in American politics. But Sinclair had nothing to do with it.

When he traveled to Europe in 1912 and then in 1913, Sinclair began to feel the tug of politics once again. He met with numerous suffragettes in England. Sinclair was also excited to find a well-developed labor movement there and to learn about the idea of syndicalism, the theory that workers should manage factories democratically and the government should monitor prices in the interest of consumers. He also met other left-wing celebrities like George Bernard Shaw and Prince Peter Kropotkin, two famous believers in socialism and communitarian anarchism, respectively, who asked about what was happening in U.S. politics. Sinclair thought that perhaps he should organize an international league of socialists ready to oppose war, even though Shaw and Kropotkin told him the idea would require too much work and have little impact. Besides, German socialists seemed to celebrate the idea of a European war, telling Sinclair that they hoped it could help topple their government, allowing them to rise up against their leaders. The excitement of these conversations prompted Sinclair to consider moving to Europe permanently. He had the first inkling that although he was an American, there was something about his views on socialism and intellectual life that made him European.

By 1913, while writing about marriage, syphilis, and divorce, Sinclair was starting to reengage with broader issues of social justice. In print, he debated Vincent Astor, a wealthy young man by accident of birth, about class disparities in the United States; the debates were held around the Christmas holidays, when people think about charity more than usual. Astor claimed that Sinclair exaggerated poverty in America and argued that moderate trade unions, led by the American Federation of Labor and Samuel Gompers, were improving the status of working-class citizens. Sinclair scoffed at the point, arguing that unions were not enough. Making an argument that Lenin was about to make in justifying Bolshevism, Sinclair claimed that labor unions were insufficient, since "a class which is opposed and ignorant may be slow in finding out the sources of its suffer-

ings." The workers needed socialist leadership beyond labor bosses. Sinclair didn't discount unions, he just put more faith in industrial unions
and more radical ones like the Industrial Workers of the World (IWW).[46]

Sinclair may have been thinking, as he debated Astor, about a series
of events in Colorado, events that pushed him back into politics.
Throughout 1913, things were heating up between miners and companies
in Colorado. In August, George Lippiat, an Italian labor organizer, was
shot in Trinidad, Colorado, prompting some miners to go on strike in
September and others to take up arms and hide in the foothills throughout the southeastern portion of the state. The demands of workers
included the "eight hour day, pay for 'narrow and dead work,' a check
weighman without interference of company officials, the right to trade in
any store they pleased, the abolition of the criminal guard system, ten per
cent advance in wages, and recognition of the union." The strike quickly
gained proportions similar to those of the Homestead Strike of 1892, in
which strikers went up against Andrew Carnegie's steel empire, only to
find themselves facing gun battles with private guards and militias and the
eventual defeat of their union. Similarly in Colorado, there was John D.
Rockefeller Jr., the son of the most powerful robber baron in history. He
was managing the affairs of the Colorado Fuel and Iron (CFI) Company
back east and pushing a hard-line antiunion message to local managers out
west. Rockefeller's toughness squared off against the toughness of the
Western Federation of Miners (WFM), who became, in the words of
Upton Sinclair's friend Louis Adamic, "the most aggressive, violent, and
revolutionary labor body in the United States" and eventually "the backbone of the I.W.W." Founded in 1893 in Butte, Montana, the WFM
organized workers who still had a certain amount of control over the work
they did in the mines, work that was notoriously brutal and dangerous. "In
1913," two historians explain, "a total of 464 were killed or severely injured
in the state's coal mines." The brutality of the work was matched by the
total control coal companies exerted over the miners' social lives. Companies owned stores where miners were forced to buy all of their goods in
local scrip, and they owned the houses miners had to rent. They controlled
the roads that went in and out of isolated mining towns. When Sinclair
protested, he pointed out that Rockefeller possessed "the domains of the
robber princes of the Middle Ages."[47]

Then the whole thing exploded. On April 20, 1914, a state militia,
made up largely of guards who had worked for mining companies, came
into a strikers' settlement in Ludlow, Colorado. They burned down tents

and "riddled" the settlement with "machine-gun bullets." "Thirty three people were either shot or burned to death." Many of the miners were still celebrating Greek Easter when bullets tore into camp, and many of the victims were women and children. President Wilson felt obliged to send troops to Colorado, even though he had his hands full dealing with a stand-off between the United States military and General Victoriano Huerta of Mexico that was boiling into war. The strikers were not ready to back down, and the country seemed prepared for a full-fledged class war.[48]

Sinclair had been following these events throughout 1913, calling publicly on Wilson to protect the WFM from the thugs that mining companies employed. When things heated up in April, Sinclair was vacationing with Mary Craig in Bermuda. Upon learning of the Ludlow Massacre, Sinclair bolted to New York City. He held a meeting at a central institution of Greenwich Village radicals, the Liberal Club, where he announced his intention to protest John D. Rockefeller's murder of innocent miners. He spoke at large events throughout the city and then started his "Free Silence Mourners" action at Rockefeller's offices. Mary Craig helped out by getting people to walk with black armbands in front of Rockefeller's offices at 26 Broadway. Here was a new style of protest. As Sinclair noted, this was not a strike picket, it was a protest picket. It was like the actions of suffragettes demanding the vote and even more like the Paterson Pageant of 1913, in which the young radical John Reed helped workers reenact a strike in the streets of Manhattan (Sinclair was in on a planning meeting of this event, so he claimed later). Sinclair chose this new form of cultural politics mostly out of desperation, fearing "a conspiracy of silence of the capitalist press." As Sinclair pleaded in a letter to John D. Rockefeller, "My voice is feeble against the powers of your hundreds of millions of dollars; but such as my voice is, I will lift it up." Thus was born his campaign of publicity and shame.[49]

The newness of this mode of protest is illustrated by a judge's declaration that it was illegal since it was based on "ridicule and insult." Sinclair was arrested and thrown into the Tombs for disorderly conduct on April 29, 1914. Craig, as Upton called her, meanwhile was trying to keep the protests going and dealing with family matters, suggesting to Meta's mother that now would not be a good time to raise issues of Sinclair's divorce (she was considering taking another step in the case), since the press would have trashed them for it. She also had to handle her own mother, who, when she heard that her son-in-law was in jail, wrote a desperate letter asking, "What shall we do?"[50]

Craig and Upton knew what to do. They'd turn up the heat. Instead of holding protests only outside of Rockefeller's offices (soon Rockefeller just stopped showing up there), they held them at his church. This was a daring move, intruding into what some might have considered a man's private life. But for Sinclair, it was precisely Rockefeller's Christianity that could serve as a wedge that could enter his conscience. So protesters entered Rockefeller's church, Calvary Baptist, and demanded of the pastor whether or not Christianity could ever justify the rich killing the poor. The socialist minister Bouck White led the protest and was tossed in jail. Failing here, the protesters then decided to go all the way to Rockefeller's home in Tarrytown, New York. These actions prompted battles over the civil liberties of protesters, especially in terms of using town buildings to hold demonstrations. But they also ensured high publicity for the cause.[51]

Meanwhile, Sinclair bought a one-way ticket to Colorado and left on May 7, sure that Craig could manage the pickets and new rounds of protests. Sinclair met with Governor Elias Ammons of Colorado, who embodied that quintessential political skill of seeming both helpless and recalcitrant at the same time. "In intellectual caliber," Sinclair would explain, he was "fitted for the duties of a Sunday School superintendent in a very small village." Ammons told Sinclair he was trying his best, having set up what he called a "mediation" committee that really turned out to be an investigative committee with little power, and Sinclair wasted no time writing Wilson to explain this. Sinclair then spoke to protesters in Denver at the state Capitol, declaring the legislature and governor "impotent or corrupt." Sinclair had now moved his sights from Rockefeller and Ammons to the president of the United States. Sinclair kept citing the fact that Teddy Roosevelt—the "warrior" to Wilson's "priest"—had threatened to nationalize the mines when faced with a recalcitrant company that refused arbitration with mining unions back in 1902. With such a precedent, why couldn't Wilson act? Sinclair even used the impending conflict in Mexico, probably not a conflict he agreed with much, to appeal to President Wilson. Standing at the state Capitol in Denver he said, "We stand on the verge of a foreign war. The fact that our troops are in Colorado instead of being at the Mexican border may any day cost us thousands of lives." Sinclair then proceeded to drum up support by making speeches across the country, arriving in Tarrytown in June.[52]

The strikers were holding out, but they knew defeat was imminent. Sinclair's own cause took a hit when it was discovered that Arthur Caron, a young French Canadian man who had been beaten up at a protest in

Tarrytown, was planning to bomb the Rockefellers' home. Though Sinclair had nothing to do with this, the threat of terrorist violence had always hurt the cause of labor (the Haymarket Affair being the most infamous case). Meanwhile, Rockefeller's steadfastness was wearing down the miners in Colorado. Wilson grew tired of handling the situation and was realizing that Sinclair was right, at least in terms of the greater need for troops in Mexico rather than in Colorado. On December 10, 1914, the miners' union accepted defeat and Rockefeller won, if not in the public's mind at least in terms of blocking unionization. Frank Walsh, the chairman of the Commission on Industrial Relations, tried to make Rockefeller break the next year during investigations, but he was negatively perceived by the public. Rockefeller hired a public relations man to improve his public image and then tried to speak with miners in Colorado's coalfields. Sinclair would later take this as a sign of victory, though not an enormous one.

At least Sinclair got a novel out of the whole situation. While in Colorado, he had interviewed victims of Ludlow, including a mother who had been shot at while taking her children out of a blazing tent. He was getting ready to write again, and this time he had three things that helped: a historical setting, lots of stories gathered from research, and an editor, George Brett of Macmillan, who forced him to take the time to develop a compelling story rather than rush ahead and make his point (Brett had earlier worked with Jack London). The novel took a while because of this, and *King Coal* would not be published until 1917. Craig had to intervene at one moment, when Brett turned testy. But in the end, it was worth it. Sinclair's novels since *The Jungle* had either focused too much on the wealthy or degenerated into replays of *The Jungle*. *King Coal*, instead, had characters from all ranks of society, many of them believable. The rich kid in the novel is an idealist who wanders into a mining town and becomes a labor organizer, eventually witnessing a strike. The story ends like the real one, with a sense of impending loss.

The most important outcome of the Colorado strike was not just a better novel but the fact that Sinclair had reentered the world of politics. The United States had changed since his last campaign against the meatpackers. Teddy Roosevelt's progressivism was now displaced by Wilson's. Wilson's political vision was less to Sinclair's liking, since he wanted to bust up big businesses rather than turn them into public trusts. But at least he was a progressive, having pushed the nation to accept the first steps toward an income tax. Sinclair had pestered Wilson over Ludlow the way he had pestered Roosevelt over meatpacking. The relationship between citizen Sinclair and President Wilson was off to a rocky start. What Sinclair didn't know at the time he was sending telegrams from Colorado and turning to write *King Coal* was that this president would soon embroil the country in a world war that was shaping up overseas. Sinclair was about to reenter politics, not just at the level of Colorado or the United States, but the world.

FOUR

WAR!

UPTON SINCLAIR'S
A MONTHLY MAGAZINE: FOR A CLEAN PEACE AND THE INTERNATION

EDITED AND PUBLISHED BY THE AUTHOR AT PASADENA, CALIFORNIA

Vol. I	APRIL, 1918	No. 1
Price Ten Cents per Copy	One Dollar per Year	Ten Subscriptions for Five Dollars

This is the hour of a world decision; the greatest crisis which ever has confronted mankind. Upon the course of history during the next few months depends your whole happiness, your whole future. No matter who or what you are, no matter what you wish to do or to be, what you wish your children or your children's children to do or to be—all depends upon this world decision.

And the decision depends upon you. No others can bring you out of peril into safety, no others can give you peace and freedom. You, the people, must know and understand. Hence this magazine—or rather this offer of a magazine; this magazine in embryo, trying to be born.

All the world is suffering from a disease; and it happens that I am an expert on that particular disease. I have lived all my life in a laboratory, where it has been under the microscope; I know the germ, and have the serum ready. So in this world decision I think that I have something to say. So I come with my offer of a magazine.

I have given the would-be publication a name which some will call egotistical. But this is no time for sham modesty. I have a certain trade-mark; I have been twenty years giving a meaning to it, and now I must make use of it. Wherever I have travelled over the world, I have met plenty of prejudice, but I have met no thinking people who did not know my trade-mark, and what it stands for.

It stands for Social Justice. I have preached it in prose and poetry, in magazine articles and strike broadsides and a string of fourteen novels. As Queen Mary said that when she died they would find Calais written on her heart, so on my heart you will find two words, burned in by the acid of pain: Social Justice!

The fundamental cause of this war was that certain youths of the ruling caste of Prussia, living Spartan lives upon a nominal salary, driven by poverty, and with no escape save by marrying the daughters of rich merchants whom they despised, conceived a dream of themselves as pro-consuls, lolling upon silken couches and drinking wine from golden cups in Mesopotamia and the Punjab. Because of this, our boys have to be shipped across the water by thousands and perhaps by millions, and drowned in mud and blood in the trenches of Lorraine.

So I come again with my message of Social Justice. If you really want to do away with the horrors of Armageddon, you have to abolish exploitation, you have to drive poverty from the earth; you have to change the ideas and ideals—not merely of German Junkers, but of American gentlemen, business-men, merchants and masters of affairs. You have to do away with the power of any man, any where, to make his comfort and his glory out of the necessities of others; you have to discredit, once and for all time, those pecuniary standards of culture, which estimate the excellence of a man by the amount of other people's happiness he can possess and destroy.

A war made deliberately by the intellectuals!

—RANDOLPH BOURNE

I think I learned something from the late war. I think
I have supported my last capitalist war.

—UPTON SINCLAIR, 1922

I N 1915 SINCLAIR WENT SOUTH WITH MARY CRAIG TO STAY AT her parents' home near Gulfport, Mississippi. They had departed from Croton-on-Hudson in New York, where Sinclair had just finished editing *The Cry for Justice*, a book of short snippets of writings from the past that most would call an anthology of left-wing ideas but that he called, in his typically grandiose fashion, "a Bible of the future, a Gospel of the new hope of the race." As Upton settled into a big house that Craig's father promised to her if they stayed, an issue he had hoped to put behind him reared its ugly head again. Meta came down to Gulfport to press for custody of David. At one point, a sheriff came to the house and seized David to ensure that, following a court order, he could spend time with his mother. It became a very sad event, with Meta and David going for a swim and then sitting on shore while the young boy took photographs to keep the memory, and newspaper reporters watched and shot their own photographs. Upton had to do what he had always done, dredge up all the bad details from the past and fling them at his ex-wife and her family, threatening to go public about events that would embarrass them. He even drafted a "letter to my friends" which opened with the line, "The woman whom for eleven years I cherished as my wife, with whom I trusted every secret of my soul, has turned into a moral lunatic."[1]

This was a terrible embarrassment to Craig's family, and it disturbed

Sinclair to find himself entangled in the same old predicaments he should have overcome by now. Fortunately, the episode passed, since Craig's father was a judge and did his best to intimidate Meta into not pressing her claims. Meta sulked away with no more rights than she had had before. Nonetheless, it probably got Sinclair to thinking of ways to get out of the South and seek out distant pastures where he would be less dependent on his wife's family. If he ever had thoughts about moving to the South permanently and settling into Craig's ancestral home, this chain of events did away with them. Besides, Sinclair hated the humidity and the mosquitoes. Craig was already starting to exhibit symptoms of neurasthenia and bad health, which would mark the rest of her life. She was not only embarrassed by Meta's invasion, she was also tiring of her mother, who was similar to Upton's own. Both mothers complained about the couple's increasingly radical politics and strange stand on social issues. Just over ten years later, Sinclair would explain to Craig's friends that her mother was still trying to convert her to "the Mississippi brand of religion." It was time to pick up and move on.[2]

But they were tired of moving. They were ready for something permanent. Sinclair recalled fondly his travels to California, and a friend told him that the southern portion of the state was especially dry and a great place to play tennis. That seemed enough for him. They moved temporarily to Coronado and permanently to Pasadena in the spring of 1916. It was an ironic location for the Sinclairs, being "a leisure class town" with palatial homes and country clubs. But Craig found cheap property. She bought run-down smaller houses and garages and then rented a trailer and carried them to her new land, where she put together a hodgepodge house that seemed to work. She went out to buy secondhand furniture and then was visited by Kate Crane-Gartz, a wealthy woman who lived close by and who admired Sinclair's novels and decided to buy the couple nice new furniture. Sinclair himself knew how to live cheaply and, unlike his leisure-class neighbors, insisted on riding a bicycle in order to get around town (the further you go up in horsepower, he reasoned, the more bourgeois you get). And as he explained to readers of socialist publications, he loved the area for its climate but could never come to accept its "cultural atmosphere."[3]

The year Upton and Craig settled in Pasadena, there was increasing bloodshed in Europe. The Great War was two years old already, but in 1916 alone, there had been the Battle of Verdun, when Germans attacked the French at a point they believed vulnerable, leaving behind 350,000 dead Frenchmen and 330,000 dead Germans. That was soon followed by a battle near the Somme River that would continue to pile up bodies. In the face of this destruction, neither side was backing down, even as soldiers and citizens were growing weary of what seemed ceaseless battle that lasted into a bitter winter. Meanwhile, though Germans had pursued submarine warfare in waters that Woodrow Wilson thought should remain neutral, and though they had even sunk ships with Americans aboard, the president wanted to stick to his campaign slogan: "He Kept Us Out of War." The British and the French prayed for the United States to enter the war, but Wilson remained aloof as he won reelection in 1916 and the calendar shifted to 1917. The submarine attacks just kept getting worse, and then in February, the Zimmerman Telegram was intercepted, in which a German foreign minister promised to Mexico lost territory (the bighorn state of Texas included) if Mexico entered the war on the side of Germany. In April 1917, Wilson asked for a declaration of war, a war that would save "democracy" from German autocracy and military brutality. The French and British prayers had been answered.

Surprising as it might sound, this couldn't have pleased Sinclair more. He saw World War I as a conflict he could support. Pasadena was about as far as you could get from Washington, D.C., and still remain in the United States, but Sinclair had acquired a taste for politics with the Colorado strike. With international conflicts now overtaking domestic ones, he was not about to let his battle for a better world lose any steam. He became a one-man army, ready to make sure that Wilson lived up to his promise that this would be a war to save democracy.

One Man's Buildup to War

Just eight years before the United States entered World War I, Sinclair had thought of war as being motivated by a search for profit. Wealthy munitions manufacturers and moneylenders would always prosper during military conflict, while the poor would die on the battlefields. Though Sinclair wasn't a pacifist who shunned all violence, he believed that left-wing intellectuals should band together to prevent war on the principle that it hurt the poor, and he made a case for peace to his friends in England as late as 1912. Sinclair's friends in Germany, though, had felt differently about war, arguing that they needed help in toppling the autocratic rulers in their own country before they could have their much-desired socialist revolution.

This argument by people willing to face guns pointed at their own country stuck with Sinclair in the years to come. If they were that desperate, why not support them, he thought. He came back to this point again and again, as he thought about his attitude toward the conflict shaping up in Europe in 1914.[4]

By 1915 Sinclair seemed ready to give his support to a war against Germany. Like many intellectuals in the United States, Sinclair saw Germany as a fount of civilization and great ideas, but by now it had become the home of militarism, Junkerism, and expansionism. "The Germans were hardly kind in Belgium" when they had invaded that small country in order to get closer to France, Sinclair pointed out to those who doubted that Germany was an aggressor. That same year, he wrote to the Committee of the Anti-Enlistment League, an organization worried about conscription of young men to fight a war overseas (they had a right to be), and told them that he was for "the allies" in their war against "German militarism," since Germany was run by "barbarians." He hoped that after the war, there would be a workers' revolt in Germany that could resist any attempt on the part of England to crush it. His public pronouncements, as was often the case, seemed much more confident in their tone. "I know that after this war there will be a revolution in Germany, which will take the nation forever out of the power of the militarists." By 1916 Sinclair was circulating a letter that endorsed the war from a socialist perspective.[5]

This put him on the outs with the Socialist Party of the United States. Sinclair's original approach to war—that it was fought in the name of profits and was against the interest of the poor who did the fighting—was much more to the party's liking, and it remained so. Many members believed it was the duty of the party to make this case to the workingman, and not too surprisingly, many workingmen who would have to go to war agreed with the point. As President Wilson announced that it was time for the country to mobilize for war, the Socialist Party called an emergency meeting in St. Louis, Missouri, and declared the war "a crime against the people of the United States" that demanded "vigorous resistance." Sinclair watched as his heroes, Eugene Debs and Victor Berger, started to slam the cause that he was getting behind. There was only one thing Sinclair could do; he would have to break with his party. It wasn't easy. As he tendered his resignation, he squirmed and suggested that he "may come back and ask you to take me in again."[6]

Sinclair found some socialist friends who were ready to make the break with him. By 1916 there was the Social Democratic League, which was both prowar and socialist. And there were many intellectuals who believed that the military defeat of Germany was necessary for the realization of socialism and that the defeat of Germany's feudalism was a necessary step in the progress toward humanitarian goals. There was Charles Edward Russell, a muckraker who had written a book about the beef trust before *The Jungle* appeared; George Sterling, Sinclair's poet friend from Carmel; and J. G. Phelps Stokes, William English Walling, and W. J. Ghent, all socialists who thought of themselves as writers too. Unfortunately, Jack London had passed away less than a year before the United States entered the war. But there was still his wife, Charmian London, who was sure that Jack would have supported the war, and she was probably right. During the beginning of the war, London had told his wife that if he ever did "go to this war, it will be to fight with England and her allies." So she signed on to the cause for herself and, she believed, for her famous socialist husband.[7]

It's sometimes difficult to understand why any American socialists would have supported a war in which the United States would stand with the reactionary power of England and would conscript young men who should have identified, as socialist doctrine goes, with their fellow working-class members, not their national leaders. At the time, though, they had their reasons, beyond just a dislike of Germany. First, they made clear that there was nothing in socialism that made it akin to pacifism and that not all socialists were "sentimental or religious non-resistants." They listened to President Wilson and thought he was right when he suggested that the war was necessary to save liberal democracy. "We believe that liberal institutions have their value as making it possible to agitate for Socialism and to progress toward Socialism without destructive internal conflict." This point highlighted not just an increased appreciation of liberal government—often cursed by socialists as simply "bourgeois" institutions that protect property rights and little else—but also Sinclair's own patriotism. He was starting to argue that the internationalist position of socialists ignored the fact that the United States was, plain and simple, a better country than Germany. To a socialist who lived in poverty and was upset by Sinclair's support of the war, Sinclair shot back, "I believe America is one of the countries where you have a better chance of escaping" your situation than places like Germany. He even claimed, "I will declare my conviction that the American people, taken in the mass, have a higher moral practice than any other nation." This didn't mean that socialists should stop worrying about things like war profiteering or reactionary politics in their own country. But their first duty was to support the war, while their second was to scrutinize the faults of their homeland.[8]

It probably seems odd to hear that the destruction of war—the bodies piled up near the Somme and the possibility that American bodies would be added to those piles—could be seen as beneficial. But the debate about the United States' entry was always more abstract than it would be in Europe, where you could see and smell the death all around. The destruction seemed far away from America, and in the end the country's sufferings were nothing compared to Europe's. At war's end, 48,000 Americans had been killed in action; 2,900 were missing; and 56,000 had died of disease. Compare that to Germany, which lost 1,800,000 men, or France, which lost 1,385,000.

So it was easier to see the war less as a tragic loss of life and more as a means of achieving liberal dreams. John Dewey, an ally of Sinclair's at this time, believed the war highlighted "the supremacy of public need over private possessions." Woodrow Wilson, before the war, had already passed anti-child-labor legislation and an eight-hour day for railroad workers. Now the government needed to ensure that the needs of the military were met (for instance, that soldiers were fed adequately and that there were enough tanks and other equipment to fight the war), and in so doing, they took over more private production. The war could be seen as the dawn of socialism in America. As the historian William Leuchtenberg explained, "The National War Labor Board guaranteed collective bargaining, mediated labor disputes, and even commandeered an arms plant; and the government took over telephone and telegraph companies, warehouses, terminals, express companies, and sleeping-car companies." Sinclair himself would grow extremely excited when the war wound down and railroad unions called for the government to retain control of the nation's railroad system and direct it toward public purposes. To America's liberals and socialists, the war seemed a lot less like death and destruction and a lot more like a utopian state triumphing over laissez-faire America. As Sinclair put it in October 1918, when U.S. participation was at its height, the war was encouraging the spread of the "social ownership and democratic control of the instruments and means of production."[9]

Such reasoning made sense, but not to all members of the American left. This included more than just the Socialist Party. Many independent progressives who came from the Midwest were isolationists, seeing the conflict as European in nature and having nothing to do with American interests. Other critics of the war were more pacifist in their opposition. One of the smartest was Randolph Bourne, a young man who had circulated in bohemian circles and Greenwich Village haunts. For him, the war wasn't an abstraction, it was a horrific tragedy. Those intellectuals trying to justify it were just building dreams around cruel realities. "Idealism," he warned, "should be kept for what is ideal." Pretending otherwise was foolish. Bourne couldn't believe that of all people it was the intellectual class, those in the business of thinking critically and analyzing things, who became so passionate in support of the war.[10]

Sinclair had likely read Bourne, and he certainly held reservations in his mind while pledging his support to the war (so too, for that matter, did the president). This wasn't blind loyalty. Sinclair struggled over his decision to support the war. As he was drafting a statement in favor of the war in early 1916, he wrote J. G. Phelps Stokes, "The truth is, that I have never been confronted with a problem which has presented so many difficulties to me personally." Those difficulties were felt throughout the war, even as he became more assured of his support. He explained to President Wilson that many people "jeer at me for trusting" you and "call me a fool, or worse, a traitor, to the radical movement." This was Sinclair seeking leverage to make his appeal to Wilson, but it was also Sinclair smarting from attacks. "For me to have supported a war and to be called bad names by most of my best friends has been a strain which only a good conscience could enable me to endure." The personal damage wasn't just psychological. At one point, an anarchist pledged to kill Sinclair over his support of the war. "We have to keep all the curtains in the house drawn and steal out the back way," Sinclair explained to a friend, "as if we were in Indian country. I am wearing out all the pockets of my clothes carrying deadly weapons." When he went out to eat or see friends, he was often harassed by angry radicals. This sort of thing bothered him immensely, but he never relinquished his support.[11]

"I Don't Like the Company I Am In"

President Wilson knew that entering the war posed a significant challenge. "It is not an army we must shape and train for war, it is a nation," he explained. There were two distinct ways to get Americans on his side. There was propaganda, the sort carried out by the Committee on Public

Information (CPI), which created posters portraying Germans as nasty brutes, sent speakers to state fairs across the country to whip up enthusiasm for the cause, and placed editorials in newspapers to make it seem that local citizens were cheering on the war. Sinclair didn't care for this effort that much, or at least not when the CPI asked him to help out, as it did many intellectuals and scholars who could provide rational arguments for the war. He explained to the CPI that he disliked the government "asking men of brains to give the use of their brains without compensation." After all, the munitions makers didn't give up their profits in order to produce for the war. If Sinclair didn't like propaganda (or not being paid for it), he was not too keen on the other means of getting public support for the war, that is, by censoring critics. This too was something Wilson pledged himself to, and it was causing Sinclair increasing discomfort.[12]

Soon after war was declared, Wilson helped support the Espionage Act, passed into law on June 5, 1917. The historian David Kennedy explains that the act "provided for $10,000 fines and imprisonment up to twenty years for persons obstructing military operations in wartime, and $5,000 fines and up to five years' imprisonment for use of the mails in violation of the statute." This was followed up by the Sedition Act of May 16, 1918, which created the same terms of punishment for those who uttered "any disloyal, profane, scurrilous, or abusive language about the form of government of the United States, or the Constitution of the United States, or the flag of the United States or the uniform of the Army or Navy" or language that could possibly generate "contempt, scorn, or disrepute" for those institutions. This was rather wide language that cast an enormous net over activities that Sinclair himself could have been guilty of. Prior to the war, there was a movement for "one hundred percent Americanism" that had called into question the loyalty of immigrants to the United States, and this sort of repressive legislation seemed intent on ensuring the sort of unity that, in the words of George Creel, the head of CPI, could provide a "passionate belief in the justice of America's cause that should weld the people of the United States into one white-hot mass instinct with fraternity, devotion, courage, and deathless determination." As Kennedy points out, both the Espionage Act and the Sedition Act are "rightly viewed as a landmark of repression in American history."[13]

Sinclair knew that war often generated nasty consequences. After all, he had written about Lincoln's violation of civil liberties in his first socialist novel, *Manassas*. During World War I, he worried openly about how the Espionage Laws were being used to silence critics of the war. Indeed, it would be people he knew and respected who felt the brunt of these laws. So he decided that in supporting the war, he would also have to criticize the way it was prosecuted. He could become an in-house critic of Wilson's policies. He saw things he opposed, and he spoke out against them. "I don't like the company I am in while I am supporting the government," he explained in a speech given at the height of the war. This provided him with a unique vantage point. "I am, so far as I know," he explained after the war was over, "unique among those American Socialists who supported the war, in that I did not lose, for a moment, my vision of the evils, both of our own country and our allies" (after all, just consider two of Sinclair's socialist cosupporters of the war: J. G. Phelps Stokes believed socialists who opposed the war should be "shot at once without an hour's delay," while Charles Edward Russell believed they should be "driven out of the country"). Sinclair wanted to chastise those "Socialist extremists" who "oppose the war" while making sure that any crackdown on these agitators didn't turn the war to save democracy into a war to destroy democracy. It was a difficult line to walk.[14]

The best way to do it was to create his own platform on which to speak, in this case, a magazine. Never a humble man, he named it *Upton Sinclair's Magazine.* "This is no time for sham modesty. I have a certain trade mark," he explained in the first issue that came out a year after the United States entered the war. The magazine started and ended as a one-man project of America's socialist celebrity, though Craig certainly helped out in ways that shouldn't be overlooked. He converted his study, a "made-over one car garage purchased for thirty dollars," into an office for the magazine. He fended off visitors to the office throughout his long workdays and continued to release the magazine, even while having his appendix removed. Sinclair sounded extraordinarily entrepreneurial when describing his magazine's operation: "My magazine will not fail but will survive just as the small sweatshop survives, because the boss works all day and most of the nights and puts his life blood into it." His normal day consisted of fourteen hours of work, followed by a night of argument with Craig about the content of the last issue and what should go in the next. He decided to make the magazine survive with no advertising, just income from sales and subscriptions. All of this was an act of love for him, and he believed the historical stakes were high. His opening editorial provided a sense of his high-mindedness for any who doubted him, "Upon the course of history during the next few months depends your whole happiness, your whole future." Sinclair would be there to help the course of history move in the right direction.[15]

This took a lot of fighting on his part, at least on paper. First, there was the issue of civil liberties, especially as it related to the press. This issue was "complex," Sinclair admitted, since he saw "both sides." On one side stood those who took an absolutist stance on civil liberties in time of war. On the other stood those who feared that the enemy might use freedom of speech in order to spread doubt about the cause of war and could therefore endorse a certain curtailment. Sinclair realized that Lincoln suppressed civil liberties during the Civil War "when he was engaged in putting down the slave powers," suggesting that sometimes the means justified the ends. Indeed, he would later cite the case of Lincoln to counteract the critics of Wilson. Lincoln "suspended the right of habeas corpus," Sinclair pointed out, whereas Wilson did not. Lincoln allowed "civilians to be arrested by the military," whereas Wilson never would have. This was not exactly a compelling case, seeing as the Civil War was fought against a domestic enemy active within America's borders, whereas World War I's enemy was international and abroad. Sinclair stood on firmer ground when he argued that there was a better way to deal with critics of war than to censor them.[16]

Sinclair grew annoyed at how far government censorship of the press went, and he expressed his annoyance in his magazine. Postmaster Albert Burleson denied affordable mailing rates to numerous publications critical of the war, thus holding up their regular mailing patterns (which then, following Burleson's circular logic, denied them the status of regular periodicals and thus the affordable mailing rates). Sinclair must have recoiled at a crackdown on the socialist *Call* and *Forward*, both magazines he had written for or read in the past. He also subscribed to *Seven Arts* magazine, a magazine that published Randolph Bourne's and John Reed's antiwar essays. Though it never suffered from Postmaster Burleson, its wealthy supporter, Annette Rankine, pulled her money out of shame. The magazine collapsed in October 1917, and Rankine took her own life soon after. Closer to home was another magazine Sinclair had written for, Frank Harris's *Pearson's*, which published both literary and political commentary. Harris, British by birth and famous for a biography of Oscar Wilde, found the "unspeakable Burleson" holding up the mailing of issues (seven issues in just one year), many of them "confiscated." Even Sinclair's own magazine would be prevented by military intelligence from being shipped to England in late 1918. Censorship and the control of the press, unlike the fighting and death abroad, was not an abstract issue for Sinclair.[17]

The most egregious case of censorship during the war centered on *The Masses*. Edited by Max Eastman, this magazine grew out of a synthesis of radical politics and cultural rebellion (feminism, free speech, free love) that marked the bohemian life found in Greenwich Village prior to the war. It was a confrontational publication that took aim at the respectable world of middle-class America. Its masthead promised "a revolutionary and not a reform magazine," a "magazine with a sense of humor and no respect for the respectable: frank, arrogant, impertinent" and a publication that would "conciliate nobody, not even its readers" (sometimes the publication simply shifted one letter and thus changed its name to *Them Asses*). Sinclair always felt odd about his relationship to *The Masses*. He believed them to be honest and sincere radicals. But he didn't like the bohemian side of Greenwich Village (Meta was haunting Greenwich Village, or so he thought). Sinclair explained to Max Eastman on March 7, 1917, that he supported the magazine except for the stories of his future biographer, Floyd Dell, stories that were "pure degeneracy" and "free smut" and not the type of "Free Love" Sinclair endorsed. He disliked the whole "Greenwich Village" feeling of the magazine and the strange modernist writing that *The Masses* published, with its "polyrhythmical" tones. But, as he also explained to Frank Harris at the time, "I disagree with both Pearsons and The Masses about the war, but I am prepared to do what I can to help maintain your right to say what you have to say about the war." So he protested the abuse they faced.[18]

On May 3, 1918, Sinclair pleaded with the federal attorney to leave the editors of *The Masses* alone. The attorney general's office shot back by saying that the magazine had gotten what it deserved and that their antiwar work had disrupted recruitment into the armed forces. So Sinclair wrote to Wilson directly, on May 18, 1918, condemning the attorney general's office and asking him to let the editors of *The Masses* go. All along, he argued that the best way to deal with the editors of an antiwar magazine was to allow them to make their case and then refute them in intelligent debate. The worst thing to do was to make them martyrs for those criticizing the war.[19]

Sinclair's protests didn't help much. By August 1917 Postmaster Burleson had held up issues going out in the mails and thus had stopped *The Masses* from being able to survive economically. But it didn't end there. In April 1918 the editors faced trial at a federal courthouse in New York City. They didn't take it too seriously, as was their style. The magazine's illustrator, Art Young, who corresponded with Sinclair, sent out notes to friends that read, "Come to the conspiracy Tuesday night. Yours, The Conspirators." Young then proceeded to fall asleep in the courtroom as the trial carried on, snoring away until his attorney poked him awake. Max Eastman, a philosopher by training, gave long monologues about questions of patriotism that baffled the prosecution. It seemed more like a humorous play than an actual trial. The jury met for a few days and then decided it could not reach a verdict. The editors walked.[20]

Sinclair kept pleading with the government to leave the editors alone, going straight to Wilson himself, explaining that the attorney general was a fool. Still, a second trial erupted in September. At this one, John Reed, whom Sinclair would label "the Playboy of the Social Revolution" since he was good-looking and always gallivanting around the world in search of the next big revolt, appeared, making it all the way back from Russia where he had been reporting on the Revolution. The trial again was a zoo. The sole testimony from a military man who subscribed to *The Masses* weakened the case that the magazine damaged morale. After all, the defense showed that this supposedly victimized subscriber had been promoted through the ranks. The prosecution closed with a speech about a friend killed in France. "Somewhere he lies dead, and he died for you and he died for me. He died for Max Eastman, he died for John Reed." Art Young, who was snoring away, suddenly woke up and shouted, "Didn't he die for me too?" The jurors burst into laughter. The prosecution's case looked silly, as if they thought people should be jailed for simply questioning the war. On October 5, 1918, the editors walked free again. But their magazine had been killed, and they had spent a great deal of time in the courtroom, arguing a case that seemed absurd.[21]

Sinclair's protest did nothing here. He would try to imply that if the government didn't look like such fools in prosecuting *The Masses* and *Pearson's*, it could stand on higher moral ground in order to prosecute the war. But Wilson did little to temper either Postmaster Burleson or the attorney general—the two officials doing the most to carry out the government's role as censor. As Frank Harris pointed out to Sinclair on August 20, 1918, he was still dealing with Burleson, who had practically put him out of business. When Sinclair got letters of reassurance from President Wilson's office that he was dealing with the matter, Harris told Sinclair, "I am afraid letters from the President do not alter the administration." Harris was right. As the historian David Kennedy recounted, Wilson might have leaned on Burleson, but not very hard. "When Wilson counseled leniency in the *Masses* case, Burleson threatened to resign. At that, Wilson reportedly laughed and said, 'Well, go ahead and do your duty.'" It was only when the more respectable magazine

The Nation was threatened in September 1918 that Wilson overruled Burleson, not out of conviction but because the situation was becoming a public relations fiasco. Sinclair could write to Wilson in October 1917, that "there is a way in which we can protect ourselves from false propaganda without so free a use of the policeman's club. The thing to do is answer it." The advice would have been compelling, if it had been taken. But Wilson had other things to do. It was like when Teddy Roosevelt told Sinclair that it was he and not Sinclair who ran the country. Except in this case, Wilson didn't even bother to take the time and write.[22]

In addition to censorship, the government threw critics of the war into jail. Most famous was Eugene Debs, a hero to Sinclair. After a speech in Canton, Ohio, in June 1918, Debs was imprisoned under the terms of the Sedition and Espionage Acts. Even worse, there were numerous conscientious objectors who lacked the cachet of Debs's name and therefore didn't get as much media attention. Sinclair condemned the retention of "political prisoners," implying it made America look as bad as Germany. He implored Wilson to release Debs, hinting that if the socialist leader died in jail (which was possible considering his age and health), radicals would commit acts of violence out of vengeance. Again, Sinclair tried to strike the nerve that seemed to work for Theodore Roosevelt's conservative radicalism; Wilson, though, was a different man. Sinclair did have some success when he heard from Newton Baker that the government was implementing a better policy for conscientious objectors, but there was no way to check whether this in fact had occurred. Nor did it do much about the general atmosphere in public that the government was creating. Local vigilantes were using the war as an excuse to attack immigrants and labor organizers. In Bisbee, Arizona, for instance, as Debs's biographer points out, "local patriots" working "in close association with state officials" rounded up 1,200 IWW copper miners and put them on railroad cars and "deported them into the New Mexico desert." Vigilantes consistently broke up Socialist Party meetings and lynched German Americans. The presidents of universities, including at Sinclair's alma mater, Columbia, fired professors who criticized the war. Sinclair might have been able to press the government, but there was very little he could do about these more nefarious forms of persecution.[23]

Sinclair learned quickly the dangers of supporting the war. There would be consequences out of his control, and though he might condemn these consequences, they could not be so easily stopped by a magazine with a subscription list of ten thousand readers. Some of his original reservations seemed to be coming back to haunt him as he watched the war being prosecuted. Wilson as war president, he believed, was witness to a "moral and intellectual collapse" unprecedented in history. One by one, all of the reasons for Sinclair to support the war vanished, and he was left with little more than doubt and anger about his original support.[24]

Take the international situation. As much as Sinclair hated German aggression, he believed the war should never be allowed to "humiliate" the people of Germany, especially when it came time to draw up the terms of peace. It was right to demand "democratization of Germany," but this required nuance and good diplomacy. Max Eastman argued with Sinclair that England would never allow Germany's democratization; its Toryism would stand in the way. Sinclair countered that there were liberals in England and that, besides, the United States would call the shots during peace negotiations. By February 1919 Sinclair was going so far as to prophesy that "Workers' councils will be in full control" of Germany "in a very few weeks." A revolt took place, to be sure, but the end result was not a workers' government but the Weimar Republic. And though this would seem to count for democratization, the diplomacy that surrounded it was not to Sinclair's liking. Wilson kowtowed to the British and the French, who wanted a punitive peace against Germany. The president even signed on with the "war guilt clause" that made Germany take responsibility for the war and pay out billions of dollars in reparations. Nothing more could have been done to "humiliate" the German people. Sinclair cabled Wilson's advisers: "All Liberals aghast at President Wilson's surrender. Urgently implore less drastic terms." But to no avail.[25]

Sinclair was also adamant that all territories freed during the war become self-governing. He telegrammed Wilson on February 3, 1917: "All territory taken from central powers in this war shall be neutralized and made forever independent under international guarantee." Wilson seemed to concur when he declared the Fourteen Points in January 1918, one of which declared the United States on the side of self-determination for all nations. But only three months later, Sinclair witnessed imperialist land grabs throughout Africa, and colonies liberated from Germany being turned over to France and Britain. Soon afterward, Sinclair accused Wilson of befriending the "reactionary forces of France and Italy and the intrenched power of triumphant British commercialism." He explained, "Every peace council has settled things on the basis that they shall take who have the power and they shall keep who can, and all the ruling class interests want to settle this war on that basis." Unfortunately, for Sinclair, the United States didn't stand up enough to prevent this. This became explicit when the Bolsheviks revealed a set of secret treaties that the czar of Russia, whom they had just deposed, had made with the Allies. The treaties handed Alsace, Lorraine, and the Saar valley—territory that Sinclair hoped would be governed internationally—to the French. Britain got much of Africa, while Japan would get some of China. These treaties embarrassed Wilson and disgusted Sinclair. The war to save democracy now appeared to be a war to save imperialism.[26]

The final blow on the international front came when the United States decided to turn its back on the League of Nations. After all, the "internation"—a clumsy word that Sinclair had incorporated into the subtitle of his own magazine—was crucial to the war's outcome, as he saw it. The League of Nations came fairly close to Sinclair's vision, so he must have been pleased when Wilson returned from Europe in order to convince Americans that their country had a moral obligation to enter this international compact. He would have been thrilled to hear that most Americans supported their country's entry. Europeans had treated Wilson as a hero when he traveled abroad, but upon his return to the United States, he met stiff opposition among politicians. He became ill in the process, suffering a stroke in October 1919, and was thus unable to fight a battle with his isolationist opponents. By March 1920 there was no chance the United States would enter the League of Nations. Once again, Sinclair's hopes were dashed; there might be an "internation," but the United States would not be a member.[27]

All of these international defeats came with domestic ones as well. The original excitement of those who thought the war would bring socialism to the United States died a quick death. Sinclair gritted his teeth when Wilson said that reconstruction at home should be carried out under the leadership of private business. Craig counseled optimism about Wilson during their late-night debates, but, as Sinclair told his readers, he "would have believed in" Wilson "if I could have believed in any capitalist statesman." He started worrying about war profits, and he condemned Wilson for turning the country back to the "profiteers" who would bust labor unions and deny bonuses to the soldiers who had done the fighting overseas. The blame fell mostly on Wilson himself. "Never," Sinclair explained in 1920, "did there live on earth a man with more genius for making the worse appear the better cause." To make himself clear, he added a week later, "I wish to repudiate the Wilson administration and all its works."[28]

Much of his disillusionment on the domestic front was Sinclair's own fault. He had not given up on his dangerous tendency to prophesy the future. He reminded readers of the "government labor bureau" he had predicted in *The Industrial Republic*. Well, he pointed out during the war, it found expression in the National War Labor Board. The point was well taken, but not this follow-up: "And is anyone so foolish as to suppose that we shall ever abolish it and go back to the old chaos of competition?" Sinclair mistook the emergency of war for a long-term change in the United States. Of course, there were people "foolish" enough to go back to the "chaos of competition." And that's precisely what happened. The reforms passed during the war that might have looked like a burgeoning welfare state were quickly scrapped after the war, including those pertaining to labor. And during the year following the war, labor unions faced resounding defeat. The only legislation that outlasted the war and that Sinclair supported was Prohibition. Sinclair championed the cause but would have a hard time arguing that it wasn't repressive in nature, even if it was the kind of repression he liked.[29]

As the progressive welfare legislation associated with the war came to an end, so too did *Upton Sinclair's*. The magazine folded in February 1919. It ended as the United States entered a new phase in its history—precisely when all of the problems generated during the war would run roughshod over the country. Sinclair ensured that he would continue to make public his growing disillusionment with the country. He cut a deal with Emanuel Haldeman-Julius, a socialist editor who lived in Girard, Kansas. The two agreed that Sinclair would hand over his subscription list and in return would do a regular column for a newspaper originally entitled *The New Appeal* (named after its predecessor, *The Appeal to Reason*), which then became, following Sinclair's example, *Haldeman-Julius Weekly*.

Red Scare

The year 1919 was one of the worst for America's radicals. There was immediate blowback from the United States' decision to extend World War I into a war against the Russian Bolsheviks midway through 1918. Two months before the war ended, eight thousand American troops entered "Archangel and into the Ukraine" and eastern Siberia, another reversal, as Sinclair took it, of a policy to allow for self-determination of all nations. Since Sinclair believed that the United States should "allow the Russian people to work out their own destiny, in their own way," he opposed intervention. But there can be no doubt that Wilson's anger about the Bolshevik decision to reveal the secret treaties had made his decision easy, as did the president's opposition to communist ideology. America's enemy changed from Germany to Russia almost overnight. Rumors spread quickly throughout the United States about what was happening in Russia. Sinclair's favorite rumor was that the state was prostituting its own women in what was called the "nationalization of women" scare. No doubt the Bolsheviks were a brutal ruling party turning into a dictatorship, but this could not justify the level of fear that erupted during the American "red scare."[30]

Some feared they saw the potential for a Bolshevik Revolution in the United States during the events that rocked 1919. That year, the first steps were taken to create a Communist Party within the United States, among the left-wing factions within the American Socialist Party. Labor union strikes increased, including one among Boston's police, who walked off their jobs, raising a fear of absolute social breakdown in the city. Attorney General Palmer promised to jail strike leaders in the coal industry. Then came the bombings. One went off at the attorney general's house in Washington, D.C. Sinclair fretted that he might be visited by authorities, as the bombings spread. Then came the shootings. In Centralia, Washington, during an Armistice Day parade, it was reported that IWW members shot four soldiers dead; Sinclair believed this to be a "frame-up." Panic had taken hold. "All over America today," Sinclair worried, "they are seizing radicals and throwing them into jail, deporting them if they are foreigners, holding them at prohibitive bail if they are American citizens, frequently beating them, torturing them under the polite formulas of the 'third degree.'" The infamous "Palmer raids" snatched six thousand radicals and arrested them. Over two hundred radicals were deported to Russia, without trial, on the Soviet Ark. And since no one on the left was to be trusted, five members of the Socialist Party, duly elected to the New York State Legislature, were expelled from office, even though they were "innocent of any offense." Some then tried "to bar the party from the ballot," as Sinclair pointed out.[31]

Much like the influenza epidemic a year earlier, which prevented Sinclair from going to the public library for a spell, the red scare of 1919 worked its way into the Los Angeles area like a virus. There were labor protests that hit essential services, including a streetcar strike and a telephone operator strike. These occurred amidst talk of a general strike on behalf of Tom Mooney, who had been convicted of bombing a Preparedness Day parade in San Francisco in 1916. Radicals like Sydney Flowers, a veteran of World War I who had lost a lung in the war, faced attack from conservative business elements in Los Angeles. None of these cases compared to California's Criminal Syndicalism Act, passed that fateful year and promoted by utility companies and conservative groups. Los Angeles had already passed an antipicketing ordinance to fight labor. The Criminal Syndicalism Act prohibited the flying of a red flag, suggesting that symbols of communism in general were banned.[32]

Sinclair steeled himself against these developments. In 1919 he explained to Max Eastman that "I packed up my intellectual baggage and made ready to move back to the left wing" of the Socialist Party. U.S. intervention in Russia angered him beyond words. The red scare made him even more angry with America. So he did what he often did: he wrote a book to express his dismay. He had already written *Jimmie Higgins*, about a normal, run-of-the-mill socialist who helped do the grunt work for the Socialist Party and then wound up fighting in World War I. Higgins opposes the war and witnesses Socialist Party meetings being broken up. After a stint as a bum and hobo, Higgins becomes a conscientious objector during the war, only to wind up serving in the war. Sinclair had expected to end the novel here, but then tacked on an ending about how Higgins goes to Russia, where he has to fight Bolsheviks. He resists and is tortured by the army for passing out Bolshevik literature and holding a Socialist Party membership.[33]

The book made obvious (excruciatingly so at times) Sinclair's anger about U.S. intervention in Russia, and his next showed his disgust at the red scare. Entitled *100%* (the term used to describe the sort of loyalty expected among Americans during the war), the novel focused on Peter Gudge, who is present at a veterans' gathering where bombs go off. He is taken in for questioning, and the police beat him and force him to become a spy. Gudge befriends Jennie, who is a Communist, and starts reporting about meetings with her back to a local detective. Unfortunately, Peter starts to have feelings for Jennie, and she for him, and she kills herself once Peter denies his desire to marry her. He justifies becoming a spy by "reminding himself that he was a 'he-man,' a 100% American, and that in these times of war every patriot must do his part." He winds up being at a meeting that is invaded by patriots who beat up participants while Gudge hides. The novel ends with Peter witnessing a Jewish man being handcuffed to a tree and whipped by members of the Chamber of Commerce and the Merchants and Manufacturers Association.[34]

Frank Harris, who had seen Postmaster Burleson wreck his magazine while Sinclair supported the war, read *100%*. Ironically, he considered it too harsh and over-the-top. At about the same time Harris told Sinclair he would have to stop publishing *Pearson's*. Here was a man who should have loved the angry reaction displayed within *100%*. After all, as Harris told Sinclair, the same forces had made it impossible for him to continue publishing *Pearson's*. As it was, Harris found *100%* too shrill. This tells us a lot. Sinclair was reacting too harshly for even those who had been victims of government repression during and after World War I. Sinclair had escaped relatively unscathed (he was never visited by federal agents the way he feared), and his magazine was blocked only from going to England, not from being published in the first place. For the first time, it seemed that perhaps Sinclair was overreacting. After all, the red scare of 1919 passed in the course of a year or so. But Sinclair was locking himself into a position based on his angry reaction to a brutal time.[35]

He was also backing himself into a dangerous political corner by defending Russia against his own country's intervention. Sinclair started as a Menshevik who believed that the early Russian Revolution against the czar was the right step to take. "I rejoiced when Kerensky came into power," he explained, "and hoped that Russia would stay in the war and postpone her proletarian revolt." Sinclair then followed the debates about the nature of the Russian Revolution, listening to the pro-Bolshevik John Reed, as well as the anarchist and anti-Bolshevist Peter Kropotkin. He himself remained a socialist who believed in an electoral path to reform, at least in the United States. He never joined the Communist Party of the United States. But he started to back down when people like John Reed told him that the Bolsheviks were the most promising agency of socialism that presently existed. "You are simply a theoretician, Upton," Reed chided him, "these Russians are practical." This must have smarted, since Sinclair was still reeling from the mistakes made involving the war. He had to admit that if there was a choice between Bolshevism and "our present system of wage slavery and exploitation, then I am a Bolshevist." Because he found himself so angry at his own country's behavior, he started to embrace its enemy. Those who should have been as angry as Sinclair, those who had been victimized by the war like Frank Harris, were starting to see a side to Sinclair that would continue to mire his political judgments.[36]

In 1919 Sinclair could still tell his critics that he hadn't been naive about the war. Sure, he still believed that the United States might break "the back of Prussianism," but he also recognized the power of "British imperialism, French Chauvinism, and the Young Snobbery of Italy, to say nothing of our old and unchastened enemy, Big Business at home." There was still a glimmer of hope. But by 1920, Sinclair would admit that he had been wrong about the war; Debs had been right. And as Debs still sat in prison, Sinclair imagined a meeting with him. It would have been a lot like the meeting between Emerson and Thoreau in jail about fifty years earlier. Emerson famously asked Thoreau why he was willing to go to jail for refusing to pay taxes that would have funded the United States' takeover of Mexico's land, including Texas. Thoreau retorted that he couldn't understand why Emerson *wasn't* in jail. Sinclair thought of himself as an Emerson who deserved scolding. This was a telling analogy. The war could have made Sinclair more tentative in his judgment, more humble in his political decisions. Instead, it seemed to harden him. By 1920 the red scare had passed, and Americans had grown tired of living in a state of perpetual tension. They were ready for a return to "normalcy." Unlike his fellow citizens, Sinclair still felt guilty for the things he had done and felt the need to seek revenge against the world for his own mistakes. Instead of coming out of the war and openly asking questions about his previous positions, he became fiercer in his beliefs. It was a point of view that made for an odd match with the decade to come.[37]

"PRIZE PRUDE OF THE RADICAL MOVEMENT"

1920–1930

*People ask me how I manage to keep cheerful in the
trying days of Coolidge, and I answer that the way
to be happy and successful in this life is to identify
yourself with some great cause, which has a future.*

—UPTON SINCLAIR, 1925

S INCLAIR WASN'T THE ONLY ONE DISILLUSIONED WITH THE WAR
and the red scare. Plenty of liberals and progressives grew distraught,
especially when Republican Warren Harding won the presidential election
in 1920 on the principle that "normalcy" should triumph over "heroism."
Harding wasn't just a conservative Republican, he seemed unbearably
dumb. H. L. Mencken described him as "a third-rate political wheel-horse
with the intelligence of a respectable agricultural implement dealer."
Harding himself came up with the term "bloviating" in describing his own
speaking. But still, it was the political dimension of his victory that really
hurt. Herbert Croly, the editor of the *New Republic*, who grew increasingly
gloomy throughout the 1920s, remarked, "The chief distinguishing aspect
of the Presidential campaign of 1920 is the eclipse of liberalism or progressivism as an effective force in American politics." The 1920s became one
of the most well-defined decades in American history, set off largely by its
political conservatism, beginning with the election of Harding, then
Calvin Coolidge, who equated business and religion, and then Herbert
Hoover, who, though more progressive than his predecessors, remained
steadfast that only voluntary activity could pull the United States out of
the Depression that hit during his presidency.[1]

The collapse of liberal and progressive ideals at the presidential level mirrored a similar collapse below. As a friend of Sinclair's, Frederic Howe, put it, "Most of the radicals of pre-war days laid down their arms" after World War I. "Tired Radicals" dropped out of politics as conservative politicians repealed Progressive Era legislation. Business reasserted leadership over society and politics, as Calvin Coolidge and others hoped it would. If government abdicated responsibility for providing welfare for its citizens, business would step in. "Corporate welfarism," as it has been called, arose. Large corporations that could absorb costs experimented with "stock purchase and profit-sharing plans, company-built housing for sale or rent, group life insurance, health and dental care for employees and their families, and improved wages and working conditions," plus "recreational" opportunities. Henry Ford famously paid his workers more while cutting their hours (in hopes they would buy his cars). King Gillette, the razor baron, even met with Sinclair during the 1920s to tell him how much his own ideas about business management were akin to socialism. None of these business leaders had to worry that muckraking journalists might be snooping about and exposing their charity as insincere. As Sinclair pointed out, the magazines that constituted the backbone of the muckraking movement—*McClure's, Everybody's,* the *American, Metropolitan, Collier's*—declined around the time of the war, abandoning the challenge of exposing wealth's corruption. This left an open playing field for business to triumph without any scrutiny from naysayers.[2]

If liberalism and progressivism seemed muzzled, socialism fell entirely off America's political map. The red scare had taken its toll, as did the economic prosperity of the 1920s. Sinclair asserted in the mid-1920s that "the Socialist movement in this country is paying the penalty of having opposed the war. Socialists are now powerless." This wasn't entirely fair, seeing as the party's membership actually grew during the war. But it was certainly true after the war. The party was racked by internal debate and fissure. In 1919 the left-wingers in the party pledged themselves to the Bolshevik Revolution in Russia, becoming at first the Communist Labor Party and then the Communist Party of the United States. They emphasized internationalism and bulked up their foreign-language federations, only heightening fear in the United States that radicalism was little more than a foreign ideology. Those who remained among the Socialist Party's dwindling ranks watched leadership move from Eugene Debs, who died in 1926, to Norman Thomas. Debs had arisen out of America's labor movement, Thomas out of the Congregational ministry. Debs knew the world of the working class, while Thomas seemed more scholarly and intellectual. Throughout the 1920s, the Socialist Party became more marginalized.[3]

Sinclair had rejoined the Socialist Party officially in 1920, repairing the bonds frayed by the war. His own reentry symbolized the party's marginality. During his first year back, he was drafted as a candidate for public office. After receiving a pitiful 20,000 votes in a run for Congress in 1920, he went on to run for the Senate in 1922. "The office sought the man," he assured his readers, "I didn't know it was to be offered to me." He admitted having "few talents" in terms of "political campaigning," and it showed in the small number of votes he received in 1922. It was hard to figure out whether he even campaigned at all. His lackluster run symbolized just how weak socialism had become. Indeed, by 1924, Sinclair didn't even vote socialist when it came to the presidential election. Socialism seemed nowhere to be found on the ballot or in the nation.[4]

With fewer political opportunities, Sinclair turned to writing, settling into a quiet life of reclusiveness and genteel bohemianism. Though he bought a car in 1918, Sinclair still lived a rustic lifestyle. He explained to Roger Baldwin in 1923, "I live very simply in a five room house. We keep no servant, and we drive a four year old Dodge car, and I wear cast-off clothing" that was passed on to him by Kate Crane-Gartz, whom he called "Craney Gartz." He tried to keep the outside world at bay in order to live quietly, but found that hard since people, especially young pesky writers seeking advice, would climb through his bathroom window if they couldn't get him at the front door. Upton and Craig even bought a second home in Long Beach in order to escape. To get out of the house, Sinclair would go to the Pasadena Tennis Club, where unsurprisingly his temper would flare at the wealthy jerks who hogged the courts. He still bemoaned the fact that he couldn't play on Sundays. He also remained interested in fasting and explored the strange medical practices of Dr. Albert Abrams, who used blood specimens and tapped on the body to try to diagnose illness. He was plagued by a wife who was constantly sick and whose neurasthenia turned his home into a "hospital." On rare occasions Sinclair would allow reporters, who were eager for updates about America's left-wing celebrity, into his home. One story in the *L.A. Record* fixated on Sinclair's small swimming pool and concluded, "Sinclair Doesn't Look Like a Radical." Though his political party had shriveled, Sinclair himself was certainly still a radical, even if he didn't look like one. He might have been marginalized now that the political situation in the United States had changed, and he sometimes appeared dated, but he was still a radical and still something of a celebrity.[5]

An Era of Wonderful Nonsense
When Mencken Was King

The sense that progressivism had died out in the United States framed the decade of the 1920s. It wasn't just the decade's conservative politics, it was how Americans seemed to throw themselves into a frenzy of diversionary fads—the Charleston, bathtub gin, fur coats—that economic prosperity offered. Terms for the 1920s as a decade were quickly invented before the decade had run out. There was the "Wasted Decade," "the Jazz Age," and "the Era of Wonderful Nonsense." "America has made a lot of money," Sinclair explained, "and spent it on idleness and futility. The mind of America is under the control of perfectly conscienceless and unscrupulous big business plunderers." Even so, it seemed to numerous social commentators that Americans were having a good time enjoying themselves while big business plundered away.[6]

Surprising though it might seem, much of American cultural life during the 1920s was indebted to changes Sinclair had helped push through before World War I. Equality between the sexes, birth control, relaxed prohibitions on divorce, the primacy of self-expression over the accumulation of wealth, a life of experimentation over conformity to preset rules—these features of prewar bohemia seemed to leave the confines of Greenwich Village and Carmel and seep into middle-class life during the 1920s. Cultural rebellion became fashionable, and this pushed radicals like Sinclair to reconsider their own radicalism. As historian Michael McGerr points out, "The emphasis on individual freedom and the pursuit of pleasure, especially among the young, left aging progressives disappointed and even aghast." This was certainly true for Sinclair, whose Puritan streak seemed to solidify as the 1920s marched on.[7]

One of the most popular symbols of American culture during the 1920s was the flapper. With the right to vote (assured by the passage of the Nineteenth Amendment in 1920), younger women started to seek parity with men in other areas as well. Some started to look more androgynous, bobbing their hair and wearing streamlined clothing that hid their natural curves. The flapper, in the words of historian Lynn Dumenil, wore a "minimum of undergarments, short skirts, filmy fabrics, and sheer hose" in order to enhance "sexuality" but also kept this "in bounds" by putting up a "boyish look." Some wore galoshes, others slathered on cosmetics. They danced provocatively while smoking and drinking—even if it was harder to find gin during Prohibition. And in face of such behavior, Sinclair grew dismayed. There was nothing radical about any of this, he thought, nothing intended to change the underlying fabric of American society. He condescended to the young female crowd, "Let me explain the flapper to herself: She is a product of a parasitic civilization," a civilization, he went on to explain, that is full of "vanity, folly, and luxury." As far as their dancing went, Sinclair sputtered: "I think that jazz dances are awkward and ugly, being imitations of savage sex dances." The "revolution in morals" that the flapper symbolized and that Sinclair noted in the generation coming of age while he puttered away into his forties was little more than a reflection of the larger society. The "freedom" of the flapper and other young people was an expression of "capitalist decadence" and little else.[8]

Sinclair's social criticism grew impudent during the decade. He laughed at how Americans embraced "youth" by living vicariously through the mindless activities of college campuses—the moblike rituals of fraternity houses or the whooping crowds flying pennants at football games. He chastised the "petting parties" prevalent among young people as well as the silent movies adults watched, which showed young women seducing rich men, promoting "lust" over "love." Sinclair documented the orgies and drunken escapades among the wealthier classes, where he saw men living "lives of unbridled lust." He coughed at cigarette smoking, plugged his ears to the sound of jazz, and let the drain run on the bathtub gin of the era. At one point, he called himself the "prize prude of the radical movement."[9]

The decade's nonsense might have been more bearable if the intellectuals hadn't surrendered to it. The innovative political thinking of the Progressive Era had passed away, as had its activism. For Sinclair, what remained was an intellectual cynicism that paralleled the escapism of youth culture. There were the writers who gathered at the Algonquin Round Table, showing off their wit in snide remarks made about their enemies. Dorothy Parker's cynical poems, one of which famously laid out different means of committing suicide, represented the mind-set of writers, as did Heywood Broun's reviews of Sinclair's work during the 1920s. Broun was a sports journalist who was edging toward Sinclair's own socialist politics. But for Broun, Sinclair was "humorless," the highest insult offered by the Algonquin wits. They sat around and drank bathtub gin and wrote for the fashionable pages of *Vanity Fair* and the *New Yorker*. They laughed a lot, fitting in with the general tone of American cultural life, as Sinclair saw it.[10]

The Algonquin Round Table members certainly laughed, but their cynicism about life was profoundly serious and reflected an intellectual tendency in the 1920s that went deep. Many intellectuals struggled during the decade with what Walter Lippmann called the "acids of modernity." As religion declined in power, Lippmann believed, mature adults had to learn how to live without any overarching meaning; they had to temper the passionate faith that religion once encouraged. Joseph Wood Krutch, a contemporary of Lippmann's who wrote *The Modern Temper*, also believed that the world was bereft of meaning now that religion had lost out to modern science. The decline of faith and the rise of "pessimism" would now leave the "soul" in a state of feeling "dry." Modern citizens, Lippmann and Krutch argued, would be like the readers of T. S. Eliot's "The Wasteland" (published in 1922). They could no longer find meaning in life, as the shards of religious belief were tossed aside. "These fragments I have shored against my ruins" offered very little, or so Eliot suggested in the last lines of his famous modernist poem.[11]

The "acids of modernity" were also captured in the novels of the "lost generation," especially Ernest Hemingway's. Injured during World War I, he drifted through Europe as an expatriate. His novels and writings seemed to embrace a life of meaninglessness. *The Sun Also Rises* told the story of Jake, who saunters from café to café, impotent due to a war injury. At one point, a man in a café describes him as an expatriate, explaining that "you drink yourself to death" and "become obsessed by sex" and spend "all your time talking, not working." The passion of romance is just another ideal thrown away by Hemingway's characters. When Jake says farewell to a woman he loved, Brett, she tells him, "we could have had such a damned good time together." "Yes," he replies, "Isn't it pretty to think so?" This coldness toward the ideal of love turned more brutal in *A Farewell to Arms*, a novel that quickly deflated military heroism by having the main character get injured while eating cheese, rather than fighting on the front lines. The book ends with the same character walking away after his wife dies during childbirth.[12]

For Sinclair, this sadness, as well as Hemingway's flatness in the way he described it, reflected the inaccurate assumptions the lost generation brought to their work. "The young fellows who went through the war are old and grim," Sinclair explained. "They write with cold precision, scorn all emotions, and deny themselves the luxury of having any ideas." In reviewing a novel by Sherwood Anderson (a writer who helped promote Hemingway's writing), Sinclair asked why it was that all of his characters seemed damaged and unhappy. In reacting against Hemingway and Anderson (as well as the playwright Eugene O'Neill), Sinclair believed he had a moral mission that could carry him through the 1920s. "We are living in a time of cynicism, a perfectly natural reaction from the war," he explained to Louis Adamic, a writer who struggled to find his voice during the 1920s, "and I am trying to save a few of the young writers from it."[13]

Adamic himself was a lot like a character in *The Sun Also Rises* who believed that "many young men get their likes and dislikes from Mencken." H. L. Mencken, the editor of the *American Mercury* and a leading literary critic and journalist, towered over the young intelligentsia of the 1920s, his celebrity status serving as an almost perfect displacement of Sinclair's prior to World War I. Mencken was an acerbic critic who felt no solidarity with the working-class Americans Sinclair had embraced. For Mencken, the American people were "the most timorous, sniveling, poltroonish, ignominious mobs of serfs and goose-steppers ever gathered under one flag in Christendom since the end of the Middle Ages." The United States was a "glorious commonwealth of morons" and an "Eden of clowns." To call Mencken's attitude cynical barely does justice to it. He thought of his magazine as a publication for "the civilized minority," and he openly embraced Nietzsche's argument in favor of an aristocracy saving civilization from the perils of democracy, which he associated with stupidity and the reign of the unbearably average.[14]

Ironically, Mencken and Sinclair became friends during the 1920s. Their friendship paralleled the earlier relationship Sinclair had with Jack London (though Mencken was about as far away from socialism as someone could get). When Sinclair went to Baltimore in 1922 in order to research a book, he looked up Mencken. Sinclair even arranged a visit to his uncle Bland's house (a place where Mencken as a boy would have been prohibited, since he was a German and thus not of the right stock). Bland and Mencken blathered on about "various brands of wines, brandies, and whiskies" while Sinclair grew bored. "Partly, of course, it was done to 'kid me,'" Sinclair explained later. Mencken wrote Sinclair a nice letter in 1925 and queried: "When are you coming East? I have" a "plan to get you off the water-wagon." When Sinclair found out that Mencken was coming to Hollywood a year later, he explained he would get a "cordial welcome" and that perhaps they could go see Aimee Semple

McPherson, a celebrity who had led religious revivals in Los Angeles at the Angeles Temple and whooped up old-time religion even though she was divorced and more like a Hollywood star (she was called "the Mary Pickford of revivalism") than a typical evangelical preacher. Sinclair warned Mencken that if they went, he'd have to "behave." When Mencken arrived, he had a fine time with Sinclair but probably even a better one getting drunk and playing a piano in a local whorehouse or going to "Hollywood parties" and "having tea with Mary Pickford" when Sinclair wasn't around. When asked later about Mencken's visit, Sinclair told people that he had tried to make a socialist out of Mencken, while Mencken tried to "make a drunkard out of me." After Mencken had passed away, Sinclair described their friendship as "a long series of feuds, punctuated by cheerful visits and vigorous correspondence."[15]

Their feuds held a wider meaning for American culture in the 1920s. For Sinclair, it wasn't just a coincidence that America's most popular writer during this decade was an antidemocrat, libertarian, antisocialist, anti-Prohibitionist cynic. It fit the larger picture for him. Though he disagreed with Mencken, Sinclair learned a great deal from him. Mencken was a thrilling writer who could turn a phrase perfectly in order to bludgeon his enemies and stir the hearts of America's "smart set." Sinclair would praise his "fighting qualities," especially when it came to debunking religion, but as he said to Louis Adamic, "scolding is not enough; you have to know what to do to remedy the affairs, and Mencken does not know." Of course, Mencken felt it was enough for a critic to say what was wrong in society; he didn't feel it necessary to outline a program of salvation. Sinclair was expecting too much from a critic, as he had expected too much from an artist (whose responsibility, in his eyes, was not just to produce beauty, but also a political message). Later, Sinclair came closer to the truth when analyzing Mencken's faults: it wasn't that his writing lacked a political solution but that it was over-the-top and altogether too insular for a self-congratulatory "civilized minority." Sinclair would argue that Mencken was a "man who would make any statement, no matter how fantastic, which would get a guffaw out of the mob which followed him." Sinclair was right to believe that Mencken fit the culture of the 1920s because his cynicism closed out hope, and Sinclair was not about to let cynicism close out hope. It might be a while before his own brand of politics came into fashion again, but he could still write with the hope that it eventually would.[16]

The "Dead Hand" Slaps Back:
Religion, the Press, and Schools

For Sinclair, intellectuals of the 1920s were making mountains out of molehills, turning the war and the red scare into issues that overwhelmed them with cynicism. To think that there was no meaning in life or that all passion was dangerous—these ideas were just plain silly. Sinclair would try to show this by waging a one-man war against the assumptions of the intelligentsia. Though he might allow his name to slip onto the ballot occasionally, his primary focus during the 1920s was writing works of social criticism that held out the hope of socialism and thereby defeated the popular cause of intellectual cynicism. Sinclair claimed he could do more by "writing my books than I can by messing in the peanut politics of our City of Black Angels." So he wrote and wrote and wrote. He learned from Mencken how to throw barbs, how to become an effective social critic in spite of his moralism. But Mencken's ironic distance from life (when asked why he remained in the United States and didn't expatriate since he hated the country so much, Mencken asked, "Why do men go to zoos?") could never become Sinclair's. Life burned with meaning for Sinclair—too much so at times. Sinclair didn't fit the intellectual feel of the 1920s, and his work would become, somewhat like Mencken's, more insular as the decade passed, albeit for different reasons.[17]

Sinclair's major project during this decade became known as the "Dead Hand" series—a group of books that took aim at what sociologist C. Wright Mills would later call the "cultural apparatus." Sinclair decided to examine those institutions that disseminated beliefs and values throughout society. The underlying assumption of all these books was that social institutions reflected the needs of capitalism: Sinclair would rip through religion, the press, schools, art, and literature and see a burrowing force underneath them all. He'd point to that burrowing force in all cases, and this made the series at times both insightful and tiresome.

The series got its start during the war. While U.S. soldiers died overseas, Sinclair published a book that would come back to haunt him throughout his life. It was called *The Profits of Religion*, and it was a book that nicely fit the mood of the 1920s. Mencken loved it, and so too did the decade's most famous novelist, Sinclair Lewis. But it was also a Marxist book in its take on religion. "Man is an evasive beast," Sinclair explained, "given to cultivating strange notions about himself." Religion is a "myth and dogma used as source of income and a shield to privilege." "The thesis of this book," Sinclair explained, as if what he had already said hadn't made the point, "is the effect of fixed dogma in producing mental paralysis, and the use of this mental paralysis by Economic Exploitation." In making this argument, Sinclair drew ideas from the rich tradition of radical anticlericalism in American social thought that ran from Thomas Paine to Orestes Brownson (a protosocialist thinker whose most famous works were published in the 1840s). The priesthood for Sinclair elevated itself above the working class; it did not work with its hands and used that to impose its power over the rest of society. Thus, religious institutions perpetuated themselves by making people intellectually lazy and justifying the status quo.[18]

Once the reader learned this argument, the rest of the book read like a catalogue of religious blunders. Catholicism, for instance, was stupid and authoritarian, its membership always attacking public schools while loathing literacy. The evangelicals, on the other hand, took the "revolutionary hope of Jesus" and turned it into the idea of a "kingdom of heaven upon earth" and a "dream of a golden harp in an uncertain future" rather than a struggle to improve social relations along the lines of Christ's ethics. Billy Sunday, undoubtedly one of the decade's more popular preachers, displayed little more than a "childish crudity of mind." After *The Profits of Religion* had been released, Sinclair would go on to attack the "holy rollers"—those "ghastly sects which cultivate the religious hysterias and have spread like a plague among the women of our lonely prairie farms and decent ranchers." But it wasn't just the more traditional religions that Sinclair attacked. He lambasted the inheritors of Mary Baker Eddy's "New Thought" gospel, which advocated the power of "mind cure." Taking a term that sounded Mencken-like, Sinclair called Eddy's teachings "unadulterated moonshine," since they justified present-day social arrangements by blaming those at the bottom of the social hierarchy for not thinking their way out of their status. Not surprisingly, Mencken considered *The Profits of Religion* to be Sinclair's best book. It was just the sort of intellectual dynamite he liked.[19]

But it did something that wound up rubbing Mencken the wrong way. It teased out the elements of religious faith that Sinclair cherished. One thing often lost in Sinclair's materialist read of religion—his argument that religion's primary purpose was to help justify social inequality—was that Sinclair was no materialist. Here again was a way in which Sinclair didn't fit the intellectual mold of the 1920s; instead, he imported the

"Social Gospel" that was popular prior to World War I in order to map out an alternative to the atheism popular among thinkers like Walter Lippmann and Joseph Wood Krutch. You could hear it in his criticism of the evangelicals; they were guilty of suppressing the revolutionary content of Christ's message—his argument that all believers are equal in the eyes of God, no matter their social standing, and that the poor were closer to God than the wealthy. Sinclair followed theologians of the Social Gospel like Walter Rauschenbusch, who believed that Christ's life—his giving alms to the poor and shedding wealth while asking forgiveness for the faithful—should serve as the model of Christian behavior, rather than the rituals of a specific church. Indeed, Sinclair celebrated Bouck White, the Social Gospel minister who had been arrested during the protests held at John D. Rockefeller Jr.'s church in 1914. Amidst the perversions of religion, Sinclair could still manage to find redemption.[20]

What better target after the churches than the press? Sinclair's next book in his series would help him seek revenge against those who had reported irresponsibly on Helicon Hall and his divorce and who had suppressed coverage of Colorado's mining wars. The Brass Check became a classic in media criticism. "It is the thesis of this book," Sinclair explained, "that American newspapers as a whole represent private interests and not public interests." Once that point was made, the rest came easy. In documenting his cases, though, some thought he was in dangerous territory. When he showed The Brass Check to a lawyer friend, Sinclair was told the book contained "fifty criminal libel cases." He dissected the way advertising dollars influenced editorial decisions and how businessmen weighed in to suppress stories. He showed that the Associated Press acted like a business monopoly that, by ignoring certain stories, could make it seem as though those stories didn't exist. Sinclair wasn't afraid to name names: the New York Times did a lousy job of reporting, he said. Many of his accusations rang true, but some read like personal sniping about the fact that what he thought was worth covering was not being covered, while what was unimportant was (including all sorts of details from his own life). This not only weakened Sinclair's argument, but also increased the likelihood of a lawsuit. The president of the Associated Press thought of pursuing one, and so did the New York Times. But Sinclair felt sure they wouldn't because it would take too much money and would give Sinclair's claims undue publicity. He was right.[21]

Though the book often read like a catalogue of bad press decisions about things dear to Sinclair's heart and thus in places became tedious, Sinclair would put into practice the principle that he had laid out for H. L. Mencken: "Scolding is not enough." There were some very basic lessons that Sinclair laid out, and it is remarkable how some of them have turned into reality today. He suggested that interviewees should be checked to verify statements before a story ran, something good journalists do now. He argued for journalists to unionize in order to get better wages and protect their profession; the next decade would witness Heywood Broun, not a friend of Sinclair's by any means, leading a successful struggle to organize the Newspaper Guild. He suggested that newspapers should refuse advertising, which was impracticable, but public broadcasting came close to this model years later. Sinclair's biggest policy proposal—public ownership without control over content—would never become a reality. Nonetheless, Sinclair rightfully stands as the godfather of media reform, a movement that lived long after *The Brass Check* was published in 1919.

Three years after his media rebuke was published, Sinclair was struggling over his next book. He planned to take on the world of education, and he decided he had enough information to fill two volumes, one on higher education, the other on kindergarten through high school. He hopped on a train and visited college campuses, arranging meetings with disgruntled professors and taking copious notes. He also did some speaking to generate publicity for his work. The president of the University of Wisconsin blocked his speech, and Sinclair—proving once again that he was a master at turning bad press into good—wound up getting two thousand students to turn out for his talk. At the University of Chicago, he pleaded for a bigger hall, and after the president there refused, Sinclair got eight hundred students to file outside to hear him speak. After both of these events and his interviews and a series of letters, Sinclair had enough material to write *The Goose-Step*.[22]

The book had its predecessors: Thorstein Veblen had already dissected trustee influence over colleges in *The Higher Learning in America* (1918); James Cattell had articulated a case for faculty self-governance in *University Control* (1913); and James Harvey Robinson had theorized principles of democratic higher education in *The Mind in the Making* (1921) and other works. Still, Sinclair managed to turn a muckraker's eye to the problem, documenting case after case of presidents, acting on behalf of conservative (and typically wealthy) trustees, firing professors at will for unpopular beliefs. Stanford University, started by railroad barons in California, remained under the control of Mrs. Stanford, who demanded that Professor Edward Ross be fired for his socialist-leaning politics.

Sinclair's neighbor at Arden, Scott Nearing, faced the wrath of the University of Pennyslvania and was fired for his unpopular beliefs. A Montana professor was fired when he released a study of how mining companies paid little or no taxes. Thorstein Veblen was not allowed to teach at Cornell University, though the course catalogues listed his name. The power of the university president didn't stop here. This sort of retribution was made easier during the red scare. The president of Harvard harassed Professor Harold Laski for supporting the Boston Police Strike of 1919. Sinclair rightfully made a big deal out of Professor James Cattell's battle with Nicholas Murray Butler, president of Sinclair's graduate alma mater, Columbia, who seized upon the war and Cattell's support of conscientious objectors to force the professor out. Sinclair focused much of his venom on Butler, exposing case after case of Butler's ruthless leadership. When asked if he worried about a libel suit, Sinclair explained, "A man like Butler has made so many enemies that he cannot face the thought of having them come on the witness stand and tell their opinions of him for publication in the newspapers." Once again, Sinclair was right.[23]

Besides megalomaniac presidents, Sinclair also took on the elevated status of college athletics, which he labeled a "monstrous cancer." Sports were a sop for keeping the alumni—a conservative force in academia, as far as Sinclair was concerned, that hoped to preserve its own experience in college—happy. They added to the overall degradation of professorial life, since many college coaches snagged higher salaries than those who taught. By emphasizing brute physical force—in the form of football, the most popular sport of them all during the 1920s—and moblike behavior among the fans, college sports destroyed what should have been its most important task—nurturing intellectual talents in students. It looked to Sinclair as if colleges were losing sight of their purpose as they catered to social pressures. On this count, he hit the mark.[24]

Once again, Sinclair set out a solution to the problem. He had met with numerous incensed professors during the research for this book. Why not, he reasoned, turn the governance of these institutions over to them? He praised the work of the New School for Social Research, organized by professors who had broken from the reign of Nicholas Murray Butler at Columbia. James Harvey Robinson, Charles Beard, and Thorstein Veblen had joined together to form a school run mostly by faculty and for the explicit purpose of educating students, even if that entailed controversial matter.

Of course, the New School was an exception to the rule, and for other institutions, Sinclair insisted that faculty should try to assert control via faculty senates or better yet by unionizing. Sinclair believed faculty were ready to unionize, although "their class prejudices stand in the way." This was precisely the reason Sinclair had documented how presidents fired professors at will. The college professor (this before tenure was instituted) had no more rights than a factory worker. What better case for employee protection, for contracts and collective bargaining? Sinclair believed that the "dignity of the intellectual worker depends upon the establishment of industrial democracy." He was coming full circle to an idea learned in his youth—that those who produce culture were not all that different from those who produced clothing or even meat in Chicago's stockyards.[25]

The book did fairly well, likely selling (or so Sinclair believed) to the disgruntled professoriate of America. It was a well-argued book, piling case upon case and then drawing out broader principles. It was stronger than *The Brass Check* because it didn't seem to have the author's personal grudges standing behind it (except perhaps the vehemence that Butler faced in its pages). But it did have a weakness that an otherwise sympathetic reader pointed out. James Harvey Robinson, having dedicated himself to building the New School for Social Research after leaving Columbia University, gave Sinclair advice on the book. When it came out, he wrote Sinclair a kind letter that included a brutal criticism. Though there might be an "unconscious conspiracy," Robinson explained, Sinclair's story overdid it. "The people we blame are hardly so individually responsible as you sometimes seem to infer. Responsibility implies much clearer thinking than those you attack are commonly capable of." Robinson's point was legitimate not only in the case of *The Goose-Step* but in all of the works of the "Dead Hand" series. Too often, the books placed blame too harshly, too conspiratorially. The enemy was known before the story was told and thus the story itself became a clutter of details.[26]

This could be seen in the next book of Sinclair's ongoing series, *The Goslings*. It was easy to figure out what Sinclair would say about America's high schools: they were training grounds for America's businesses. After all, the founder of public schools in America, Horace Mann, had argued that smarter students could become better employees. In Sinclair's time, the National Association of Manufacturers, the Chamber of Commerce, the American Bankers' Association, and the National Industrial Conference Board all pushed for schools to focus on business-minded schooling; they had a victory with passage of the Smith-Hughes Act, which promoted vocational education in secondary schools and was passed during

World War I. Businesses wanted docile employees who would learn regimentation in the schools that they would then apply at the workplace. But business did not want just good employees, they also wanted good consumers. Sinclair pointed out how textbook companies racked up profits by taking advantage of their captured audience of students. The schools became an extension of the business society they fed.[27]

The story grew sad at times. Even the National Education Association (NEA), the professional organization that was supposed to represent teachers and the public interest, was in bed with the administrations of local schools. The high number of female teachers, Sinclair believed, allowed the profession to be pushed around and helped prevent unionization. Across the country, public school system after public school system fell prey to the demands of businesses and conservative forces. At one point, Sinclair wrote: "We go from city to city, and I wonder, will you grow tired of reading the same things over and over?" This passage betrayed the problem of this book and the others in the "Dead Hand" series: They became wearisome. And it seemed that perhaps Sinclair himself was growing weary. What was the purpose of documenting case after case of the same exact thing? Sinclair seemed tired, and, as often happened, his desire to move beyond writing and to change the world in concrete ways took hold. For a moment, he dropped the "Dead Hand" series (though he would return to it) in order to reenter the world of activism.[28]

A Respite in the Form of Activism

Sinclair's return to activism showed how much things changed politically during the 1920s. He wound up being a staunch defender of civil liberties and the right to protest during a very conservative age. As it had been in the past, labor-union organizing galvanized his activism. A strike in San Pedro, a harbor town near Los Angeles, generated backlash by the police, who Sinclair believed were acting on behalf of the Merchants and Manufacturers Association, who hoped to smash the strike. Sinclair always admired the IWW, the union leading the strike, but he seemed less aggrieved by the issues provoking the strike than by the violations of civil liberties it had prompted. Sinclair rarely spoke about the actual demands of the strikers, and he didn't seem to be acting the way he had during the Colorado strike, when he lobbied Wilson to settle the strike the way Theodore Roosevelt had, by threatening to nationalize the mines. Instead, he stood up for the protesters supporting the strike and their civil liberties. He did this the best way he knew how—he got arrested.[29]

Sinclair went to San Pedro in order to support the strikers and read the Constitution and emphasize its support for free speech. The chief of police, Louis Oaks, was ready for him, arguing that Sinclair was "more dangerous than 4,000 IWW's." Sinclair was promptly arrested on private property for being a nuisance. When Sinclair cited the Constitution, the aggravated police chief supposedly screamed at Sinclair, "Don't pull this Constitution stuff on me!" Sinclair was taken to jail and denied access to legal help. Craig was frantic, trying to get her husband out of jail, and once she finally tracked him down, he was released. But instead of letting it go there, he worked with the American Civil Liberties Union—then just a few years old—to hold public meetings to condemn his arrest and the action of Police Chief Oaks. The meetings drew five thousand people to one rally and two thousand to another in May 1923. They succeeded in drawing attention to the case. As far as the strikers were concerned, they faced fewer attacks, but eventually, they returned to work and remained without a union until the 1930s.[30]

The longest-term result of all this was the formation of a Southern California American Civil Liberties Chapter. The public meetings helped generate interest, and Sinclair, realizing that he couldn't run such an organization by himself, spent a few months forming committees that dealt with membership, finance, literature, and recruiting speakers. He also helped recruit Clinton Taft, who had been a Congregational minister, to lead the organization successfully. As a national organization, the ACLU had been galvanized by World War I and the red scare. Its leader, Roger Baldwin, had formed the National Civil Liberties Bureau during the war, working on the issue of conscientious objectors and their political status. Jailed during the war for his activism, Baldwin was released and formed the ACLU on January 20, 1920. Baldwin hoped the organization would spread throughout the United States, and bringing the ACLU to the West was no small feat for Sinclair, considering the legacy of frontier justice and the antiunion sentiment that generated the original attack on the San Pedro workers.[31]

Sinclair remained involved, doing what he was good at—publicity. He not only established, but wrote regularly for, the *Open Forum*, which was the organization's newspaper. He helped the ACLU create "an open forum at the Fine Arts Hall in Los Angeles every Sunday evening" which drew about "a thousand people" each meeting in the early stages, declining to about five hundred people in the later months of 1923 and then tapering off from there. Whenever a high-profile case arose, Sinclair was the first to suggest the ACLU take the lead in the fight. He suggested that the ACLU protest the "Long Beach refusal of the Municipal Auditorium to [Eugene] Debs," who had been released from jail by President Harding and was now doing a speaking tour. He also defended an organizer of the Communist Party, Charlotte Anita Whitney, who was being sent to jail due to the state's infamous criminal syndicalism act. Sinclair hoped this case could generate "a state-wide campaign to rouse public sentiment against this law." He argued that he didn't support the Communist Party and that the state threatened to raise the party's profile by making its leadership into martyrs. His case for Whitney went down to defeat, but he continued to fight nonetheless, protesting the American Legion's invasion of Socialist Party meetings during the late 1920s and early 1930s and the Criminal Syndicalism Law as well.[32]

Much of this activism seemed rearguard in nature. Sinclair wasn't helping the cause of labor or socialism, just the right of the cause to exist and vocalize itself. He still believed there was a positive political philosophy undergirding his activism and that he wasn't just attacking government or mobs for infringing freedoms. He philosophized that his civil liberties work nurtured an "active constructive citizenship" as the basis of American democracy. The Bill of Rights protected citizen activism and thus nurtured a public sphere of debate and participation that could then flourish, as seen in the ACLU's defense of both the left and the right, including the organization's defense of the KKK in Boston and the Salvation Army in Los Angeles. If it wasn't necessarily rearguard in nature, it was certainly motivated by Sinclair's residual guilt from supporting America in World War I and the repercussions of the red scare that he felt ill prepared to face.[33]

Indeed, Sinclair never seemed to leave the red scare behind. It was a constant reminder for him of America's nastier side, the one that the Bill of Rights had tried to temper. If Sinclair's activism during 1923 into 1924 was dominated by civil rights cases (as was his continued activism surrounding the publication of his novel *Oil!*), his writings from this period that were not a part of the "Dead Hand" series also expressed the legacy of the red scare. There was *They Call Me Carpenter*, published in 1922, a novel that updated the Jesus story by having Christ reborn in Los Angeles, siding with the IWW during a strike, and then assaulted by mobs. There was *Hell*, a play about radicals being tossed to the devil. There was his 1924 play *Singing Jailbirds*, whose central character, Red, is placed in jail for labor activism, left to hallucinate in an isolation tank. Sinclair's political and literary activism seemed dominated by one grand mea culpa: Please forgive me, my radical allies, he seemed to be saying, for the mistakes I made a few years back.

Taking On the Culture Producers

When not worrying about the red scare's legacy or forming a new chapter of America's leading civil liberties organization, Sinclair was pondering the state of culture in the contemporary United States. He took up his "Dead Hand" series once again, this time taking on artists and writers and their culpability in the sad state of affairs that constituted America during the age of wonderful nonsense. The first stab in this direction was *Mammonart*, published just one year after his activism with the ACLU was settling down. The book put artists in the Western past through Sinclair's now well-established grinding machine, showing capitalism at work in just about every case. "All art is propaganda," Sinclair wrote, shocking no one at this point. "The path to honor and success in the arts," he explained, "has been through the service and glorification of the ruling classes." With this simple thesis, Sinclair then wrote a simple book. Even by his own standards, it wasn't very well researched. He explained to a friend, "It is merely as much as I could do on the basis of my present knowledge. I did not have the time to study up other artists than those I happened to know well at the present." This says nothing about the simplicity of the thesis itself.[34]

While Sinclair once saw the artist—including the young poet that lurked in his own past—in constant rebellion against mammon, he now turned artists into whores. The change could be seen, perhaps in its most ridiculous form, in his treatment of Shakespeare, an artist who lived before the onslaught of industrial capitalism and whom Sinclair once admired. Now Shakespeare was portrayed as a pawn of class society. He pointed out that Shakespeare's plays about the upper class were classed as "tragedy," and plays about the lower class as "comedy." Sinclair tore through the rest of the Western pantheon of artists—Raphael, Michelangelo, Beethoven, Coleridge, Dostoyevsky, Tolstoy, Zola, Ibsen, Nietzsche—with similar cheap insights, taking little time to develop his argument, and rarely entertaining alternative interpretations. When he got closer to his own day and age, his criticisms remained cheap.[35]

There was one thing that Sinclair was onto in the book as he moved forward on the time line, and it drew from his hopeful side. Sinclair believed that the decadence gripping American writers and artists during the 1920s was historically doomed. His grand historical perspective might have shown a recurrent debasement of art by mammon, but it also showed that history changes. So too might be the case with the present. The bohemians of Greenwich Village—sloppy free-love advocates like his ex-wife or the libertarians living for free expression over any other social obligation—were descending into "the Slough of Despond" that could be seen "in the bottom of the coffee-cups in which Greenwich Village now gets its bootleg gin." But not all was lost for Sinclair; there was reason to hope, even in the nebulous terrain of culture. "This I do believe: a time will come, and not so far in the future, when American youth will react from the hip-pocket flask and petting party stage of culture." Artists might just be able to give them something more to believe in. Though it would take longer than Sinclair might have expected, and it would take something as devastating as the Great Depression to bring the message home, Sinclair was right to hope that artists would someday merge their work with the greater cause of social justice and that it wouldn't be far from the time of this writing. He was ready for this.[36]

To show his readiness, he wrote yet another book, this one solely about writers. *Money Writes!* was surely one of Sinclair's worst books ever. He explained to Haldeman-Julius that he was going to turn to "muckraking of the authors both ancient and modern." It's an interesting admission, that he wasn't muckraking institutions the way he had the Chicago meat-packing industry, but rather individual authors. This is what made the book seem more of a moralizing sermon against individuals than a strong work of literary or social criticism. He got his digs in nonetheless. Jack London's alcoholism and George Sterling's drinking problems were broadcast again. Sinclair Lewis had ditched his radicalism for literary success and refused to write what Sinclair thought he should have—a "labor novel." Harry Kemp, not exactly someone Sinclair should have been making literary judgments about, faced his wrath: "What had been the pure ecstasy of art became all at once the poisoned brew of sensuality." Mencken got hit: "The darling and idol of the young intelligentsia has no message to give them, except that they are free to do what they please." And of course, money governed everything about every writer.[37]

The book became the last in Sinclair's series on the cultural apparatus, and for good reason. No one seemed to like this one. Floyd Dell, just then writing a biography of Sinclair that proved favorable, accused him of becoming "a reckless slinger of hysterical foolishness" in *Money Writes!* H. L. Mencken, defending Sherwood Anderson, one of many writers attacked in Sinclair's book, lampooned his friend's peculiar line of reasoning: "Instead of filling his reports with Marxian indignation, Anderson resorts to the lewd quackeries of Freudism, which is a madness of Greenwich Village, which, as everyone knows, is an outhouse of Wall Street." Heywood Broun believed that Sinclair ignored the fact that creativity as such was an act of rebellion in a society as materialistic as America's and that Sinclair had gone searching for political arguments where good stories would do. A reviewer for the *New Yorker* praised Sinclair as a novelist but, as a literary critic, saw him as "prey of delusions of persecution" or "a confirmed belly acher." His take on other writers besides himself could be summed up this way: "their purses are fat, their livers white, and their tongues black with boot-polish." It goes without saying that none of the reviewers recommended the book.[38]

Sinclair had to self-publish all of the books of the "Dead Hand" series—except for *Money Writes!* He became, in the process, a bona fide cultural craftsperson, turning his house into a small business. His life became swamped with translation rights, book shop orders, credit management, and the printing of books. When necessary, he turned salesman, churning out circulars announcing the next book due out soon. He'd talk up the "combination offers" he had in store: if readers bought two books instead of one, they would get a real bargain. Sinclair was in constant battle with his printer (located in Indiana), and Craig was always worried about how much debt Sinclair racked up. After all, Sinclair wanted to keep his books as cheap as possible. Though he sold a number of copies of *The Brass Check*, he hadn't priced it high enough to get any return. As he explained to his readers, self-publishing was a "constant strain and worry." He even considered hitting the road for a lecture tour in 1925 in order to raise money for his self-publishing, even though he knew that this would create a hardship for Craig.[39]

At one point, he considered putting his book business on a "cooperative basis." He thought that since his books were not created for the purpose of profit it would be good to express that in the way they were made. Sinclair wrote to J. P. Warbasse, a leading expert on cooperative businesses, to inquire about the possibility, and Warbasse came back with a negative recommendation. Cooperatives should be joint ventures, Warbasse counseled, and not centered on one person. "A cooperative society which is confined to the publications of a single individual is apt to be static. Moreover, with all respect to yourself, no individual is a sure thing while he is alive." Around the same time, Sinclair also lobbied the American Fund for Public Service to help him create a not-for-profit way to publish his books. He called the plan his "Two Foot Shelf," since that was how wide his books stacked on a shelf at the time. This didn't work any better. So he experimented by trying to get his readers to lend him money that would be returned in discounts on the books he would continue to self-publish.[40]

Sometimes it sounded as if Sinclair was desperate for any way to get his voice heard. But self-interest was not the only motivation at play here. Sinclair wanted to find ways to create culture that didn't involve profit. He celebrated the creation of Vanguard Press during the mid-1920s, a small publishing house that made "cheap books for workers." When Emmanuel Haldeman-Julius pledged himself to printing five-cent blue books that would reproduce classics in Western thought (from Shakespeare to Karl Marx) for a working-class audience, Sinclair praised him. He believed that books offered intellectual nourishment not found on the radio or in the movies or in the jazz music of the era. He honestly sought out ways to ensure that open access to culture—his own and that of others—would never pass away.[41]

Assessed!

The challenges of self-publishing, plus the deteriorating quality of Sinclair's own books, started to show up in diminishing sales. His books sold less and less throughout the decade. By 1924 he figured he had sold 135,000 copies of *The Brass Check*; 25,000 of *The Goose-Step*; and 10,000 of *The Goslings*. He explained six months later that he had printed 9,000 copies of *Mammonart* and sold only 5,000. It's no wonder he found a way to get out of self-publishing at this moment by signing a contract with Boni and Liveright for *Money Writes!* It seemed as if the decline of the Socialist Party during the decade of the 1920s was paralleling the decline of Sinclair's books. Or perhaps his social isolation, as Craig became sicker throughout the decade, mirrored his intellectual isolation. Whatever the case, Sinclair was in danger of becoming an underread crank.[42]

There's a story about Sinclair that offers insight about his state of mind during the 1920s. It involved the *Little Review* magazine—a modernist journal that became famous for publishing James Joyce and other writers experimenting with literary technique. Margaret Anderson, the editor, recalled a correspondence with Upton Sinclair that probably occurred right as the red scare hit. It went something like: "'Please cease sending me the *Little Review*,' Sinclair wrote. 'I no longer understand anything in it, so it no longer interests me.' I replied, 'Please cease sending me your social-ist paper. I understand everything in it, therefore it no longer interests me.'" This tells us something about the problems of Sinclair's mind-set during the 1920s—he had stopped asking big questions and started instead to fit all of his observations into a predetermined formula. This was reflected in his "Dead Hand" series, and it was fast becoming the impres-sion of his contemporary critics.[43]

Sinclair seemed to want people to assess his literary and political career by the beginning of the decade. In 1921, he released *The Book of Life*, a two-volume work that set out his philosophy of life, especially on matters of diet, marriage, and political philosophy. The book seemed to bellow out, "I am a phenomenon, recognize me as such." It rambled and intro-duced complex topics without doing them much justice. He had also published *Upton Sinclair: Biographical and Critical Opinions* in 1923. For this slim volume, he solicited flattering remarks from fellow writers and strung them together into an incoherent whole. It was if he now consid-ered himself a figure warranting the sort of treatment that usually comes after death.

He got it. In 1927, the George Doran Company released *Upton Sinclair: A Study in Social Protest* by Floyd Dell. It was an interesting choice for an author. Dell was fresh out of the Greenwich Village bohemian scene, having worked at *The Masses*. Sinclair had condemned Dell's own novels as grotesque explorations of free love. He might have had some trepidation about the final product. He shouldn't have if he did. Dell wound up comparing Sinclair to Mark Twain and Walt Whitman, cer-tainly flattering company. Though a Puritan, Dell believed Sinclair should not be judged too harshly, since he had "far transcended in his writings the limitations of the Puritan point of view." Dell offered a fine biography of Sinclair, showing how the writer had moved beyond his difficult childhood and his youthful phase as an alienated poet to become a realist author with well-founded socialist beliefs. But Dell saw limitations and couldn't help concluding on an ambivalent note. "His future literary career may bring surprises," he wrote at the end; "the poet in him may yet overwhelm the propagandist." The implication here was obvious: the propagandist in Sinclair was killing off the poet in him.[44]

While Dell was kind, Walter Lippmann was not. Lippmann was one of America's most famous journalists, and one who happened to have cut his teeth on the Intercollegiate Socialist Society that Sinclair had started. He reviewed Dell's biography and took the chance to skewer Sinclair as a self-marginalized figure—representing the overall fate of socialism in the United States at this time. Lippmann and Sinclair had been friends, but their relationship grew strained as Lippmann denounced socialism and then told Sinclair that *Sylvia's Marriage* was a horrible novel. It all came out in Lippmann's review: "Upton Sinclair's writing is insulated against experience. He has erected a structure of theories in front of his eyes, which is so dazzling that nothing in the outer world is clearly visible to him." These words were written soon after Sinclair had spent most of the 1920s trying to document the world outside his eyes—the press, churches, schools, and colleges of the nation. Lippmann went on, "He simply used the socialist philosophy to barricade himself more elaborately against the world whose contamination he dreaded" as a puritanical child. Though Lippmann got one thing wrong—he said he hadn't read any of Sinclair's novels since Debs first ran for president, which would have meant that he had read none of Sinclair's novels—the central message stuck. Sinclair had barricaded himself from society and could see the different institutions of the cultural apparatus only through the lens of socialism. When Sinclair responded to Lippmann, he pointed out Lippmann's one mistake, as he was prone to do, and then said that Bolton Hall, not necessarily someone whose name would be recognized, recently sent him a complimentary letter, as if this did away with Lippmann's characterization.[45]

Lippmann was not alone. Lawrence Morris, writing for the *New Republic* in the same year, argued that Sinclair is "writing books today with the wealth of detail of a man of fifty and the thoughts of a youth of twenty-five." Repeating Lippmann's claims, Morris argued, "His mind has remained tied to the mile-post it reached in his twenties." This created a "shrillness of a tirade" in his more recent work. Essentially, Morris suggested, Sinclair had stopped doing what any good intellectual should do—learning about the world and approaching it afresh. Added to the resoundingly bad reviews that met *Money Writes!* Morris and Lippmann might have made Sinclair nervous, if he hadn't taken refuge in his tendency to see all criticism of his work as reflecting his critics' conservatism.[46]

Surprisingly, none of Sinclair's critics pointed out his attitude toward Russia. For here was a subject in which Sinclair's limitations became more explicit as the 1920s proceeded. The embarrassment Sinclair felt in the face of U.S. intervention in Russia closed Sinclair's mind to any criticism of Lenin's revolution and the rise to power of Joseph Stalin after Lenin's death in 1924. Though Sinclair never joined the Communist Party in the United States, his defense of Russia pushed him into a corner. "I am not a Bolshevik, and I have opposed the Bolshevik movement," Sinclair explained in 1918. Nonetheless, he refused to listen to critics of Lenin if he thought they had ulterior motives. To Sir Arthur Conan Doyle, the creator of Sherlock Holmes, Sinclair would explain, "I oppose the terror" in Russia. "Nevertheless, I cannot blind myself to the fact that the revolutionary forces have a great bulk of the right on their side and are bringing a new stage of civilization into birth." As early as 1919, the fateful year of the red scare, he would declare Russia a "working class government" and a "democracy" at least in terms of industry. Just as he had refused to become a sucker for U.S. propaganda after the war, he became more of a sucker for his enemy's enemy. Sinclair should have known better, since numerous leftists were pointing out how Lenin was imposing a dictatorship over the country. J. G. Phelps Stokes, who had sided with Sinclair on the issue of World War I, now attacked him. Upton answered that the Bolsheviks were still better than the czars who ruled prior to them. Sinclair had a similar debate with another socialist, George Viereck, and another with Alexander Berkman, an anarchist who reported on Emma Goldman's disillusionment with the society she found herself deported to on the infamous Soviet Ark during the red scare. By 1929, Sinclair would celebrate John Dewey's visit to Russia and argue that Russia possessed "the greatest intellectual and moral awakening in the history of the human race." His opposition to U.S. intervention in Russia kept him from seeing the reality—that Russia was fast becoming a cruel dictatorship, much more like the czars of the past than Sinclair could imagine.[47]

Oil!

If nothing more, Sinclair must have worried about the drop in his sales. Certainly Craig worried about it. When Floyd Dell told Sinclair that *Money Writes!* was an embarrassment, that too must have stung. Neither

The Spokesman's Secretary (1926), a story about a ditzy woman who didn't care about anything beyond beauty parlors, or *Letters to Judd* (1926), another disquisition about socialism's merits, promised a way out of his problem. Sinclair was in desperate need of a story. It had been a long time since he had developed characters and plot lines, the way he had with *King Coal* ten years earlier. He knew he was at his best when aiming for an epic story, even if he couldn't quite hit that mark. So Sinclair must have been hopeful about the novel he was finishing as Dell's biography was released. It was a novel that might provide a way out of the dead end of the "Dead Hand" series.

As a novel, *Oil!* grew out of the grand historical epic of U.S. history during the 1920s as well as the smallest detail of Sinclair's own life. In 1924 Senator Robert LaFollette, the man Sinclair would vote for as presidential candidate that year, exposed the Teapot Dome scandal. What he found during his investigation was shocking: Secretary of the Interior Albert Fall had signed over public lands in Wyoming to private oil companies. This sort of privatization of public goods was typical of the Harding administration. What was more shocking in this case was that Fall had taken enormous kickbacks in order to prosper himself. Fall received a year in jail, becoming "the first cabinet officer in history" to receive such a fate. Around the same time, Craig had decided to make investments in real estate around the Los Angeles area in order to shore up her and Upton's financial security. Pursuing property in Long Beach, California, Craig found out that some of it had oil on it. Upton drove her to meetings with other property owners in the area who were trying to figure out the best way to sell to an oil company. He took notes of the meetings and marveled at the participants' greed. Craig sold the property, and pretty soon, Sinclair had the basis for a new novel.[48]

Oil! told the story of Bunny, the son of an oilman who grew up during a boom in the industry. Bunny would go hunting on the ranch property of the Watkins family, a group of poor fundamentalists whose son, Paul, is becoming a radical in politics by organizing workers in the oil fields. Paul befriends Bunny and tells him his father is corrupt. Meanwhile, Bunny falls in love with Eunice Hoyt, a flapper who is liberated from sexual prudery and a good dancer who enjoys the occasional petting party. Paul is shipped off to World War I, returning even more of a radical, while Bunny becomes a budding socialist who goes off to college only to become bored with it. Bunny's father continues to hold to his Republican politics, praising Harding as a president who will do good by the oil industry.

While his father is trying to work out political favors, Bunny starts his own labor college, where he hopes to put into practice his socialist politics. He also has an affair with Vee, an actress who travels in Hollywood circles, but this cannot last since Bunny, turning socialist in his politics, turns her off with his newfound seriousness. Paul goes Communist, and Bunny tries to help him in his political evolution, while breaking up with Vee. Bunny then falls in love with Rachel, a Jewish girl who works at the labor college with him. This ecumenical love affair seems to offer a hopeful message, though the novel ends with the tragedy of an oil fire and the death of its major characters. The book was over five hundred pages long. As Sinclair explained to Horace Liveright, who rejected the manuscript, *Oil!* "is so long because I have taken the trouble to invent sufficient story to carry my ideas." There wasn't too much new ground broken for Sinclair. The story was one of capitalist society turned rotten, as usual, and a young idealist—the sort who was at the center of *King Coal*—trying to change it for the better.[49]

Sinclair's lucky break came when Reverend J. Frank Chase of Boston condemned *Oil!* as a work of pornography. In May 1927, the book was banned in the city. Sinclair leaped into action, feeling a righteous combination of self-interest and the need to defend his civil liberties. The next month, Sinclair was in Boston selling copies of the book with the purportedly dirty sections blacked out by a fig leaf and with "two cardboard fig leaves hanging from my shoulders." The books sold like "hotcakes." Meanwhile, a judge who had only read the dirty parts of the novel issued a warrant for Sinclair's arrest. When the police approached Sinclair, he offered to sell them a copy of *Oil!*, but when they took him to court, they found out they had been sold a copy of the Bible. "The only way to fight this law," Sinclair explained in justifying his street theater, "is to make a monkey of it." Sinclair pressed to have a show trial where he could raise issues of civil liberties and censorship, but unfortunately for his sales, the issue quickly died away. And soon Sinclair was face to face with another controversy in the city of Boston that he said was "too serious" to justify fighting this personal cause of the fig leaf.[50]

The End of an Era: Sacco and Vanzetti

Just two months after Sinclair visited Boston to sell his fig leaf copies of *Oil!*, two Italian immigrants were executed in the electric chair. Nicola

Sacco and Bartolomeo Vanzetti were poor Italian immigrants arrested for robbing a shoe company and murdering a paymaster just outside of Boston in 1920, right on the heels of the red scare. They proclaimed themselves anarchists but denied involvement in their alleged crime. A year after their arrest, Judge Webster Thayer, who had referred to Sacco and Vanzetti as "those anarchist bastards," sentenced them to death. There were immediate appeals, and some liberals hoped Sacco and Vanzetti might be let off if they exerted enough pressure. The answer came that fateful summer of 1927. Before their electrocution, Sacco celebrated anarchism and Vanzetti restated their innocence, crying as the electricity coursed through his body.[51]

Like most progressives and liberals, Sinclair had followed the case since its beginning. He wrote about the case as early as 1922, the same year he visited Vanzetti in jail to learn more about the anarchist's philosophy and his self-declared innocence. The next year, Sinclair declared the Italian immigrant an idealist and a romanticist who could never have committed a murder or descended to petty crime. He renewed this argument three years later and then turned desperate with concern in 1927 when the last appeals were failing to clear the two immigrants. Sinclair pleaded with Governor Alvan T. Fuller of Massachusetts that he met Vanzetti in jail and thought him an "idealist, remote from the possibility of selfish crime." As the death penalty's date was announced, Sinclair frantically tried to plan a pageant where a "grand jury of thirty or forty well-known persons" would convene to "vote a formal indictment against the Commonwealth of Massachusetts for murder in the first degree." The pageant, which Sinclair would explain two years later was proposed to generate "publicity," never materialized, and the day after the execution, Sinclair declared to a friend that "all we can do now is to try and make the noble lives and example of these two men count with the future, and I am sure I can give of a very real and important help in this way." Not surprisingly, this took the form of a book.[52]

Sinclair went back to Boston in September 1927 to gather information for a historical novel about the case of Sacco and Vanzetti. He wouldn't even bother bringing up the issue of *Oil!*'s censorship; there were more important things to do. On his way back from Boston, he stopped in Denver, where he was suing (unsuccessfully and some might suggest hypocritically) the *Rocky Mountain News* for libel in calling him a pseudo-radical (a charge that he hated, though his case lost). There he met with Fred Moore, the radical labor lawyer who had defended Sacco and

Vanzetti up until 1924. Moore, like Sinclair, had a gift for publicity; he also had doubts about the nobility of the cause. He admitted to Sinclair that he thought Sacco was guilty. Sinclair had begun to think the same thing, knowing that Sacco had possessed literature on bomb making. As Sinclair continued to research the matter, the picture became grayer. He explained to Robert Minor on February 8, 1928, that he believed both Sacco and Vanzetti knew about the holdup, even if Vanzetti was less guilty than Sacco. Sinclair admitted his confusion about the matter: "The problem I am now confronting is how I am going to handle this story and what is going to be the effect upon the movement." It had gotten out among Communists that Sinclair was going to declare both Sacco and Vanzetti guilty as charged. Sinclair tried to settle the score with Mike Gold by claiming, "I am not going to say that I know they were innocent, because I do not know that. But I am certainly going to say that they were not proved guilty." This wouldn't have satisfied numerous Communists who wanted to turn Sacco and Vanzetti into innocent martyrs for the cause of immigrant laborers.[53]

The whole thing was becoming more difficult than Sinclair had planned. He admitted that *Boston*, as the novel was called, was "the most difficult piece of work of my life, the most dangerous and the most exhausting." He knew that "the friends of the defense are more than upset and distressed, because I insist in stating what I know: That there was a great deal of perjury on both sides in the Dedham trial." But what made it more difficult was also what made the novel better. Sinclair was starting to inject complexity into his portrait of America. This meant the novel was taking longer to write than he had planned. He had wanted it out by the first anniversary of Sacco and Vanzetti's death, in August 1928. But that became "suicidal," as Sinclair explained to his publisher. By October 1928 he had traveled to New York City—showing his determination to do right by this project—in order to help work the novel through its final stages and watch a performance of his play *Singing Jailbirds* being performed at New Playwrights Theater.[54]

Sinclair's sweat and struggle over the novel showed. It was a finer piece than *Oil!*, and it led some to believe that his skills as a novelist had returned. The novel centered on Cornelia Thornwell, a member of Boston's aristocracy. *Boston* starts off a bit unbelievably with Cornelia dropping out of her family's comfortable background and looking for a job in a mill. She winds up rooming in the same house as Vanzetti, who she discovers is a vegetarian and an opponent of alcohol (both beliefs Vanzetti really subscribed to). Cornelia gets to know the political culture of anarchism while rooming in the house, and she hangs out with Vanzetti, learning of his anger at the failed strike of workers at the Cordage Plant nearby. While discovering this new world, Cornelia's granddaughter visits and expresses excitement at her grandmother's increasing radicalism. Then Sinclair returns to the historical narrative, showing Vanzetti leaving for Mexico in order to avoid fighting in World War I, and Cornelia and her granddaughter Betty engaging in the suffragette struggle.

Not surprisingly, Sinclair spent a great deal of time setting the stage for the red scare, describing the bombings that Sacco and Vanzetti were associated with. Spies are sent into the Boston anarchist community, and Vanzetti goes into fish selling to survive the backlash. Sinclair describes the Boston police strike, the Soviet Ark, and the Palmer Raids. This helps contextualize Sacco and Vanzetti's entry into jail. Cornelia observes all of this, and knowing Vanzetti (as Sinclair did), she believes he's innocent, while she is unsure about Sacco. The trial is described, as is Judge Thayer's comment about "anarchist bastards." Sinclair also makes these Italian immigrants into heroes of the American dream. Sinclair considers it "an odd turn of fate, that this Italian seeker of liberty should have been convicted within sight of Plymouth Rock." He also documents the growing movement forming around Sacco and Vanzetti's case. "Lee Swenson" takes up the case and suggests that the defendants prepare to lie (Fred Moore, as Sinclair knew, had accepted a certain amount of perjury). Swenson's realism battles against Cornelia's idealism, symbolizing, no doubt, Sinclair's own internal battle. The novel climaxes with the announcement of the death sentence, and the "war" for "public opinion" that followed. Then comes the Lowell Commission—headed by Harvard president A. Lawrence Lowell, a man Sinclair utterly despised, as was made clear with *The Goose-Step*—which upholds Judge Thayer's decision. The death sentence is defended, and protests follow. The novel ends with ten thousand people showing up at the funeral, but the novel's message seems captured in Lee Swenson's worry over the case. Swenson declares, "A terrible world to live in! A world full of tangles impossible to unravel, or danger impossible to foresee!" This captures Sinclair's attitude toward the end of the novel. He can portray what was wrong and unjust about the case—Judge Thayer's prejudice, the collective rush to judgment, the prejudice common among Boston's aristocracy—without turning Sacco and Vanzetti into innocent martyrs.[55]

Boston appeared at the end of the 1920s, and it seemed to mark the end of the decade as far as Sinclair was concerned. His hard-fought battle against the cynicism of America's intelligentsia was starting to bear results. Though the Sacco and Vanzetti case was safely lodged within the decade of the 1920s, it was really a foreshadowing of a shift in American intellectual life—away from intellectual cynicism and Mencken's dominance and toward political reengagement. The future literary editor of the *New Republic*, Malcolm Cowley, explained, "For a time it seemed that Sacco and Vanzetti would be forgotten, in the mist of the stock market boom and the exhilaration of easy money. Yet the effects of the case continued to operate in a subterranean way, and after a few years they would once more appear on the surface." Indeed, two members of the Algonquin Round Table were profoundly affected by the case. Dorothy Parker, the cynical poet who admitted to not voting, would march for Sacco and Vanzetti, as her 1920s cynicism melted away into 1930s engagement. She would eventually support Upton Sinclair's run for governor of California in 1934. The same was true for Heywood Broun, who lost his writing position over his support for Sacco and Vanzettti. He too would continue to drift left as the United States entered the 1930s. And even some of the expatriates of the 1920s would come home during the 1930s to commit themselves to social justice.[56]

For Sinclair, the Sacco and Vanzetti case would be the basis for his best work of the 1920s, and the questions it raised would add a layer of complexity to his thinking. Sinclair questioned the sanctity of the cause while throwing himself into it, and in this book he prefigured a realist dimension to his politics. Though he would remain uncritical of Communism for some time, he tempered his assuredness a bit when he saw how quick the Communists were to criticize any introspection on his part about the case. It would take the impending Depression to reach a climax for things to change entirely, forcing him to get more practical about politics. But Sinclair had traveled quite a distance from World War I to 1929. The world had grown more complex, and so too Sinclair's ethics. This became abundantly clear as he took the next step in his life, the attempt to reach broader numbers of people in the United States.

SIX

A BRIEF INTERMISSION—
UPPIE GOES TO THE MOVIES

1930–1934

Well, [Fox] and I know that it's you who are the showman,
leader, and prophet. You Upton, not Fox.

—LINCOLN STEFFENS TO SINCLAIR, 1933

O N THURSDAY, OCTOBER 24, 1929, THE STOCK MARKET CRASHED. Frightened traders scampered around Wall Street, trying to figure out what to do. Some considered shutting down the stock exchange. The crash began to shake Americans' confidence in the prosperity that had marked the 1920s. President Hoover immediately denied that anything was wrong with the country's economy, calling it "sound and prosperous." But rising unemployment and failing banks made the claim sound hollow. So did "Hoovervilles," with their rickety structures housing families whose mortgages had gone into foreclosure, and the growing lines at soup kitchens across the United States. So did farmers who could not find markets for their products, and the factories who were forced to slow down production. The year 1930 was destined to be the first year of the nation's greatest economic depression.[1]

Little of this seemed to affect Upton Sinclair. For sure, 1929 had been a difficult year for him, but not because he traded on the stock market (he wouldn't consider it). The writing of *Boston* had burned him out. The book was a hard act to follow. And he started to fritter about, going to the dentist more often than not and having teeth pulled. He also spent more time with Craig, whose neurasthenia continued to keep her barricaded inside the home. She started to believe she had powers not possessed by most. Sinclair would have her sit in one room while he sat in another. He would draw a picture, and she would guess what it was. She was making a large number of correct guesses. She was also able to get a book down from the shelf, place it on her solar plexus, and tell Upton the title. So Sinclair decided that this behavior merited a book. He called it *Mental Radio*. "Regardless of what anybody can say, there will never again be a doubt about it in my mind. I KNOW," he declared and then proceeded to tell stories about his wife guessing what he had drawn or the titles of books that lay on her stomach.[2]

There were also the séances. The Sinclairs had their own medium, Roman Ostoja, popularly known as Nostradamus, whose roadshow included being buried underground in a casket and coming out alive. He was dark and mysterious, claiming to be a Polish aristocrat, though he was really from Cleveland, Ohio. Sinclair watched as Ostoja put a nail through his tongue and went into trances and performed séances. If Ostoja wasn't available, Sinclair would call upon other mediums, including the more famous Arthur Ford. At one séance, Jack London's ghost appeared and talked a moment with Sinclair. Sinclair would invite skeptics to these séances, including Theodore Dreiser, who unfortunately was drunk and proceeded to fall asleep once the lights were turned off. Sinclair also invited one of his newest friends, Albert Einstein, the father of modern physics, who happened to be visiting the California Institute of Technology. Einstein admired Sinclair's socialist politics and was willing to entertain his friend's belief in telepathy and spiritualism (after all, there were mysteries in physics that Einstein admitted to not understanding). Einstein even wrote a nice preface to *Mental Radio*, though he never said whether he actually believed in the stuff.[3]

There was also mind cure. This too was a gift that Craig believed she had. Ironically, over the years, she had embraced a school of thought that Upton had lampooned during the 1920s—Christian Science. Upton seemed willing to change his mind about the doctrine now that Craig had cured a nasty case of the uncontrollable hiccups with it. Hiccups were something Sinclair suffered from himself, making him eager to believe in a cure, and he didn't think there was that much of a mystery behind what was happening here. He tried to explain it to Mencken, "There are constructive forces in the subconscious mind which build and maintain the body and these same forces have the power to remedy any abnormal condition in the body." Mencken was the last person Sinclair should have told about this. He wrote back and told Sinclair, "A glass of beer would have probably cured your hiccoughs in two minutes." Another one of Sinclair's intellectual comrades, Emmanuel Haldeman-Julius, simply called all of this Upton's "spookology."[4]

But it was more than this. It was part of Sinclair's worldview and one that related back to his socialism. His spiritualism helped him look beyond present-day social arrangements to a world where all souls were equal. "I feel sure that this universe is not an accident," he once explained, "and that an intelligence guides it. I feel that every living creature has a personal relationship with that intelligence." Believing in something beyond the present-day world helped him believe in change. He didn't think that Craig's ability to guess pictures was just coincidence, but rather a sign of that same thing that pushed him to think beyond what was currently going on in his world. It was a source of his hope, no matter how bizarre some of his friends might think it. When Mencken laughed at him, it undoubtedly confirmed his belief. Mencken, after all, didn't believe there was anything beyond the miseries of the world he currently inhabited.[5]

While experimenting with Craig and séances, Sinclair continued to write, but nothing that took too much time or stress. He couldn't do another *Boston*, but he could whip out a novel like *Mountain City* in two months. It was a story about a ranch boy who grows rich, and though it included details about Henry George's single-tax theory, it was not a very interesting or compelling book. His son David's wife, Betty, told him so. Sinclair admitted she might be right but then explained that his books had brought joy to "millions of people all over the world, and I hope also they have brought them a little instruction." Instead of "subtleties and sophistication," he believed he offered stories that were "simple and elemental." Maybe his books wouldn't satisfy the "New York intellectuals," he told *Time* magazine two years later, but so what. He was becoming a middle-brow writer who could please the reading public of America. This was his ambition: to reach ordinary people. These people probably didn't care for the ponderings of James Joyce or T. S. Eliot, and they may not read much at all. Therefore, Sinclair wrote simply and even thought about starting a radio station. He was serious enough about the idea to raise thirty thousand dollars for the venture, even though it never came to fruition.[6]

He then wrote a book he originally entitled *Roman Interlude*. He had a hard time selling it to publishers, but John Farrar eventually accepted it. It was a story about the owner of a car corporation who has an accident and is transported back to ancient Rome, where he recognizes parallels to his own time. It was a story that seemed made for the movies, with its magical journey between the past and present. Sinclair even sent it to a friend who was connected in Hollywood, suggesting he might especially like it. It wasn't clear in this case if Sinclair was aiming to write a movie in the form of a book, but it was certain that he dreamed of breaking into the world of Hollywood. In a little more than a year after *Roman Holiday* was published, he would have success on this front. It wasn't this book that would do it for him; it was, of all things, his prohibitionism.

"Going Hollywood"

Back in his New York City days, Sinclair had tramped the city's streets and seen nickelodeons with long lines of working men waiting to get in. He thought movies provided a marvelous opportunity to reach the working class. His first attempt came when August Thomas contacted him about making a movie version of *The Jungle*. Sinclair immediately consented, and the movie was made in 1913 and released the next year. It "ran for a several weeks in New York," Craig later claimed. Sinclair even got a cameo as the speaker of socialist ideas at the end. He thought the film a "really honest version" of the book. The posters released for it show a man falling off a ledge backward into a vat, using the most sensational part of the story as a major advertising hook. Sinclair was so pleased with the film that he constantly tried to get the movie rereleased in an improved version, which wound up becoming a frustrating, and finally fruitless, project.[7]

Just four years later, right as the red scare was about to take hold over the United States, Sinclair contacted labor unions to see if there would be interest in a film he thought would take the country by storm. It seemed remarkably similar to D. W. Griffith's epic movie *Birth of a Nation*, but instead of being about the Civil War, it was about labor conflicts and World War I. The premise was simple: It would show a railroad strike and focus on the wealthy owner's family and a poor family, locked in battle against one another. Then the film would show two young men from both families fighting together on the front lines of World War I. The message would be clear: the nation needed to unify and get along in industrial matters just as much as in military matters. He sought the support of the Railroad Brotherhood, the union trying to maintain nationalization of the railroads once the war was over. Though Sinclair offered to write the entire thing for just a thousand dollars, it never materialized.[8]

All of these attempts to break into the "flickers" (what movies were called back then) should not cover up another aspect of Sinclair's world-view. Like most writers, Sinclair had a profound distrust of the seductive world of imagery that the movies pioneered. For instance, in 1916 he argued that movies propagated lies about how easy it was to make wealth in this country. During the 1920s, as the movies reflected what he took to be the decadent values of the jazz age, Sinclair grew more hostile. In 1920 his own novel *The Moneychangers* was turned into a movie, and when Sinclair saw it, he went berserk. A novel about J. P. Morgan causing the panic of 1907 became a movie about drug trafficking in Chinatown, show-ing wealthy members of society doing good work through charity. Sinclair demanded that the movie change its credits to say it was "adapted" from his novel. Ben Hampton, who helped Sinclair get the contract for the film, told him, "Personally, old fellow, my thought is that you are making a grave error in not extending your area of influence." This gave Sinclair pause, no doubt, and he was soon proposing to Hampton that they make a movie version of *100%* that would star Charlie Chaplin (it never happened). But just two years later, Sinclair declared, "My own experiences with the moving picture industry have been varied, and have so disgusted me that I have given up all idea of ever using the medium to express my ideas."[9]

There's an irony here. Just as Sinclair was saying this, the world of Hollywood was consolidating, just around the corner from his home. From 1914 to 1920, Hollywood became what it is today, and already by the 1920s just about every film made in the United States was shot and dis-tributed here. The world of independent nickelodeons, with their own small-fry filmmakers, was gone, and the studio system—Paramount, Loew's, Warner Brothers—and "block booking" (where theaters were forced to carry all of the movies made by a specific studio) became a real-ity. Suddenly, writers were moving to Hollywood to get jobs, and with the founding of Rob Wagner's little magazine *Script* in 1929, Hollywood even started to get a reputation for having something that most never thought it would—intellectuals. *Script* was, in Sinclair's own words, a "beacon of light" for the "the intellectuals of the movie colony." As the Depression hit Hollywood, some even began to think that perhaps the studios might turn to serious subjects, even if that was hoping against hope.[10]

During the 1920s, Sinclair was hobnobbing with Hollywood's elite. First and always, there was Charlie Chaplin. The man who created the character of the "little tramp," whose humble virtues stood out against the prejudices of others, had always been the love of intellectuals, the saving grace for decadent Hollywood, a touch of genius where few expected it. As early as 1922, Sinclair called Chaplin a "great actor" and "a man of culture." In hanging out with him, Sinclair claimed that Chaplin constantly groused about the capitalist businessmen who funded his movies, and Chaplin claimed that Sinclair taught him about socialism. So it seemed natural for Sinclair to think Chaplin would be sympathetic toward his dreams of making movies. Soon after moving to Pasadena and meeting Chaplin, Sinclair pitched him scripts, one for *The Hypnotist*, in which Chaplin would play a man who ran a hypnosis parlor and is kicked out because he couldn't afford the rent. He winds up at a millionaire's palace, where he hypnotizes a rich young man who looks like him. Chaplin would then pose as the wealthy young man and wreak havoc on the palace. Unfortunately, the clothes he stole would be too tight, and Chaplin would no longer be able to breathe after a while, so he would leave the palace and live on the streets once again. The film had potential, but Chaplin was too much his own man to take leads from Sinclair. Nonetheless, later when Sinclair had a "negro helper" work on his house, he swore to Chaplin that he was the "living image of you." Why not put him on the screen since it "it would raise a howl," Sinclair reasoned to his friend.[11]

Chaplin would introduce Sinclair to a Hollywood star who possessed even more cachet than Chaplin himself. Douglas Fairbanks was known as a swashbuckling hero in movies about the Three Musketeers and Robin Hood. He was good-looking and athletic enough to do his own stunts. He also happened to be married to the actress Mary Pickford, who was even more famous than Fairbanks (with Chaplin, the three of them formed United Artists Studio). People would stand outside the Fairbanks-Pickford mansion, hoping to see the couple float their boat out onto what was one of the largest swimming pools ever built. But even with his wealth, Fairbanks was interested in Sinclair's socialist politics, and he suggested they make a movie together about a future socialist utopia. As with the suggestions Sinclair made to Chaplin, this one never happened. But when Fairbanks visited Russia in 1931, Sinclair spoke proudly of the actor's belief that good culture required a foundation of social justice.[12]

None of these contacts got Sinclair into the movies. That still required a good story that appealed to a studio executive. During the summer of 1930, Sinclair wrote up an interesting idea for a movie. It would be about a young man getting drunk and killing someone. There would be a trial, and Sinclair would write the prohibitionist side of the argument. He wanted someone else to write an argument for the defense. He first thought of Mencken, and when he said no, Sinclair considered Sinclair

Lewis and then settled for America's most famous lawyer, Clarence Darrow. Of course, it was foolish to think that anyone would be willing to
write this part, since it was obviously a setup for defeat. Darrow was no
fool and told Sinclair that he was turning down the offer. By that point,
Sinclair had abandoned that version of the project and was transitioning
into writing a novel about Prohibition, his first since *Roman Holiday*.[13]

The Wet Parade was a defense of the Eighteenth Amendment and a
call for tougher prosecution of the amendment's violation. It opens in the
South with the character Maggie May watching as her father's drinking
ruins his life. The young son of the family, Roger Chilcote, leaves the
South for the North to pursue a career as a playwright and to rebel, Sinclair explains, against "Puritanism." He gets a job in journalism and meets
up with, among others, Kip, a newspaperman who refuses drink and eventually becomes an agent for the prosecution of Prohibition. Not only was
the novel a Prohibitionist tract, it tried to highlight the populist side of the
cause, tying it into Sinclair's dream of social justice. At one point, Sinclair
pointed out that New Yorkers liked to think of the "rest of America as 'the
sticks' or the 'Bible belt,' 'Hicktown,' or 'Boobville.'" And the young intellectuals who rebelled against "Puritanism"—including the central character of Roger Chilcote—were turning their backs on the better half of the
country. "The young intellectuals of America," Sinclair wrote, "were making a practical protest against 'Volsteadism' by spending all their spare
time and money abroad." Prohibition was not just a good policy because
it saved people from drink, it was an expression of the hopes and dreams
of the virtuous folk who, unlike intellectuals, lived outside of the confines
of New York City and cared about things besides booze and hedonism and
thereby transcended the decadence of the 1920s.[14]

It shouldn't come as a surprise that the novel pushed all of Mencken's
buttons, even more than Sinclair's Christian Science. "Mr. Sinclair,"
Mencken wrote in *The Nation*, "undertakes a feat unprecedented in
swell letters. He makes a Prohibition agent his hero." That wasn't all. "His
cunning as a literary artist does not diminish," Mencken went on.
"His dialogue is highly polished. "'Please, please, Papa!' cries Maggie May
to her wine-cursed father, Mr. Roger Chilcote. "Do not drink any more!"
"Oh, little girl, little girl," he replies, "what can Papa do? I cannot give it
up! It is a fiend that has got to me!"'" Mencken could never stand for a
novel in favor of a policy he thought had failed, especially not one tinged
with such populism.[15]

Mencken's attack helped Sinclair find an unlikely ally in turning the novel into both a play and a movie. The First Methodist Church of Pasadena contacted Sinclair about turning the novel into a play, and it opened on May 15, 1932, with crowds of people turned away. The church's leaders spoke out in defense of the Eighteenth Amendment, which was under attack and soon to be repealed. The popularity of the play was likely due to the version Hollywood had already released. Sinclair's friend Edgar Selwyn, who happened to be a lawyer with Hollywood connections, helped negotiate a fine contract to turn *The Wet Parade* into a movie. By 1931, Metro-Goldwyn-Mayer (MGM) had optioned it, and on March 1, 1932, the movie premiered at Grauman's Chinese Theatre, perhaps the most famous theater in the city (Douglas Fairbanks and Mary Pickford both had their footsteps permanently engraved on the sidewalk in front of it). Sinclair was happy with the film, which stuck closely to the central story. He tried to get his books sold in the lobby. It would seem that he had arrived.[16]

Sinclair received twenty thousand dollars for the film. In Depression-era America, this was big money. Tiring of the ramshackle house she had built in Pasadena, Craig seized the opportunity. She knew there was cheap real estate in Beverly Hills, and she bought fast. For Sinclair, a house in Beverly Hills made a great deal of sense. He was now working with Irving Thalberg of MGM on another movie sketch. Thalberg's job was to work with writers, whom he called a "necessary evil" for the film industry. Nothing came of Sinclair's sketch; by this time studios began churning out all sorts of products—scripts, sketches, promos—that never culminated in actual movies. But this didn't prevent Sinclair from feeling that he had made it in Hollywood, nor did it prevent the slow move to their new mansion in Beverly Hills. From September to November 1932, they moved "just a little bit at a time and mostly in our own car." Sinclair wrote his daughter-in-law Betty that he was still planning to use his money from *The Wet Parade* to fund the Socialist Party, and he knew his socialist son might be embarrassed to hear about the relocation to Beverly Hills. He pleaded, "I hope the comrades will excuse this, and not think I have 'gone Hollywood.'"[17]

Fox Presents

Around this time, Sinclair was working with another big name in Hollywood, William Fox. As with other businesses during the Great Depression, the Fox Corporation wasn't doing terribly well, and Fox had a plan. He wanted Sinclair to write a book about his company, explaining the financial tribulations he had faced recently. As Sinclair watched *The Wet Parade* move into the theaters, Fox was often found sitting in the Sinclairs' living room. Sinclair wrote to Betty in April 1932 that "one of our great captains of industry" has been "dictating to a stenographer in our home for about three hours every morning." Fox wanted Sinclair to take these interviews and make them into a book. But he didn't want the book to hit the stands before the November election. Fox feared his story about "a Wall Street banking group" that acted nefariously might suggest that the American economy really was in trouble—something that would hurt Fox's favored candidate in the election, Herbert Hoover. Sinclair was now in the position of writing a vindication of a Hollywood robber baron who hoped the Republicans could win in 1932. The challenge was certainly made easier by the fact that Fox paid Sinclair twenty thousand dollars up front for his services. All the more reason to believe Sinclair had arrived.[18]

William Fox was a Hungarian refugee and a Jew whose life seemed to fit the rags-to-riches formula in American history. He started selling lozenges on the streets of New York City and then went into the movies, building up, in Sinclair's words a "chain of moving picture 'palaces' of all sizes in and about New York." The Wall Street Crash of 1929 devastated him financially, as did an investigation by the Justice Department and also a car accident. By the time Fox was visiting Sinclair, he was an insecure man who swept tufts of hair over his head to hide his baldness. He hated the chiefs of other studios for destroying his business and had it in for Sinclair's own employer, Louis B. Mayer. He must have seen in Sinclair a meticulous researcher who enjoyed telling stories about the darker side of America's business misadventures.[19]

By the summer of 1932, Sinclair was going through the details from the interviews and trying to get things right about stock prices. One of his interviewers did a lousy job, because Fox talked too quickly and she was afraid to slow him down, so he'd write Fox, who was then on Long Island, and ask him to clarify things. Sinclair wanted to get this thing right. By June he was writing five thousand words each day about Fox. It made him nervous that Fox wouldn't comment on the book until the whole thing was done. He wanted to make sure that the thing was moving in the right direction and that he wasn't fudging facts; it angered him that Fox wouldn't respond to his letters. Fox's silence should have told Sinclair something about the project, but it didn't. Sinclair believed Fox when he started saying that his diabetes was acting up, making it difficult for him to look at the drafts Sinclair was sending toward the end of the summer. By September the book was finished, and Sinclair was waiting for the bald and insecure man suffering from diabetes to write him back from Long Island. Nothing came. He wrote pleading letters to Fox's wife. Still nothing.[20]

By the end of the year, Sinclair got fed up and asked his friend Floyd Dell to see if he could find out why Fox wasn't getting back to him. Dispatched like a spy, Dell went to Long Island and found out that Fox was not ill at all. Fox had been heard using the Sinclair manuscript as a threat in order to get those who bilked him to hand back his properties. So Sinclair contacted a lawyer friend to see what would happen if he were to publish the book himself; he was told that this was not a very good idea. But that rarely stopped Sinclair. Betty pointed out that if the things Fox told interviewers were false and they were published under Sinclair's authorship, that could prompt a libel case against her father-in-law. Sinclair explained to her that Fox swore everything he said was true. In other words, Sinclair was willing to take a risk that a man who had lied to him was not a liar. The twenty thousand dollars he had already received just wasn't enough. And so he shipped the carbon copies out to his printer, and the book became what he hoped it would be—a sensation in Hollywood, with Fox screaming mad about it. At least it wouldn't affect the election, which had tipped significantly against Fox's wishes.

The book was an excellent exercise in business reporting. It told the tale of a man building a monopoly. Sinclair made a direct analogy between Fox and the Chicago meatpackers who had bought out independent butchers to build monopolies (Fox didn't like the comparison). The book then told of Fox's difficulties in 1929 and how his business had been taken over by shady Wall Street speculators. Sinclair could work with Fox's materials and not stray too far from his socialist roots. After all, it was Thorstein Veblen who pointed out the destructive tendencies built into the American business system by the fact that financiers and the actual owners and producers were separated from one another, causing conflict and tension between the principle of efficiency and profit. Even Henry Ford could agree with this line of reasoning. Sinclair simply told the story in a way that both Ford and Veblen could understand. So too Fox, even if he was throwing a tantrum at the time.[21]

Sinclair had exposed the business element behind a world that liked to think it lived for dreams. Though he was too beholden to his subject's desires, it seemed closer to Sinclair's heart to write an exposé of Hollywood business than to write scripts for Irving Thalberg. As he pointed out in his book about Fox, it still seemed to him that Hollywood was making movies that will "never tell anyone that there is anything fundamentally wrong with our social system." So behind the darling antics of Shirley Temple, the buxom humor of Mae West, the snide outlook of W. C. Fields, the gangsterism of James Cagney, and the gonzo humor of the Marx Brothers, Sinclair suggested there lurked the power of what always lurked behind everything in America—money. He even made some while making the point.[22]

Battleship Eisenstein

As much as Sinclair was making money hand over fist in 1932, he was losing it just as fast, and not just on his anti-Socialist mansion in Beverly Hills. This was thanks to someone Charlie Chaplin had introduced him to. His name was Sergei Eisenstein, and he was the most famous moviemaker in the Soviet Union. Eisenstein had believed and fought in the Russian Revolution, though he had doubts about Stalin. He was also a member of the international avant-garde. By most reports, he was gay and certainly a bohemian artist who had experimented with theater and then moved into movies. His film *Battleship Potemkin* was a masterpiece of modernist film, and Sinclair thought it, rightfully, a work of artistic genius. It used ordinary people rather than professional actors in order to re-create the mood of the Russian Revolution. Eisenstein also used montage, patching together scenes that conveyed the simultaneity of historical happenings and generating a riveting whole. Having become enamored of the technical sophistication of American movies—sound had already been introduced as far back as 1927 by Hollywood—Eisenstein wanted to come learn more about Hollywood technique and, in the process, make a movie version of Theodore Dreiser's *An American Tragedy*. In October 1930 he arrived in Hollywood, but Paramount quickly fired Eisenstein from the project, and he was cut adrift. Thus began what Mary Craig Sinclair recalled as the "greatest blunder" she and Upton "ever made."[23]

The original approach to Sinclair should have clued him in. After all, it was Charlie Chaplin who suggested that Eisenstein ask for financial help from Sinclair so that Eisenstein could go to Mexico and shoot a film. Charlie Chaplin, one of the richest men in Hollywood, was suggesting that a socialist author help fund Eisenstein's film? That should have given Sinclair pause, but he was not a man given to pause. He rushed in to help Eisenstein, believing him to be an aggrieved artist shunned by the wealthy Hollywood studios. By November 1930 Sinclair was frantically going around to friends trying to raise money for Eisenstein. He met with Eisenstein, and they planned the trip to Mexico. Sinclair was a bit nervous about the whole thing, so he contacted Craig's brother, Hunter, and suggested he go south with Eisenstein. Here was an interesting plan: a southern man nursing a drinking problem would go to Mexico to keep a Russian Jew and avant-garde director on schedule. Sinclair told Hunter that he couldn't drink while in Mexico, and in a manipulative venture told Hunter that Eisenstein had overheard Sinclair talk about Hunter's drinking. Thus, Eisenstein would be on the outlook for his drinking, so Hunter had better behave, Sinclair suggested. Besides, "Craig has staked everything she owns on this venture." Hunter would never want to ruin the life of "sister," as he referred to Craig reverentially, and so he went to Mexico in preparation to oversee a movie entitled *Que Viva Mexico*.[24]

The problems began immediately. When Hunter arrived with Eisenstein and his trusty cameraman, Edward Tisse, in Mexico, the police promptly arrested them and took their papers. Then came the earthquakes, which upset filming. Back in the United States, Sinclair was busy writing *The Wet Parade* and desperately raising gobs of money. He struck it rich with Otto Kahn, a wealthy banker who threw money Sinclair's way, but there was always the need for more. The reports coming back from Mexico were worrisome. Hunter explained in February 1931 that "a group of men" had "threatened" them because they believed "our cameras were machines that enabled us to look through the women's clothes." All of the problems resulted in more headaches for Sinclair, all of them financial. By summer of 1931, Sinclair was prepared to raise seventy thousand dollars for the film, much more than he had originally intended, but he was starting to wonder why he hadn't seen any actual film being sent back to the States.[25]

So Eisenstein sent back some film, which made Sinclair only more nervous. By August, he wrote Eisenstein saying that the film looked random and chaotic, not very promising. "You keep calling for more—and what am I to do?" This tone of exasperation captured Sinclair's mood at the time. Nonetheless, he upped the amount of film sent to Eisenstein. He was writing to his ailing mother, whose doctor was demanding more money for her treatments, and telling her he couldn't worry about her situation now, since the Eisenstein affair was swallowing all of his money and time (she passed away a few months later). Sinclair was especially worried now that banks were collapsing across the country. He knew that as winter approached, there would be less cash to raise. By fall, Sinclair was suffering health problems due to the stress. When he got out of the hospital, he came home to a frightening letter from Hunter that foresaw doom. "I am positive that" Eisenstein "has not the slightest regard for the interest of the investors or for you and sister," Hunter bemoaned. "He is thinking only of his artistic triumph." So Sinclair started putting limits on the project; he refused to raise any more than the extra ten thousand dollars Eisenstein had just demanded. He even telegrammed Stalin asking what he should do with this wayward artist. Stalin telegrammed back and said that Eisenstein should return to the Soviet Union and stop messing around in Mexico. This sent Sinclair into a tailspin.[26]

Eisenstein prepared to return to the Soviet Union, where he would continue to work on the film. Sinclair explained to his friend William Woodward that "Moscow will know a good deal more about managing Eisenstein than we do." Eisenstein was misbehaving by sending dirty pictures through customs and telling people that Hunter had a drinking problem. Things couldn't seem to get worse. Then Sinclair made another fateful decision. He had invested his own money and had bought the film, as he didn't trust Eisenstein any longer. So, he reasoned, why not take the film that had been shot so far and edit it himself? By the end of 1932, when Eisenstein was safely back in the Soviet Union, Sinclair made a deal with Sol Lesser, a man who, like Fox, had climbed up the hierarchy of the movie business during the 1920s. Lesser quickly set to work to make what was now to be called *Thunder over Mexico*. The job was done, and by March 1933, Sinclair was showing it to his friends Charlie Chaplin and Douglas Fairbanks. They liked it. It's easy to see why: The final version was beautiful, depicting bullfights, men farming milk from cacti, and peons struggling for dignity, all in a dreamy format. And so Sinclair decided he wanted to "give the high-brows and reading public a chance to learn that the picture is worthwhile" by having openings in Los Angeles and then New York City.[27]

On May 10, 1933, the film showed at the Carthay Circle Theater in Los Angeles. Sinclair spoke, as Communists protested in and out of the theater, arguing that Sinclair had stolen the art of a great Soviet artist. Some protesters threw stink bombs. Then Sinclair hauled himself out to New York City, where he and Lesser were planning to show the film at the Rialto Theater on Times Square. Craig, paranoid as usual and with the debt stacking up making her that much more so, began to think that Lesser wanted the film to do poorly so that he could take complete control over it and rake in a profit. So Sinclair was on guard and worried about the Rialto showing. The film opened at the Rialto on September 22, 1933. Lesser had done nothing to sabotage it; the only ones who wanted to do that were the Communists who showed up again. This time fights broke out, and people had to be removed from the theater.[28]

Sinclair stayed out east for six weeks. He had numerous battles to pursue. The movie pleased no one. The right thought it revolutionary, while the Communist left attacked Sinclair for stealing Eisenstein's art and making a "fascist" film. Some radicals believed Sinclair had purged the film of its radical content. *The Daily Worker*, the Communist Party newspaper, and the *Modern Monthly* attacked him along these lines, the latter blaming him for "the destruction of Que Viva Mexico!" The editors went on to say that it was the responsibility of communists to "reveal the fascist character of" Sinclair's "ideology and deed." This confused Sinclair, since a leading Communist had told him earlier that "the ideology" of the film "will be satisfactory to Moscow." He painstakingly showed how no radical scenes were cut, while claiming the film was essentially not a revolutionary work of art, just a work of art. Sinclair could have pointed out that Stalin had doubts about Eisenstein, but he never wanted to do anything that might make the Soviet Union look bad. So he just absorbed the Communist attacks and went on.[29]

The hostile reaction to the film posed problems in getting it distributed. For once, Sinclair's skills at publicity failed him. The Soviet Union was unwilling to help distribute the film, for obvious reasons, and Sol Lesser was running into problems finding anyone in America interested in touching such a hot potato. Showings were sparse after the first few, and the money coming in was tiny. After a little more than a year, Sinclair tallied up the whole thing and figured out that the film cost $94,000 to make and had grossed $30,000. Sinclair's attempt to become a movie producer was an abysmal failure. He should never have listened to Chaplin.[30]

By 1934, as he watched his debts shoot up after a brief stint of being flush, Sinclair could at least say that he had broken into the world of Hollywood. In two cases, he had been played the sucker—by both Fox and Eisenstein. But he tried his best to persevere in both cases. There was still a question about whether he had "gone Hollywood," as he feared when writing his daughter-in-law in 1932. By 1934, as he was turning his attention from entertainment back to politics, Sinclair had a movie version of *The Jungle* that was quickly turning to dust; a movie credit for *The Moneychangers* that embarrassed him; a success in *The Wet Parade* that aggravated many of his friends; a failed script at MGM sitting in the file cabinet of Irving Thalberg; and a movie that some thought a colossal violation of Soviet artistry. Sinclair had made some important friends in Hollywood, including Charlie Chaplin. But he had also made his fair share of enemies, and they were ready for revenge, which they got of the sweetest kind. One of them was Louis B. Mayer. He had gone along with the making of *The Wet Parade* but clearly didn't care for Sinclair's book about Fox. Nor did he care for Sinclair's socialist politics (which were barely disguised in *The Wet Parade*). He was poised and ready to do something to ruin Sinclair. And he did so in the fateful year of 1934.

SEVEN

I, GOVERNOR OF CALIFORNIA

1934

OVERLEAF:

Ship with pro-Sinclair banner, 1934

American conditions require American thinking
and American methods of action.

—UPTON SINCLAIR, JULY 1934

You will have to be citizens not merely for flag waving
and listening to speeches on the Fourth of July, but for
education and organization and hard work.

—UPTON SINCLAIR, AUGUST 1934

You know what Mark Twain said—that a lie
can travel all the way around the earth while the
truth is putting on its boots.

—UPTON SINCLAIR, OCTOBER 1934

BECOMING A SOCIALIST RIGHT NOW," JOHN DOS PASSOS, A friend of Upton Sinclair's, explained in the year 1932, "would have just about the same effect on anybody as drinking a bottle of near-beer." Waldo Frank, another friend, believed that the "world" was "in crisis" and that there was "no time to lose" in pledging his faith to Communism. Desperate times demanded desperate acts, even on the part of writers. More than words were needed. Revolution was needed, even if it had to be modeled on one that had occurred miles away in Russia, under circumstances very different from those that the United States faced in 1932. So Dos Passos signed his name to the pamphlet *Culture and the Crisis* and made it clear he was voting Communist in 1932. Other writers followed. With Sinclair's pronouncements on the Soviet revolution plus the deepening crisis of the Great Depression throughout that year, it might have made sense for him to have joined his writer friends. After all, he had done everything he could, even when Eisenstein was driving him crazy, to shield the Soviet Union from criticism. He sometimes sounded as if he thought the Soviet Union was the only source of hope for the world. Still,

Sinclair never joined the Communist Party and refused to associate his own radicalism with it. He remained, truly, an *American* radical seeking indigenous solutions to his country's problems. While Dos Passos and Frank rushed to join the Communist Party, Sinclair left the Socialist Party for the oldest political party in U.S. history—the Democrats.[1]

Desperation can make people act in strange ways. Instead of making Sinclair a revolutionary, the Great Depression made him a realist and a reformer. If ever there was a reason to become apocalyptic—to think about taking up guns and rushing over to the posh mansions in Pasadena and Beverly Hills—a 25 percent national unemployment rate, which had set in around 1932, was it. But Sinclair didn't become desperate. When he became a Democrat and decided to run for governor, believing he might actually win, Sinclair explained, "I am not talking utopias but about keeping starving people alive." The problem of starvation forced Sinclair to pose constructive solutions that were viable and could garner political will behind them. Sinclair was never content chitchatting about revolution, or pretending that the American working class was ready for Leninism. Like Dos Passos and Frank, Sinclair believed it was time for action, but not the sort that merely made intellectuals feel good about themselves, or that stoked their anger to equal the level of desperation setting in nationwide. Certainly Hoovervilles, soup kitchens, and riots among veterans demanding their bonuses from World War I demanded anger, but it had to be an *American* anger capable of mobilizing people for action that was responsible and productive at the same time. And, ideally, the sort that could win votes.[2]

In 1930 Sinclair had run as a socialist for political office in California. That time, it was for governor, and again, it was lackluster, much like his earlier campaigns for the House and the Senate. "My friends," Sinclair told an audience during the campaign in his typical pull-no-punches style, "I will tell you a secret—I really don't believe I am going to be governor this time." He was right. Running on a platform of socialism, tenure for schoolteachers, a heavier inheritance tax, and a single tax on land, he received fifty thousand votes. He at least got a laugh when he was accidentally listed as the Republican candidate in early state documents, but this was about all the fun there was. The rest was the same old thing: make a few speeches and then sit and watch his votes fail to exceed 3 percent of the electorate. When Heywood Broun asked him to consider running for president as a socialist in 1932, Sinclair was flattered but ruled it out. What was the point in pretending about politics any longer?[3]

But then a new approach came, this time not from a journalist living in New York City but from a Santa Monica hotel owner named Gilbert Stevenson. The man knew California politics and figured it wouldn't be difficult to take over the Democratic Party and point it in a more radical direction. The party was weak, having become, over the years, a party of feeble opposition and little more than a shell. Sinclair could probably win the nomination for governor if he drew new people and new energy into the party. Sinclair worried that Craig would object (which she did), but he also believed the times demanded action. He changed party affiliations on September 1, 1933. He tried to rationalize it by saying that he had been born a Democrat (he didn't mention that few white southerners weren't born Democrat), but his real rationale came when he explained that there was a long tradition of activists taking over parties and pointing them in new directions—the way politicians like Teddy Roosevelt and Robert LaFollette tried to push Republicans in a progressive direction. When asked if he was selling out, Sinclair explained he had always tried to change the system from within, and that he had, after all, "written appeals to Vincent Astor and John D. Rockefeller," that is, to the wealthy leaders of American society. Besides, being a socialist wasn't cutting it any longer. Perhaps people would listen to him if he replaced the word *socialist* with *democrat*. "So long as I was a Socialist," Sinclair explained to his son, David, who objected to his father's abandonment of the Socialist Party, "I was just one more crank; but when I call myself a Democrat, I become a man worth listening to."[4]

Part of Sinclair's new political affiliation was due to the man who had impressed nearly everyone at the time—the president of the United States, Franklin Delano Roosevelt. By the time Sinclair registered as a Democrat, Roosevelt had responded to the Great Depression in bold ways. He had provided relief to the banks, passed the Federal Emergency Relief Act, put young men back to work by creating jobs for them in America's public parks, helped refinance failed mortgages on farms, brought electricity to impoverished areas of the South, and started to encourage businesses to self-regulate in order to encourage confidence in America's failed economy. All of this in his famous first "hundred days." Though Sinclair wrote FDR in April 1933 saying, in his typically condescending manner, that the president needed to do much more, he was also willing to cut the president some slack. He explained to David, "I have no certainty as to what" Roosevelt's administration "will do and can only note the facts and tendencies day by day." It was not just FDR's policies, some of them bold and some not so, that Sinclair admired, but his style of leadership. As the historian Michael Kazin points out, "Not since Lincoln, had a president combined so deep a compassion for ordinary people with so fierce and visionary an assault on their well-to-do enemies." Even if Sinclair was hopeful, he was not naive. He knew that FDR, like any leader, needed to feel pressure from below if he was going to move in a direction to Sinclair's liking. So Sinclair pushed by running for governor on a platform that was more radical than the first steps taken by the New Deal. Thus he would help show the United States the way out of the Depression.[5]

EPIC: Sinclair's Own American Plan

Others were pushing FDR at the same time. Sinclair's old ally John Dewey helped form the League for Independent Political Action, which tried to galvanize labor organizers, farmers, and middle-class Americans around a third party. They had a magazine, *Common Sense*, and an intellectual guru, Alfred Bingham, who talked about a "cooperative social ethic" replacing capitalism. The Farmer-Labor Party, an independent third party riddled with Communists, had successfully elected Floyd Olson as governor of Minnesota in 1930. The governor's rhetoric and action swerved to the left by 1932. In the words of one historian, Olson "mixed endorsements for some of Roosevelt's policies with criticism of the New Deal for not going far enough." Meanwhile, labor organizers like John L. Lewis were organizing industrial sectors of the economy, pushing beyond the conservative American Federation of Labor (AFL) that limited its sights to skilled laborers. Lewis's United Mine Workers (UMW) believed that the government could do more to support its goal of building a vast industrial army of organized citizens.[6]

While some organized, others dreamed of better worlds over the horizon and told their fellow Americans that they should as well. Father Charles Coughlin, a parish priest from Detroit, went on national radio on a regular basis to tell Americans that Christianity supported not just the New Deal but even more radical steps in the direction of "social justice." Francis Townsend, a doctor who lived close to Sinclair and who happened one day to be shaving and looked out his window to see old people rummaging through the garbage for food, started to argue for a pension plan for the elderly in America, and many read his arguments in national newspapers. Most important of all was Huey Long. This "messiah of the rednecks" condemned the New Deal for being too favorable to business and offered his own plan, known as "Share Our Wealth." His idea was simple: he'd tax the wealthiest members of society in order to ensure that every man could have a "homestead" or "enough for a home, an automobile, a radio, and the ordinary conveniences." Long didn't just talk about these things; he promised to make them come true once he moved from being senator of Louisiana to becoming president sometime in the future, as he hoped.[7]

Gilbert Stevenson and the others who counseled him to run believed Sinclair would have to stand for something that could attract voters and make clear he wasn't a traditional Democrat. Anyone who had read his books would have known this already, but now it was time for him to explain what he stood for in the context of California politics and the Great Depression. Thus was born End Poverty in California (EPIC). It was a straightforward set of ideas, "so obvious that a ten-year-old child can understand it," Sinclair explained. Essentially, Sinclair believed that the state government should buy up idle factories and abandoned farmland. These properties would then be leased back to unemployed citizens who would use them to produce for themselves and their fellow citizens the goods necessary to pull them out of the Depression. He called this "production for use" and argued it was grounded in "good morals and sound public policy." Meanwhile, as unemployed citizens put themselves back to work with the help of the state, the government would abolish the sales tax and accrue revenue instead from a heftier income tax. The consumer would no longer be punished for consumption, and this too would help resuscitate the economy.[8]

Not much of this was new, at least not in terms of Sinclair's own thinking. In one of his first articles written after joining the Socialist Party in 1903, Sinclair used the phrase "production for use" to explain his social and economic philosophy (a term that other socialists used at times and that had heavy overtones of Thorstein Veblen's economic thought). As far back as 1920, he spoke of the end of the American frontier and how idle acres of land abandoned by settlers could be used more fruitfully if managed by the government. The ideas that served as the backbone of EPIC had been swimming around in Sinclair's mind for some time now, many of them going all the way back to reformers who were struggling to make capitalism more humane when Sinclair was still in knickers. These ideas were also finding a receptive audience in the state of California as it entered the Great Depression during Sinclair's adulthood.[9]

The central ideas behind EPIC flowed back to the thinking of Eugene Debs in the earliest years of the twentieth century, and from there back to the Populist Party activism of the 1870s and 1880s, and even further back all the way to the political thought of Thomas Jefferson. Debs, for instance, came to socialism during the 1890s not by reading Karl Marx but by hearing his fellow laborers talk about the pride found in their craft—working with one's own hands to produce wealth that couldn't be measured in stocks or bank notes but only in the physical creation of actual products. Debs loved the pride of "citizen-producers" who wanted nothing more than to own their own farms or small shops where they could produce for the good of the community. He had learned from the populists who had organized throughout the southern and western portions of America after the Civil War in order to protect the small farmer from rapacious lenders. Populists didn't just believe that ordinary people were better than bankers, they had built up an alternative system of cooperative warehouses where they could store their goods and then have them reenter the market when prices went up. Collective action, they believed, could protect the small independent farmer. As these populists watched their cooperatives being trounced by banks and by railroad rates that grew exorbitant, they started to believe that the federal government needed to support them in their work. The government could help extend credit to small farmers and their cooperatives, and this would save the small farmer from the more predatory aspects of capitalism. In the end, Thomas Jefferson's egalitarian dream of small farmers—the "chosen people of God," as he referred to them—serving as the backbone of the nation would survive into the twentieth century.[10]

For Sinclair, the populists' Jeffersonian dreams lived on in the cooperative movement of the United States. Like numerous socialists, Sinclair knew a great deal about cooperatives. Right after he arrived in Pasadena in 1916, Sinclair helped out a local cooperative, but he was saddened as stores in the area undersold it and made it go broke. He considered putting his own publishing company on a cooperative basis during the 1920s, though he was warned against it. Then as the Depression hit California, Sinclair grew amazed at just how much cooperative enterprising was going on in the state. There was Oakland's Unemployed Exchange Association, which had 1,200 members; closer to home, there were numerous food cooperatives around Los Angeles. Though most of these co-ops wanted to stay out of politics, Sinclair drew upon their energy, noting that the Great Depression had driven some people to develop creative barter systems that saved them from economic despair. Sinclair took a page from the populist playbook by suggesting that EPIC would extend credit to existing co-ops throughout the state, the way the populists had wanted to create a subtreasury that could extend credit to farmers banding together in cooperatives. The "citizen producer" that Debs had championed could find political support from EPIC. Following that logic, Sinclair believed "I Produce and I Defend" was a good slogan for EPIC.[11]

Once he became governor, Sinclair thought, land colonies would take off. Because they relied upon state funds, they would originally be indebted to the state, but as they became more productive and capable of generating their own income, they would become "self-governing groups" though still "conducted under a charter from the state." These land colonies would serve as a potent critique of FDR's agricultural programs under the New Deal. Like many Americans, Sinclair could not understand why farmers were being asked to destroy their products while people starved. Of course, Roosevelt's idea was to keep products off the market and thus drive prices up in order to save farmers, but when pictures of farmers burning crops or dumping milk were teamed up with pictures of migrant farmer families with starving children, Americans began to wonder what was happening. For Sinclair, keeping productive land "out of use" was wasteful; the thing to do was make it productive and reemploy those without jobs. The state government would also help get "farmers' products to the cities," and thus by coordinating production and consumption would ensure that all citizens' needs were met. Land colonies would employ doctors and dentists who would receive a salary but be free to work elsewhere. And colonies would become communal enterprises that would have "cooperative kitchens" as well as libraries, theaters, and even moviehouses.[12]

Sinclair's ideas sounded utopian to many—and distinctly Californian. By the Great Depression, California was known less as the land of milk and honey and more as the home of "crackpotism." Utopian dreamers could be found everywhere, by some reports. There was, for instance, the Utopian Society, whose members had read Edward Bellamy's *Looking Backward* and believed society could be organized in such a manner that everyone would go to college until age twenty-five, work three hours a day from ages twenty-five to forty-four, and then retire into prosperity at age forty-five. Such a precise plan for everyone's life wasn't really the strange part; the strange part was the organization's "secret rites" and cultish practices. In addition to the Utopians, there were the Technocrats, part of a wider national movement that had sunk roots deep in California's soil. They believed, drawing upon the thinking of Thorstein Veblen, that if experts were put in charge of the government, and if the government managed the economy, waste and inefficiency would be eliminated and economic prosperity would flourish. No doubt, when Sinclair called for putting "the technicians in control of the state" and argued that government was often more efficient than private industry, Technocrats cheered.[13]

Sinclair welcomed support from every quarter, but it is unfair to characterize him as a California crackpot. The land colonies that EPIC would create would eventually manage themselves after they became financially viable. "Such local self-government," Sinclair pointed out, "is directly along the lines of our American tradition." His EPIC plan would simply unleash the natural energies of citizen-producers, and in doing this, the program fell in line with the ideals of America's founding fathers. "We are seeking to do in the realm of economics exactly what our ancestors did in the realm of politics," he argued.[14]

This might explain why the idea of EPIC resonated with large numbers of Californians and even caught on outside the state. Sinclair knew that he had to speak in an American idiom if he was going to offer practical solutions to getting out of the Great Depression. This required more than outlining policy proposals, it required explaining how his faith and the American dream were in sync—how it could be that Jefferson's ghost might smile at a man calling for self-managing cooperatives aided by the government. Sinclair did not talk about socialism when he outlined EPIC; instead, he talked about "self-reliance, initiative, frugality, equality, neighborliness." He didn't just chastise those hording wealth, but explained why the United States was a "middle class" nation and needed to continue to be if it was to hold on to its national greatness. He didn't speak of Marx but of Jefferson.[15]

He also emphasized the conservative dimension of EPIC. If there was one thing Sinclair hated, it was the "dole"—providing welfare and giving away something for nothing. "If we start to make the unemployed self-sustaining, we stop the dole," Sinclair explained. "Our plan," he wrote, will "put the unemployed at productive labor, letting them produce what they are going to consume and thus taking them from the backs of the taxpayers." Sinclair despised the "idleness" encouraged by welfare handouts. Nor did he think the dole fiscally responsible (nor, it should be pointed out, did FDR). Sinclair believed the New Deal was less prudent than EPIC, since the former would wind up taxing and giving money away while the latter expected something in return from the people receiving public support. Sinclair took what sounded like very conservative ideas and made them into a part of his progressive EPIC package. "The dole, by enabling the poor to buy goods, constitutes a government subsidy for private business," Sinclair explained. Such a plan would "bankrupt the government. Let the unemployed produce what they consume and the problem is solved." Thus, EPIC ensured relief for the unemployed in a manner that was in line with American ideals of democracy and even fiscal conservatism. As *Time* magazine admitted, while some claimed Sinclair an "agent of Moscow," he was really "as American as pumpkin pie."[16]

Run, Uppie, Run

Armed with arguments that EPIC was a logical extension of American democracy, Sinclair leaped into the primary. The original advice he had received proved right: The Democratic Party was a shell and it didn't take much for him to win the nomination. The party had been out of power for a generation, and what Sinclair did was draw in supporters who thought the party should adopt new leadership and ideas. He needed only one hundred signatures from members of the Democratic Party to get his name on the ballot, and anyone who wanted could become a member of the party, even switching prior affiliation if necessary. Sinclair's only real opponent during the primary was George Creel, who had headed up the Committee on Public Information (CPI) during World War I and who had influence within FDR's administration. Creel said that Sinclair had "the brains of a pigeon," but that didn't stop Sinclair's large voting base in Los Angeles from trouncing Creel's smaller base in San Francisco. During August, the month of the primary, Sinclair grew more optimistic as positive reports came back from precinct workers and as volunteers poured in to support him. The results showed: Sinclair won 330,216 votes to Creel's 206,001 votes. And all it cost him was $674.60.[17]

As he moved from the primary to the general election, Sinclair faced two opponents—the incumbent, Frank Merriam, and a third-party progressive candidate, Raymond Haight, who had run for the Republican Party nomination. Sinclair thought his chances looked fairly good, especially since Merriam didn't receive as many votes in the Republican primary as he had in the Democratic primary. There was an immediate problem, though, in that the longshoremen whom Sinclair had originally supported during his fights for free speech during the 1920s went on strike again, and this time it turned much more violent. Merriam squashed the strike, believing it threatened California with an onslaught of radicalism. This gave an otherwise lackluster governor some strength (just how lackluster can be seen in this *positive* assessment of Merriam by the *Los Angeles Times*: "Just a bald head; a pair of clear, business-like glassless eyes; a firm handshake, and one belongs to the lodge"). Merriam's actions during the strike solidified support for his candidacy. "The best gauge of the Governor's real public service is to consider what might have happened had this sturdy, rugged American not been in office at Sacramento. Nothing short of chaos would have been invited if not actually precipitated by weakness or indecision," the *Los Angeles Times* explained. It was no surprise that the *Times* would support Merriam over Sinclair, but what should have worried Sinclair was just how quickly the campaign became framed around a growing fear about impending radicalism. Sinclair felt hemmed in, afraid to support the longshoremen too strongly, thus garnering attacks from the left as well as the right in this case. This foreshadowed the course of the campaign. Though he might have been as American as "pumpkin pie," he had a hard time convincing enough Californians that this was really the case.[18]

He also fell into problems with the Democratic Party. What had been Sinclair's strength during the primary became a weakness during the general election. The Democratic Party split, with numerous old-timers bolting. This problem went all the way up to the national level. James Farley, chairman of the Democratic National Committee, would waver in his attitude toward Sinclair, causing the candidate numerous headaches and embarrassments throughout the course of the campaign. Sinclair decided that it was best to go all the way to the top and try to get the president to endorse him. He hopped a train on August 30, just on the heels of the primary, and traveled east to visit FDR, who had already made it clear he couldn't get involved in state politics and didn't want to talk politics with Sinclair. Nonetheless, Sinclair left Hyde Park beaming with satisfaction, telling reporters that Roosevelt agreed with the idea of production for use and would say so publicly when he had the chance. Sinclair also had a good meeting with James Farley, who was, like Roosevelt, a master of mixed messages. Then Sinclair proceeded to meet with members of Roosevelt's own administration, including Henry Wallace, who seemed to like EPIC, and Harry Hopkins, who liked it too. The *New York Times* reported that Hopkins's favorable attitude toward Sinclair reflected a split within Roosevelt's administration. There was no chance in hell that Roosevelt would have endorsed Sinclair; nonetheless, that left plenty of room for mixed messages on the part of the administration and faulty conclusions on the part of Sinclair.[19]

Sinclair returned to California flush with optimism. He proceeded to campaign hard, making speeches everywhere he could. There were big turnouts at his rallies; twelve thousand people heard him speak at Dreamland Rink in San Francisco and then another nine thousand in Oakland. California is a big state, and when he wasn't busy speaking, he was driving, or answering letters or going on the radio. "I am now no longer a writer," he admitted. "I am making a sacrifice of my own talents." Not just his writing suffered; so did his diet. He was down to eating a cup of custard or ice cream when he had the chance. The hard work was paying off, though. At the Democratic Party convention on September 20, the EPIC platform was adopted. Even a former enemy like George Creel was willing to throw in with Sinclair.[20]

The campaign brought out Sinclair's better side. He remained on message, never allowing himself to be deflected, and he always responded quickly and decisively against attacks. He had a remarkable ability to defuse people during meetings, especially hecklers. He once asked a heckler if he believed in democracy, to which, of course, the heckler responded yes. Sinclair then polled the audience as to whether they wanted to hear him or the heckler; the vote went overwhelmingly to Sinclair, who then proceeded to speak while the heckler sulked off. Sinclair also took questions at every speaking event, answering his critics forthrightly, by most accounts. When he said this "had never before been done in politics," he was exaggerating, but not by much. Sinclair knew not to talk about religion or other matters that divided people on the campaign trail. He told his fellow campaign workers that when asked about religion, they should "tell the people that Jesus denounced poverty" and that EPIC would end poverty no matter what a person's religion was. That would settle the matter, and there was no need to go any further.[21]

Sinclair was the type of leader who knew that a successful campaign required grassroots initiatives. "The people are doing it all," he explained toward the end of the campaign. "I don't even know their names; it is just a blur of faces to me." At the center of the campaign were locally managed EPIC clubs that coordinated outreach and raised money. Starting in January 1934, there were 289 active EPIC clubs in California; by March there were 600; by June, 800; and by the end of the campaign, over 2,000. Grassroots initiatives didn't necessarily translate into a free-for-all democracy. Sinclair worried that too much democracy could dilute his message; it was bad enough that there were all the books he had written that could be pilfered for embarrassing quotes. Sinclair didn't need some local yokel getting off message. So, as Greg Mitchell points out, Sinclair's campaign manager Dick Otto "appointed all of the chapter secretaries. The End Poverty League's board of directors, known as the Twelve Apostles—ten men and two women—held daily meetings in L.A. (rarely attended by Sinclair) to decide policy, with little input from outside." Nonetheless, the clubs still provided the energy behind the campaign, getting the word out and raising money from bake sales, rummage sales, picnics, dances, and even rodeos. Sinclair believed that grassroots organizing was the only way to defeat the influx of big money into politics. By going directly to the people, he could dampen the media onslaught he would face throughout the campaign.[22]

EPIC kindled its own movement culture. Symbols sprouted up everywhere: The "I Produce and I Defend" slogan was accompanied by a picture of a bee that was replicated throughout the state (symbolizing the capacity to produce and sting if necessary). EPIC workers set their own lyrics to popular songs and then taught them at local club meetings. This one was sung to the tune of "Glory Hallelujah!":

> Our eyes shall see the dawning of a great triumphant day!
> Want and hunger shall be swept from us, as hosts of people pray!
> Farm and homestead shall be sacred and one's home one's own shall
>   stay
> When Sinclair is marching on
> Glory, glory hallelujah! Sinclair is marching on
> We'll make Sinclair our Governor and joyous bells will chime
> End Poverty. End Poverty. And now's the happy time!
> Free Americans are destitute and hungry, that's the crime
> But Sinclair is marching on

Another was sung to the tune of "Over There":

> EPIC Plan—EPIC Plan, On the air, everywhere, EPIC Plan!
> Vote for Upton Sinclair, He's always "been there" with plans to help
>   his fellow man.
> We'll Colonize and Factorize; There's work for all, Food for all,
>   If we're wise.
> We'll elect him! May God protect him! Sinclair for Governor,
>   California's EPIC Plan!

Sinclair himself contributed a play, *Depression Island*, to the cause. It told the story of three people on an island and how one started to exploit the others after winning a contest. The other two then try to unify and beat the winner and are accused of "Red stuff"; then the island occupants discover there is "an American way" to solve the problem. Sinclair even got Charlie Chaplin to speak at a fund-raiser where the play was performed. As a Chaplin biographer pointed out, "Chaplin paid for the rental of the theater and appeared on stage at the rally, where he forgot his nervousness and delivered a rousing speech." In addition to single events such as these, EPIC published a newspaper that, at its height, reached two million readers on a weekly basis. Sinclair's message was reaching people through song, print, speeches, and radio, and it seemed that people were listening.[23]

Attacked!

He should have seen it coming. The first to attack him were the usual suspects. It was no surprise when the Chamber of Commerce rallied against Sinclair or when real estate salesmen worried openly about his election. As far as the Realty Board was concerned, this wasn't just about self-interest on their part but defending the American way of life. The board's president argued that Sinclair "ridicules our religion, our schools, our business and about everything else we love." Then came the churches. They had read *The Profits of Religion* or at least the scarier outtakes that the *Los Angeles Times* made sure to publish in its pages. Ministers preached anti-Sinclair sermons. One Presbyterian church posed a potent question, "The arm of 'Red Russia' is Long: Is it to be Merriam or Moscow in California November 6th?" To drive home the point, the church put Upton Sinclair in a league with the Four Horsemen of the Apocalypse and the Anti-Christ. Then came the Mary Pickford of religion, Aimee Semple McPherson. Twice divorced and with a public scandal about disappearing in order to have an affair, she still posed as the paragon of virtue. McPherson set up a pageant built around the theme of "America Awake! The Enemy Is at Your Gates!" She threw a red flag into a burning cauldron just to make sure people got the point. And for a last-second blast to rally the troops, someone gave fifty dollars to every African American preacher who would sermonize against Sinclair the Sunday before the election.[24]

Sinclair was clearly putting California, and more specifically Los Angeles, on the map in ways that embarrassed the city's elite. Many believed the *Los Angeles Times* when its headline bellowed, "Hordes of Jobless Swooping on State." If true, then it seemed right to drive poorer people off the voting rolls, since they might not even be residents but outsiders from Oklahoma or some nearby state. Some Republicans went to work trying to disenfranchise those they suspected had flooded into Los Angeles in order to vote and then live high on the hog off of Sinclair's planned programs. Some investigations turned up false registrations, and around half a million voters found their registration challenged. One court summoned twenty-one thousand registered voters and found only the eight who showed up were legitimate and allowed to remain registered. Try as they may, Democrats had a hard time opposing this sort of blatant intimidation, though Sinclair supporters eventually blocked the most egregious attempts to drive voters off the rolls.[25]

The *Los Angeles Times* led the charge that Sinclair posed a danger to California. Harry Chandler, "perhaps the richest man in California," ran the paper and had a personal vendetta against Sinclair. Chandler never failed to point out that he wasn't alone, since, by his own calculations, 90 percent of the press in California was against this rabble-rouser. But the *Los Angeles Times* still wound up playing a special role, culling through Sinclair's writings and taking controversial quotes, often out of context, and slapping them into black boxes in just about every issue up to election day. Every quote made Sinclair sound like a lunatic. Even the paper's more traditional reporting about the election dripped with venom toward Sinclair. When the candidate sought refuge from the campaign and went to Kate Crane-Gartz's house to read through mail and relax a bit, the *Times*'s headline read, "Sinclair Taking Vacation: Candidate for Governor Retires Temporarily to Luxurious Mansion of Crane Plumbing Heiress." The story read, "Worn by the labors of his candidacy, which he says is purely in the interests of the downtrodden, the ex-Socialist Democratic gubernatorial nominee is living luxuriously." The paper printed just about any anti-Sinclair letter it received, since in these, it had no obligation to truth. One letter writer feared that if Sinclair were elected, people would be herded "into great barns or tents, sleeping on the floor or ground." Worse than that, each morning a person would get "a cup" and stand "in line" to be given coffee while "great pots of mush cooking" would be nearby. People would then be forced to eat out of "troughs."[26]

The *Los Angeles Times* helped generate a rumor mill that took on a life

6

of its own. In the minds of some California citizens, Sinclair had supported "everything from nudism and free love to Bolshevism." He had trampled the flag when at San Pedro—though he had really upheld the Constitution—and was present at the bombing of the San Francisco Preparedness Day parade that Tom Mooney was blamed for, even though Sinclair had just moved to Pasadena at the time and was nowhere near San Francisco. Sinclair had illicit love affairs and was a Moscow agent. He was known as "Upton Éclair" and "Saintclair" and "Sincliar." He was reportedly a millionaire and making buckets of cash off the campaign. Communists called him a "Social Fascist," which meant an enemy on the left, while those on the right printed pamphlets that read, "Sinclair Dynamiter of All Churches and All Christian Organizations." He had a "Free Love Farm" and his political activism was better described as "SEPTIC," with "Santa Claus for Governor of the State of California" and the slogan "abolishing all unpleasantness." Whenever polls came out, they reported Sinclair losing at a margin far above anything that seemed feasible. Typically, these polls were conducted by phone, a luxury item at the time, meaning that mostly wealthy people who would never have thought of voting for Sinclair responded.[27]

It was Hollywood that did the most to destroy Sinclair. Louis Mayer, "the highest salaried executive in the country" and vice-chair of the Republican Party, had his revenge on the man he hated. He returned early from a European sojourn in order to map out an anti-Sinclair campaign, and provided money to United For California—the lead anti-Sinclair organization. By the time Mayer had returned to the United States, studio executives had already threatened to move to Florida if Sinclair won (Sinclair shot back that once an actress was stung on the nose by a mosquito in Florida, the studios would move back). Mayer had bigger plans than to threaten a move. He encouraged Irving Thalberg, who had once hired Sinclair to write scripts for Mayer's studio, to make nasty newsreels attacking Sinclair. Thalberg was more than ready to do so. Two of these newsreels, shown throughout California's moviehouses, had an "inquiring cameraman" ask random people on the streets who they planned to vote for. It seemed that all of the nice-looking people were planning to vote for Merriam, and the dirty, scroungy ones with bad accents were going to vote for Sinclair. Sinclair supporters were always asked follow-up questions, and they often appeared ignorant when asked about the reasons for their vote, while Merriam supporters were treated more cordially. Thalberg also filmed people coming off trains for his final "Bums Rush" newsreel.

When one actor who supported Sinclair told Thalberg that this was "the damnedest unfair thing I've ever heard of," Thalberg supposedly replied, "Nothing is unfair in politics."[28]

Other studios got in on the act. Some raised money by either intimidating employees or simply docking their pay and putting it directly into a fund for Merriam's reelection. Some posted warnings at the time clocks where employees punched out that read, "If you expect to punch this two weeks from now—don't vote for Sinclair." Sinclair threatened to press for a grand jury investigation into the movie industry's intimidation of employees, but to no avail. *Variety* magazine had an editorial that galvanized the anti-Sinclair troops by stating it was time to "stop moaning" about the man and instead to start "whipping friends and employees into line." The *Hollywood Reporter* crowed, "This campaign against Sinclair has been and is DYNAMITE. It is the most effective piece of political humdingery that has ever been effected." Some movie stars threatened they would leave if Sinclair was elected, believing taxes would get too high. There were a few Sinclair supporters in Hollywood, but they were ineffective against the blitz.[29]

The *Los Angeles Times* and Hollywood worked in tandem against Sinclair, creating a kind of synergy. Both were ready to pounce when Sinclair made any mistake. And it was certain that Sinclair would make a mistake, given that he was an inexperienced candidate, at least in terms of a high-profile campaign like this. On September 26, Sinclair gave his enemies what they wanted by making his worst gaffe of the campaign. He was tired that day, and Craig thought, as usual, that he should rest, but instead he took questions from reporters. Recounting his visit to Washington, D.C., Sinclair said, "I told Harry Hopkins in Washington that if I am elected half the unemployed of the United States will come to California, and he will have to make plans to take care of them." He made other comments that were just as controversial throughout the conference, but this was the one the *Times* reporter fixated on. He knew full well that the fear of losing one's job was a fear that could be played upon. The quote appeared the next day in the *Times*, and soon after, it appeared on billboards posted throughout the state. Soon after that, Irving Thalberg's newsreel was released featuring the "Bums Rush." The comment had ricocheted and found itself in an echo chamber perpetuated by Sinclair's enemies.[30]

While the "lie factory," as Sinclair called it, churned on, Merriam stayed in the background. Not that it seemed to matter, but Merriam didn't like that what *he* stood for was getting lost in the clutter of negative billboards and personal rumors spread about Sinclair. Merriam tacked to the left, even though he was a traditional Republican taking advice from Herbert Hoover. He praised the New Deal and endorsed Townsend's call to provide pensions to the elderly. Merriam spoke highly of FDR and even of the co-ops that Sinclair believed were the backbone of his own campaign. No matter what Merriam did, though, his handlers would continue to go negative. So he lurked in the shadows. He was a nonentity in a campaign that was mostly about his opponent's weaknesses.[31]

The Victory of Defeat

The last week of October was an especially bad week for Sinclair. It became clear that FDR's promise to say something good about production for use over the radio wasn't going to happen. James Farley denied that a letter that seemed to give support to Sinclair was really meant to do so. George Creel bolted the campaign and condemned Sinclair publicly, saying that while the New Deal thought of unemployment and economic depression as temporary conditions of capitalism, Sinclair believed them permanent. At the same time, Creel called Merriam "medieval," leaving this onetime candidate "stuck between epilepsy and catalepsy." A *Literary Digest* poll that showed Merriam way ahead got a lot of play at the same time all of this happened. Of course, the *Los Angeles Times* reported all of this dutifully. If it weren't for his grassroots support or his utter hatred of the opposition he faced, Sinclair would have probably called it quits at this point.[32]

Things went from ugly to bizarre the first few days of November, right before the election. Raymond Haight, who seemed less of a presence during the campaign than even Merriam, had tried to convince Sinclair that he should drop out of the race, leaving him to win the progressive vote and thus win out over Merriam. After that failed, Haight started making noise suggesting that no matter if Merriam or Sinclair got elected, there would be class war and the need for military rule over California. The day before election day, violence did break out: somebody threw a rock through the windows of Sinclair headquarters. Sinclair believed gangsters were roaming the streets, prepared to stuff ballot boxes for Merriam. Both Merriam and Sinclair had lawyers out searching for election fraud. Some citizens feared there would be civil war on the streets of Los Angeles and other cities on election day; there was even talk of calling out the military. None of this could prevent 70 percent of registered voters from turning out; nor could it prevent a psychotic businessman from buying a gun to shoot Sinclair the next day if the candidate happened to win against all odds.[33]

Fortunately for Sinclair's own life, Merriam won handily. He received 1,138,620 votes to Sinclair's 879,537. When the news came in, Craig broke down and wept out of relief. Sinclair himself felt relaxed. When Adlai Stevenson lost his run for the presidency in 1952, Sinclair wrote to him and recounted his experience of 1934: "One half of me" wanted to "win in order to punish a vile and corrupt opposition and the other half of me" prayed for "relief from a nightmare." With all of the work done on the campaign, EPIC could claim only two state senators in 1934. Nonetheless, a message had been sent. Sinclair's showing was not bad, especially considering the attacks he had faced. If under these circumstances he could come this close, who was to say what might happen in the future?[34]

The first thing to consider after the election, Sinclair believed, was to "keep our political organization intact" by continuing to publish the EPIC newspaper and educating the public about EPIC principles. But without a candidate or an election to get behind, EPIC was doomed to failure. Immediately after the election, divisions within EPIC appeared. Dick Otto, Sinclair's trusted campaign manager, battled Culbert Olson, who had supported EPIC during Sinclair's run, but who now wanted to tone down EPIC planks in the Democratic Party platform and get Sinclair's supporters behind more traditional Democratic Party candidates. Some tried to unseat Olson as state chairman of the Democratic Party, with the support of Sinclair. There were also debates over whether to support Townsend's pension plan, with Sinclair worrying that it was too dependent upon a sales tax. Tensions came to a head at a May 1935 EPIC convention. Communists had tried to take over EPIC, as they had done with numerous organizations during the Great Depression, and Sinclair railed against their efforts—upsetting even many non-Communists with his anti-democratic techniques. Sinclair decided to write to EPIC members: "Immediately after the election, when our people were discouraged and exhausted, there was an enemy drive to break up our headquarters; and factional disputes broke out at the same time. To avoid the complete disruption of our organization, it was necessary to maintain our original set up until the air had cleared and our people had recovered." Now Sinclair suggested that these issues could be settled more democratically at the convention, a suggestion he wound up regretting. Communists turned up again and started demanding that EPIC become a third party and bolt the Democrats for a more radical alternative. Sinclair went berserk and got up on a chair and chided the Communists.[35]

This event increased Sinclair's disaffection with EPIC. He continued to consult with the organization's leaders, but he grew frustrated at the crises that emerged within the organization. Writing to a colleague in September 1935, he outlined a new problem in EPIC and then stated, "There always is" a new problem, "of course." A few months later, Sinclair simply hid out from EPIC's leadership, refusing to answer telephone calls or return letters. He kept writing for the EPIC newspaper, but even this became distasteful by January 1936. He watched the subscription numbers continue to plummet and grew depressed. Total disintegration had set in. "My efforts to keep a headquarters going have been defeated by lack of health, lack of time, and lack of money—more especially the last." By December 1936 Sinclair could write to someone and admit, "I do not know how the movement is going." He felt that if he gave advice, he would be accused of being too autocratic, and if he receded, he would be accused of being too tolerant. Better, he decided, not to get involved at all. And so EPIC slowly disintegrated.[36]

Sinclair's own life held together better, but still, the campaign had taken its toll. "Upton was ten pounds under weight and had a headache every other day," Craig explained to a friend of hers after the election. By April 1935, Sinclair complained that he was "flat on my back with severe lumbago." His diet had disintegrated badly, which probably caused more physical ailments. Craig's illness, as expected, grew worse under the stress of the campaign. Sinclair used the summer of 1935 to get better, but his weight loss and back problems were not easy to overcome.[37]

At the same time that his health deteriorated, the campaign had boosted his national reputation and profile. *Time* magazine had noted, "Rarely has a state campaign evolved more national attention." By the end of 1934, Sinclair reported receiving ten pounds of mail per delivery. When he debated Hamilton Fish on the constitutionality of EPIC, ten thousand people showed up. He even planned to make a movie about EPIC (it never came out). Instead, he spoke at a showing of "King Vidor's picture, 'Our Daily Bread,' which dealt with an agricultural cooperative along the lines of EPIC." The film had been made by the time of Sinclair's campaign, but the studio had refused its release, at least in California, until after the election was over. There was too much fear it would help Sinclair. Because the message of EPIC was finding its way into movies and debates and national magazines, Sinclair felt assured the program's legacy would last, even if the organization itself floundered.[38]

Sinclair could take some credit, though certainly not all, for political developments the year after his campaign ended. In 1935 FDR moved to the left. The president grew disgruntled with business chafing at his legislation. He grew especially disgruntled as the Supreme Court found the National Industrial Recovery Act unconstitutional. Instead of moving to the center, he moved in Sinclair's direction, although he never endorsed the idea of production for use. In 1935 FDR helped pass a spate of progressive legislation, including the Social Security Act and a soak-the-rich tax. He also gave more power to labor unions by making the Wagner Act "must" legislation. There was no mistaking what was happening; FDR had heard the "thunder on the left," as some historians have called it. Sinclair's good showing in the election had contributed something to the thunder.

Sinclair was pleased with FDR's move, although he still had doubts about the New Deal. He felt that EPIC had accomplished a great deal, especially in providing support for more radical solutions to the problems of the Great Depression. Sinclair's greatest hope was that people could collectively organize and demand political power based on a program grounded in American ideals of equality and Jeffersonian democracy, and his campaign bore this out. Nonetheless, he knew his own political career was over. He had been the wrong candidate to carry a progressive message. As he pointed out, he was "an author of too many books trying to be a politician." He decided it was more important for him to write books than to muck about in the dirty world of politics. He would remain political, of course, but only in the realm of words, not action.[39]

EIGHT

BEYOND CALIFORNIA, TOWARD A POPULAR FRONT

1935–1939

It is the very essence of a faith in Democracy,
that there are in the people reserves of power and
intelligence and honesty, and that in a desperate crisis
like this men will come forward and take up the burden
and carry it, men who are not merely job seekers
and lovers of power and applause, but men of conscience,
and true believers in government by popular consent.

—UPTON SINCLAIR, 1935

What's your proposal? To build the Just City? I will. I agree.
Or is it the suicide pact, the romantic Death? Very well, I accept,
For I am your choice, your decision: Yes, I am Spain.

—W. H. AUDEN, "SPAIN," 1937

IN 1935 SINCLAIR FOUND HIMSELF IN THE SAME POSITION AS many other Americans. He was out of money and on the road. But unlike the Depression's faceless masses, the Okies escaping the Dust Bowl and migrant farmers scurrying around the country in search of jobs, Sinclair hit the road as something of a celebrity—a man who had come close to being California's governor and could share his stories about the fight and the cause. Once again Sinclair had been propelled into the ranks of stardom, and it seemed the right moment for a national lecture tour to recoup his financial losses. After all, the campaign had put him ten to fifteen thousand dollars in debt. Looking over his personal accounts, he desperately searched for a way to sell his Beverly Hills home, approaching John DeKay, a wealthy man who had befriended Sinclair during the EPIC campaign. Unfortunately, not too long after Sinclair approached him, DeKay had a mental breakdown, appearing at Sinclair's home with cuts all over his face and talking about communicating with Martians. So Sinclair had to turn to the things he knew better—writing and lecturing—and use them to get out of the red.[1]

As usual, Sinclair merged his personal life with a larger cause. His lecturing could not just be about the dough. So it became, in large part, about launching a national EPIC movement. He didn't think this would take that much, seeing as candidates had already run on EPIC principles in numerous states outside of California, including Louisiana, New York, Kansas, and Colorado. Sinclair would simply have to explain why more people should take up the call of EPIC, which now stood for End Poverty in Civilization, an "American plan in line with our traditions of self-help and self-reliance." There will be no "foreign words" or talk of "class struggle," Sinclair counseled as he planned to move throughout the United States preaching the new national gospel. First, he took his road show to the Pacific Northwest in July 1935, tracking five thousand miles with Craig. Then, traveling through a nasty "heat wave," he headed east, starting in the upper Midwest, where Governor Floyd Olson introduced him in Minneapolis. He was then bested by a Communist during a debate in Detroit. Sometimes his lectures degenerated into little more than sales pitches for his books: Sinclair reading from his books and pausing while salesmen walked through the audience hawking the book being read. The traveling could be difficult, what with "several break-downs and one smash up." And, of course, Sinclair had to worry about Craig's health, which made him decide to cut the tour short.[2]

Driving all that way, Sinclair saw a lot of gas station attendants. He had a particularly strong reaction to them and the other faces he saw. "Always when I go out among the people and see their hard work and their cheerfulness," he explained, "I renew my regard for them, and my pity at their harsh fate." It was as if Sinclair experienced, up close and personal, the primary art form that cultural expression took during the Depression—namely, the documentary photographs of the poor, the displaying of faces etched with poverty. The photographs of Dorothea Lange (most famously "Migrant Mother") and Walker Evans (especially his pictures of southern tenant farmers) still provide some of this country's strongest memories of the Great Depression. These images denote clearly to viewers, who might have scant historical memory, the decade of the 1930s. Sinclair's reaction to the poor faces that blazed by him as he drove across the country and lectured in various towns and cities was precisely the sort that Lange and Evans hoped to produce. These photographers intended to depict the poor realistically in order to generate sympathy but also to provide a spiritual sense of the American "people," writ large, as beaten down by circumstances but possessing an inner strength that would pull them through this crisis.[3]

This was a broader theme of Depression-era culture, especially during the second half of the 1930s. Artists and writers wanted to express the power of ordinary people, capturing their ability to persevere in the face of tough odds, showing them as stronger, and certainly more noble, than America's elite. Consider John Steinbeck's *The Grapes of Wrath* and the film version of the book made by John Ford, both depicting Okie migrants struggling against the plight of poverty. "We're the people," Ma Joad says at the end of the movie, showing resilience after her family has searched hard and long for work they cannot find. Or take John Dos Passos's trilogy, *USA*, the last entry of which, *The Big Money*, was published in 1936. The novel has ordinary Americans presenting their individual stories and tries to capture the way people speak, while intermingling their experiences with broader themes and events in American history through the occasional literary "newsreel." Dos Passos hoped to capture, in his own words, "the speech of the people." Or examine any mural painted by Thomas Hart Benton, America's most popular painter during the 1930s, with its panorama of ordinary citizens—farmers and industrial laborers— creating, with their own hands and sweat, the wealth that made America great and that Benton thought deserved praise and reward.[4]

Much of this cultural expression received support from the federal government. Under Roosevelt's watch, the government encouraged artists to move into communities to teach ordinary people how to create art and employed writers to document America's folklore (everything from jokes to spirituals). This was a time when the Federal Theater Project, an initiative Sinclair always praised, supported plays performed and written for working-class people who had never set foot on Broadway before. It was a time when the struggles of hardworking Americans entered literary works like James Agee's *Let Us Now Praise Famous Men* and Carey McWilliams's stories about migrant farm workers in California's Imperial Valley. It was a time when writers not only wrote about ordinary men and women but thought of themselves as sharing their plight. During the 1930s, writers would march in New York City's May Day Parade, and they believed, rightly or wrongly, that their cause was the cause of the workingman. This was a time when labor unions like Heywood Broun's Newspaper Guild and Hollywood's Screenwriters' Guild made clear that cultural producers were in need of collective bargaining rights just as much as industrial producers who were then banding together in the Congress of Industrial Organizations (CIO). With the organizing of white- and blue-collar workers in tandem, the 1930s became known for a "Popular Front," that is, literature and art that not only represented the people but that saw the needs of writers and artists themselves in line with the people being represented. Sinclair, though not as fully as Steinbeck, Dos Passos, or Broun, contributed to this cultural struggle for political change. Though he refused to run for political office again, he sought ways that, as a writer, he could strengthen movements for social justice and help push the country to the left, further than where FDR was taking it.

Writing His Way Out of Depression

An internal dam burst after the governor's race, and out flooded all of the writing that Sinclair had suppressed during 1934. After losing, Sinclair went into a writing flurry. Some of this was an attempt to make money, but most was to make up for lost time. After writing two books about the governor's race itself and then publishing the play *Depression Island*, performed during the campaign to raise money, Sinclair still felt that he had one score to be settled from that difficult year. Attacked as a godless atheist by people whose religious devoutness he must have questioned (Aimee Semple McPherson comes to mind), Sinclair wrote a new book on religion. Called *What God Means to Me: An Attempt at a Working Religion*, it made clear that Sinclair was no atheist or materialist but a spiritualist at heart—the sort that grew out of his faith in telepathy and mind cure. Sinclair's was a thoroughly tolerant and loving God, in his own words, a "democratic God, a Father who loves us, a comrade who works with us." Sinclair believed God could be reached through the human subconscious and intuition. His own passion and emotions suggested that there was something beyond his material body. "I feel in me a spiritual sun, something which glows and burns and gives out energy." This sort of assertion symbolized the central weakness of the book. Though it broached serious theological questions, it never mustered the intellectual strength to answer them without resorting to emotional exhortation.[5]

So the literary dam broke, but it often gave way to things that might have been best left dammed. Two years after *What God Means to Me*, Sinclair would write yet another exegesis on religion, *Our Lady*, which told the story of the virgin mother Mary propelling herself into the future and growing disenchanted in the face of established Catholicism. The book was dull and hastily written. The fact that it was, in Sinclair's own words, "rejected by forty publishers" never frustrated him. He always reverted to the idea that the world was out to reject his writings, in this case because people could not deal with his anti-Catholic message, not because the writing was poor or done too hastily. Much of Sinclair's work after the governor's race and throughout the rest of the 1930s faltered in this way.[6]

It often seemed that Sinclair couldn't quite put the governor's race behind him as he tried to write his way out of it. It was his golden moment, and it demanded reflection. He wrote the novel *Co-op* to express his faith that behind EPIC there stood a "huge sprawling movement for self-help, by and for the unemployed." The book centered on the story of Sig Soren, a man who believed in co-ops as the best way to approach socialism in America, and a man whom Sinclair modeled after Hjalmar Rutzebeck, his bodyguard during the EPIC campaign and a leading member of a Santa Barbara co-op. The novel is set during the Great Depression, and it traces the advent of a fictionalized co-op, starting with its first meetings and committee formation. Sinclair shows the co-op benefiting those who would otherwise starve, especially women who improve their lives through collective kitchens and social networks that help them raise their children—a lesson that Sinclair believed was visible earlier in Helicon Hall. Sinclair then tells of debates within the co-op movement about becoming more political, and he even merges the story of his fictional co-op with the rise of EPIC. Eventually, Sig himself goes to Washington, D.C.—much as Mr. Smith would three years later in Frank Capra's film *Mr. Smith Goes to Washington*—to plead for federal loans. Some senators then ask him to draft a bill in favor of co-ops, and then FDR asks Soren to help him figure the best way to support the cooperative movement. The message couldn't be clearer: not only was EPIC right and grounded in real experiments carried out by ordinary citizens, but it should have gone all the way to the White House. This was a point that Sinclair never ceased to make throughout the Depression.[7]

When Sinclair put EPIC behind him in his own writing, things sometimes turned strange. Having traveled through California's redwood trees on his way up north in 1935, Sinclair wanted to capture the beauty of that place. He decided to take a crack at writing a children's book, entitled *The Gnomobile* and released the same year as *Co-op*. The story focuses on a little girl, Elizabeth, who meets Glago and Bobo, two gnomes who inhabit the redwood forests of California. The gnomes are having a hard time of it, since logging companies are hacking away at their forest home. Though Elizabeth tries to protect her new friends, a profiteer steals Bobo, who winds up performing in a circuslike show. He then quits and decides to rejoin his fellow gnomes in another forest, and Elizabeth pledges herself to saving the forests from further logging. The book had illustrations, and Sinclair, once again, thought it would make a perfect movie. It wasn't for almost another thirty years that Walt Disney took him up on the prospect, making a movie that was even goofier than the book.[8]

Next up was *Wally for Queen!*, a short play that Sinclair produced quickly in order to take advantage of an accident of family history. It seemed that a cousin of Sinclair's had wound up seducing the king of England, Edward the Eighth. Sinclair's cousin, Wallis Simpson, was divorced and a coquettish southern belle, and Sinclair told the story of royalty breaking up over love (a theme that Sinclair would take up again in a lackluster play about Marie Antoinette published three years later). Sinclair managed to slip in a few criticisms of England's royalty, but its sixteen pages or so failed to create a sensation or a very good play at that. The writing flurry—represented by *What God Means to Me, Co-op, Wally for Queen!*, and *The Gnomobile* all coming out the same year—started to look like little more than a flurry. "I wish I could report to you that my books have large sales and are highly praised by our literary critics," Sinclair explained to a friend in 1936, "but unfortunately, neither of these statements can be made."[9]

Political Coaching from the Sidelines

The writing seemed a form of sublimation, an attempt to replace the fury of his prior political engagement. Sinclair would never seek political office again. He explained, "I am out of politics in California and elsewhere for the rest of my life. I shall never again run for any political office. I am out because neither my health nor that of my wife could stand another political campaign." But this didn't mean he stopped caring about politics; his passion for public life surged after 1936, once his initial writing flurry calmed down. He poured this passion into his political commentary written for *EPIC News* as well as other journals. Now that EPIC was to be national in scope, he would coach from the sidelines, pressing for a viable left-wing vision of politics that might not put him in political office but that would win the minds of his fellow Americans.[10]

His first concern was continuing to push FDR to the left. That had, after all, been one of EPIC's primary aims. He tussled intellectually with FDR's administration, recoiling at punches it threw his way and pointing out when it pleased him. His fight was rooted in a very simple premise: "America is moving to the left; and Franklin D. Roosevelt can remain the leader, only if he too keeps moving." So in May 1935, as the Supreme Court killed FDR's farm mortgage plan and his National Industrial Recovery Act, Sinclair pounced. Now was the time, Sinclair counseled the president, to do what he had promised in their private meeting—to endorse the concept of "production for use." Nothing of the kind happened, of course, but Sinclair could at least take some comfort in FDR's support for Social Security, the Wagner Act (which put the federal government behind labor union organizing), a higher tax on the wealthiest bracket of Americans, and stronger public works projects. Sinclair continued to worry that taxing and redistributing wealth didn't really confront the underlying problem of a system that produced for profit rather than human need. At the same time, though, he was becoming more of a realist, knowing that FDR's enemies were strong, having felt their brunt during his own run for governor.[11]

The question about supporting the president sharpened as the presidential election neared and FDR prepared to run again. Some in the EPIC movement and throughout the nation pressed for Sinclair to form a third party. But he said no. "It is better to get a half loaf than nothing at all," he explained, "and Roosevelt is much to be preferred over Hoover." When Francis Townsend's and Father Coughlin's supporters bolted for the Union Party, Sinclair called their move what it was, stupid and unrealistic. By now he was thoroughly disenchanted with Coughlin (who had gone back on his support for Sinclair during the governor's race and who was tending toward fascism), and Townsend had backed Merriam for governor in 1934, so he was no friend in the first place. Sinclair's call here might have been personal in part, but it was spot on, seeing as the Union Party polled next to nothing in the election. Sinclair was more willing to accept the idea of vote swapping. If someone lived in a state that FDR was guaranteed to win, it was fine to vote for a third-party candidate, ideally Norman Thomas, Sinclair counseled, so long as that person could convince someone in a less-certain state to vote for FDR over a third party. Sinclair believed that strategic voting like this could send a message without putting conservatives into office.[12]

After FDR won handily, Sinclair grew less enchanted with the president, as did others on the left. Sinclair knew FDR to be a masterful politician, but he worried that conservatives had his ear as much as progressives. Especially dangerous was Sinclair's own home region, the American South. Deep South Democrats were too quick to protect the region's capacity to "exploit the labor of the poor whites," especially sharecroppers. Sinclair also knew that conservatives on the Supreme Court would stop at nothing to push FDR to the right. When that push, started in 1935, heated up again in 1936, and FDR pushed back by floating the idea of adding more seats to the Supreme Court (seats that he himself would appoint), Sinclair thought it not such a bad idea. This "court packing" scheme, as it became known, created a sore point for conservatives worried about an overextension of executive power. But for Sinclair, it seemed a legitimate political move. After all, there had been a long tradition of distrusting the judiciary in America—going all the way back to one of Sinclair's heroes, Thomas Jefferson. The executive had been voted in by the people, so why shouldn't the president have the majority of influence and power? It may not have been an ideal move, Sinclair reasoned, but court packing didn't bother him.[13]

His real concern was over the conservative wing within FDR's administration. Treasury Secretary Henry Morgenthau, who Sinclair believed supported him in 1934, was pressing for FDR to balance the budget. Sinclair had a certain fondness for fiscal prudence himself, but in this case, he sided with the left wing of the administration, especially Harry Hopkins and Harold Ickes. These two high-profile New Dealers thought balancing the budget would swallow up funds for public works and other spending that was drastically needed, especially as the economy was once again faltering in 1937. Sinclair worried that FDR was growing "feeble" and moving to "the right" as he listened to Morgenthau. When FDR started talking openly of balancing the budget, Sinclair condemned the president: "You have bowed before your conservative critics." Sinclair still believed that FDR might turn back to the left, but he started to show sympathy for third-party activists in 1937. A year earlier, he had praised Floyd Olson's governorship and the Farmer-Labor Party for pushing FDR to the left. So Sinclair teetered on a fence between his prior Democratic Party realism and his third-party idealism. Finally, he fell off the fence, turning against his own arguments against a third party, as he learned about the National Progressive Party formed by Phil LaFollette—a party with roots in Midwestern progressivism. Sinclair supported Raymond Haight in his run for governor of California as a Progressive Party candidate in 1938, but it wasn't entirely clear whether this was full-fledged support or anger about California Democrats, including Culbert Olsen, pulling EPIC planks out of the Democratic Party platform a year earlier. Whatever the case, it was not a long-lived escape from the Democrats, seeing as neither Sinclair's decision to leave nor the Progressive Party itself—at least this version of it—lasted much longer.[14]

If Sinclair was never entirely clear on the appropriateness of third parties in American politics, it reflected a larger confusion about what leverage progressives could muster to have their voice heard. For instance, should progressives ally with the Communist Party or with independent leaders on the left? On both counts, Sinclair had done a fair amount of political thinking. He counseled that a Popular Front between progressives and the Communist Party would be impossible, since the Communist Party never formed alliances other than to pursue its covert agenda. Sinclair still held to his earlier Socialist Party animosity toward Communists, and he grew even more sickened at their attempt to invade EPIC in the wake of his governor's run. Nonetheless, his own ideals started to merge with the Communist Party's own push for a Popular Front during the mid-1930s. After all, he believed in an alliance between white- and blue-collar workers, the sort espoused by Lewis Corey, a leading Communist theoretician, who argued that the Great Depression had turned the middle class into little more than exploited proletarians. Sinclair called for a United Front among all workers, "whether of hand or brain." He also remained committed to a left rooted in American values, and by 1936, the Communist Party was proud to declare that "Communism is Twentieth Century Americanism." Sinclair's own attempt to make Abraham Lincoln and Thomas Jefferson into heroes of the left would be echoed by numerous communists at this time. Nonetheless, though he shared the Communist Party's new philosophy of middle-class Americanism during the 1930s, Sinclair still believed the Communist Party could never become the foundation for a viable political movement.[15]

The Communists were not the only ones Sinclair worried about. He grew concerned about independent leaders who continued to push FDR to the left the way he did. Everywhere he looked, Sinclair saw demagoguery—a dangerous threat to a republic coming apart during the Great Depression. Sinclair had already expressed reservations about Coughlin and Townsend, as they threw in with the Union Party. Coughlin was especially dangerous, not just because he had so much influence over the radio but because he was growing increasingly anti-Semitic and allying with Gerald Smith, whom Sinclair considered, correctly, an

American fascist. There were others too. In 1938, Sinclair considered writing a historical pamphlet about "crazy experiments" that would include Huey Long, who by then had been shot to death, as well as "Father Coughlin, Dr. Townsend, and now the '$30-Every Thursday plan.'" The latter plan, known popularly as "Ham and Eggs," was a strange pension scheme created by Robert Noble, a radio announcer once active in EPIC. It would have given every Californian thirty dollars every week, but as Sinclair pointed out, it would have also drained the public coffers and hurt public-sector employees the most. It would do nothing to change America's political culture. Sinclair didn't endorse giveaways, since EPIC had intended to put people to work so they could produce for themselves rather than rely upon government largesse and, in the process, learn the virtues of "industrial self-government." Needless to say, Sinclair worried that wrongheaded ideas might appeal during desperate times.[16]

Sinclair believed that demagogues were making headway because the New Deal was growing weaker from 1937 to 1938. FDR had offered fewer and fewer reforms, as he spoke of balancing the budget and changing the composition of the Supreme Court. There was need, Sinclair argued, for a serious alternative to the New Deal, which he now argued was not creating "a planned economy" but rather "a hodge podge, a political dispensation of governmental charity, and in no wise economic democracy." This description might have been true, but Sinclair also knew that the political realities of America made it hard to articulate a feasible alternative—demagoguery itself serving as testimony, along with the power of the American South. Sinclair also admitted that the New Deal had helped build up a national public sector that critics shouldn't scoff at. "We have built some important public works," he explained, "and the CCC boys have done a lot of forestry work; the people have a lot of new school buildings and roads, and also some very interesting plays have been produced." He explained that the New Deal "represents the best that our people will stand for at present, and every step towards social control of our economic affairs has to be taken in the face of those bitter attacks of reactionary forces." Nonetheless, Sinclair still believed in pushing beyond the New Deal, and now as FDR was shifting rightward, Sinclair wanted people to protest and offer alternatives. The problem was finding those who had enough power and influence to turn his exhortation into real policies.[17]

There was a source of hope on this front. Sinclair witnessed organized labor getting its act together, and he hoped to help out. In 1935 the

Congress of Industrial Organizations (CIO) formed, the same year that FDR supported the Wagner Act. The CIO would take the lead in organizing the industrialized and largely unskilled sector of the American economy, precisely the areas that the AFL had left behind, much to Sinclair's frustration prior to 1935. In many ways, the CIO became the grassroots power base for the New Deal, pushing FDR's administration to adopt social legislation that reflected the interests of the working class. One of its leading unions was the United Auto Workers (UAW), whose rank and file, taking their cue from rubber workers in Akron, Ohio, pioneered a "sit down strike" in Flint, Michigan, on December 30, 1936. Instead of picketing outside the plant, the workers decided to take it over and sit down inside in order to prevent the company from using "scab" (nonunion) employees. General Motors "surrendered," as one historian put it, and the UAW went on to win more victories. Sinclair was elated. "For seventy five years big business has been sitting down on the American people," Sinclair explained, "and now I am delighted to see the process reversed." He now knew what he could do. He could help the UAW do what it hoped to do next—organize the recalcitrant Ford Motor Company.[18]

In June 1937, just as FDR was figuring out how to balance the federal budget, Sinclair was at work on a new novel entitled *The Flivver King*. It told the stories of Henry Ford, starting off with his days as a young inventor, and Abner Shutt, one of Ford's early employees. Sinclair documents the growth of the Ford Motor Company, describing the assembly line, Ford's famous five dollar day (one of the most prominent examples of corporate welfare), and his Social Work Department, which examined the private lives of workers to ensure they were moral and upright. Abner is fired and then directly approaches Ford, whom Sinclair depicts as increasingly isolated while union organizing erupts at his company. Abner gets his job back, and then the story shifts to Tom Shutt, a labor organizer, fired for his pro-union agitation. The novel ends with an alarming juxtaposition between a lavish Ford dinner party and Tom Shutt getting beaten up by thugs Ford had employed to break up union drives. The message couldn't be clearer: Ford was a tyrant. "Henry was more than any feudal lord had been," Sinclair wrote, "because he had not merely the power of the purse, but those of the press and the radio; he could make himself omnipresent to his vassals, he was master not merely of their bread and butter but of their thoughts and ideals."[19]

Sinclair finished the story during the summer of 1937, and by August, the UAW was running the story serially in its newspaper. It was then printed in book form, and the UAW agreed to take 200,000 copies of *The Flivver King* and use it as a recruitment tool in trying to organize Ford's recalcitrant company. Ford's workers often placed copies of the book prominently in their back pockets in order to symbolize their affiliation. The book made Sinclair an intellectual who tied his work directly to the growth of one of America's most militant unions. Its leader, Walter Reuther, not only admired Sinclair but consistently called on the federal government to support progressive legislation. Sinclair was so excited about offering his help to the UAW that he proposed turning *The Flivver King* into a movie. His plan was to have workers buy tickets in advance in order to fund the making of the film. The plan, as with many of Sinclair's, never came to fruition. And Ford did not unionize until four years after the appearance of the book.[20]

Sinclair believed he could replicate this initiative. He turned to the industry that caved in to union demands right after General Motors. In March 1937, U.S. Steel, which had resisted negotiations with the Steel Workers' Organizing Committee (SWOC) for years, suddenly did an about-face and settled a contract. No doubt part of the reason was the UAW's victory at General Motors. In the wake of its success, SWOC turned its attention to "Little Steel," those companies, like Bethlehem and Youngstown Sheet and Tube, that were smaller than U.S. Steel, which was an enormous consolidation going back to the Gilded Age. SWOC pushed, but was quickly squashed by, steadfast business leaders. Not surprisingly, Sinclair entitled his next novel *Little Steel*. He was proud of it, since it was published on September 18, 1938, which happened to be his sixtieth birthday. *Little Steel* also happened to be his sixtieth book.

It told the story of Walter Judson Quayle, an owner of a small steel plant who resists a union drive on the part of SWOC. Ironically, his daughter, Genevieve, grows sympathetic to the Communist Party during the time he ruthlessly suppresses a strike. Genevieve and Charrie, her boyfriend and a journalist, join the labor movement. Meanwhile, Quayle grows tired of business, considers selling out his portion of the company, and then decides to embark on a camping trip to leave it all behind. He winds up traveling to Red Hills, Georgia, where a strike has erupted. While camping, Quayle is arrested for vagrancy, is thought to be a Red, and winds up in jail. Here the novel ended, with no speeches or overt message making. Sinclair explained to his publisher, "You see I have ended so many of my books with preaching and I was particularly glad to end one in a way that would put my social criticisms into the reader's mind without seeming to do it." He wanted the book to provide "one chuckle after another" for his reader. Sinclair believed this would allow the novel to reach the widest audience possible.[21]

Sinclair suggested to Philip Murray of SWOC that he should do with *Little Steel* what the UAW did with *The Flivver King*. This never happened; instead, and ironically, the Communist Party serialized the story in *The Daily Worker*. Sinclair grew upset that once the book was published, much like *The Flivver King*, it received little attention in newspapers or journals of opinion. Sinclair complained to Irita Van Doren, an editor at the *New York Herald Tribune*, that his books about the governor's race and *The Flivver King* never received reviews from highbrow papers. She explained that his books were perceived as pamphlets rather than serious works of literature. Sinclair's ire was raised by this, and he accused her— as well as the broader ranks of highbrow critics—of elitism. As he reasoned, why couldn't a book be literary even if it was intended for the mass consumption of working-class readers?[22]

Both *The Flivver King* and *Little Steel* symbolized Sinclair's hopes for the labor movement. More so, they symbolized his desire to make his intellectual work play a meaningful role in social change. This he considered the highest aim for any author; propaganda was not such a bad thing, he reasoned, nor was tying oneself directly to the movements that served as the audiences for a writer's books. Though Sinclair didn't have the UAW dictate the content of *The Flivver King* and didn't write *Little Steel* with anyone from SWOC looking over his shoulder, he knew what the labor movement wanted—stories about selfish, shortsighted business owners who were idiotically resisting what was best for their employees. This was something a writer, especially of popular novels, could do better than labor union organizers or the rank and file.

Sinclair had spelled out his vision of the intellectual's role in political change at the Western Writers Conference held in November 1936, his speech being reworked and printed in 1937. The American Writers' Congress, a Communist Party organization that attracted big-name writers to its ranks, had held its first meeting in 1935, and Sinclair parroted many of the sentiments of those participants who had looked for a way in which writers could engage with progressive movements. Sinclair argued that "art is what you are used to, and propaganda is anything new and disturbing." He obviously thought of his role as creating propaganda more than art—a point he had made countless times. Sinclair used the speech to describe his friendship with Jack London, a novelist whom

Communists were quickly championing. All of this was par for the course. But then he made a new and bold statement. He argued that the biggest threat to writers in 1936 was not capitalism but the rise of fascism. Sinclair had worried about fascism before, but now he connected it to his search for an intellectual's role in changing the world for the better. He was starting to look outside at the larger world and was starting to think that international developments were more urgent than domestic ones.[23]

International Antifascism (with a Blind Spot)

To a friend in 1933, Sinclair wrote, "That Hitler thing has made me realize the seriousness of our danger." That "Hitler thing" now meant the dawn of the Third Reich. Sinclair knew of Hitler's anti-Semitism, and it became all the more real as his own German publisher, Malik-Verlag of Berlin, had to shut down since its owner was a Jewish pacifist. Sinclair explained the severity of the Nazi revolution: "The seizure of the German state by a band of desperadoes called Nazis has changed all my thinking about social questions. I consider it the most dreadful event in modern history, and I consider that every civilized country in the world should devote itself first and foremost to the task of keeping that nightmare from spreading." He worried that Hitler could find supporters in the United States among anti-Semites and southern racists who lynched blacks in his homeland. He worried about Gerald Winrod, who ran for governor of Kansas as an open anti-Semite and won fifty thousand votes. He worried about Gerald Smith and the legacy of Huey Long, whom Sinclair now labeled a fascist "demagogue." When backlash against FDR erupted within the ranks of the wealthy, Sinclair was sure that this could be the first step toward fascism in the United States. He especially worried that as the middle class became threatened by the Depression, it might turn desperate like Germany's middle class and become susceptible to fascist appeals.[24]

But Sinclair's biggest fear was international. He fretted as Italy, under the fascist leadership of Mussolini, invaded Ethiopia in 1935, and as Germany took over the Rhineland in 1936. By that time, Sinclair imagined a line being drawn in Western Europe. It was a line that was intended to contain fascism in Germany and Italy—preventing it from gobbling up Spain and France. He zeroed in on the Popular Front government of Spain that had won power in February 1936 (soon thereafter, a Popular Front government was elected to rule France). Spanish fascists were mounting a war against the republic, and Sinclair believed that this battle captured the symbolic future of Europe. "If the Spanish people lose the war," he warned ominously, "and a Fascist state is set up in Spain, the fate of all the people of the world is altered." He was right, of course, to foresee World War II's imminent future in Spain, what with Hitler and Mussolini supporting Franco, the leader of the Spanish fascists, with full knowledge that France was next. Spain would become the cause célèbre of the international left, and Sinclair was ready to throw in with the cause.[25]

One of the most famous works of literature that captured the spirit of this new international cause was Ernest Hemingway's *For Whom the Bell Tolls*. Though written after Spain had fallen to fascists, the novel is set during the battle to defend the Spanish republic. In fighting there, the novel's central character explains, "If we win here we will win everywhere." That sentiment was echoed among many writers of the time. George Orwell, having gone over to report on the war, wound up joining "the militia, because at that time and in that atmosphere it seemed the only conceivable thing to do," as he put it in his *Homage to Catalonia*. André Malraux, the famous French writer who flew fighter planes in Spain, wrote an epic novel about the civil war entitled *Man's Hope*, and then made a film. He also came to Los Angeles to speak in favor of the Spanish Republicans at the Shrine Auditorium; Sinclair was there and tried to publicize the event, disappointed that the press didn't turn out. He was also at the Philharmonic Auditorium showing of *The Spanish Earth*, a documentary made by Archibald MacLeish, John Dos Passos, Ernest Hemingway, and Joris Ivens. Hemingway, having reported on the war, went out to speak in favor of the Spanish republic, often at Communist Party venues, trying to raise money and to recruit soldiers to be sent overseas and fight as members of the International Brigades. Sinclair, never a big fan of Hemingway as the "lost generation" writer of the 1920s, now had nothing but praise. Sinclair recognized that the fighting in Spain had changed Hemingway from a hedonist to a committed writer. The observation could be generalized. As Malcolm Cowley explained it, "People of my sort," meaning left-wing intellectuals, "were more deeply stirred by the Spanish Civil War than by any other international event since the World War and the Russian Revolution."[26]

Sinclair made his own commitment; he was too old to go to Spain as Malraux, Orwell, and Hemingway had. So he did what he was expected to do: he wrote a book in support of the cause. Paling in comparison to *Man's Fate*, *Homage to Catalonia*, or *For Whom the Bell Tolls*, Sinclair's *No Pasaran* was a short novel intended to recruit young people to join the

International Brigades recruited to fight on the side of the republic. The novel takes place in New York City, which allowed Sinclair to depict a variety of ethnic groups living side by side. There are two central characters: Izzy, a Jewish supporter of the Spanish republic, and Rudy Messer, a Nordic young man from a wealthy family whom Izzy tries to recruit to the cause. Rudy's cousin, Ernie, is a fascist who rails against the New Deal as a Jewish conspiracy and who scolds Rudy for attending meetings where socialists and anarchists congregate. Rudy decides to go to Spain to fight, following the lead of Izzy, who dies in battle. The moral of the story is obvious: people of different ethnic backgrounds with different political opinions need to band together against fascism in Spain. *No Pasaran* was truly, in Sinclair's own words, a "united front" book that "could be used by all the different groups" on the left "for the benefit of the Spanish cause." Anarchist, socialist, communist, Jew, Nordic—none of this mattered in the battle against Franco. Though it would be hard to prove that *No Pasaran* actually recruited anyone to fight in Spain, it's clear the book directed itself toward the right audience. Among the three thousand Americans who went to Spain, the typical recruit was young, urban, working-class, and politically on the left.[27]

By March 1937 Sinclair had finished the novel and printed fifty thousand copies that he would distribute himself at his own expense. He immediately searched for organizations that could help use the book as a recruitment tool—an international equivalent of the UAW. He thought he found it in the North American Committee to Aid Spanish Democracy, an organization littered with Communists that sought to send goods and men to Spain. He believed *No Pasaran* could serve as "an advertising or promotion circular" for the organization's work. The relationship was rough at first, with the organization getting cold feet (perhaps because the book was a bit too tolerant of different political philosophies). Sinclair got so frustrated at one point that he wrote a friend complaining that all anti-fascist organizations seemed to want to do was raise money for food to be shipped to Spain rather than raise consciousness about the issue. Sinclair was upset that his offering of a recruitment tool wasn't greeted with open arms. He must have been more upset when his contact at the organization wrote him in April 1937 to say that the book wasn't very good and didn't sell well. Fortunately, the next month took a turn for the better, and by July forty thousand copies of the book were sold. Sinclair got especially excited when he learned later that the South African government had banned *No*

Pasaran, believing this might boost sales. It didn't, and all copies of the book sold at under cost. Sinclair had just gotten out of debt from EPIC when he was back in the red over *No Pasaran*. Becoming an engaged intellectual was an expensive and nerve-wracking business.[28]

Spain put Sinclair in debt to banks but, even more importantly, to the Soviet Union. Many writers on the international left tended this way: Hemingway, in the words of his biographer, became a "darling of the Stalinists" since he spoke at so many Communist Party events when he came back from Spain. Malraux was even worse than Hemingway in the slack he cut the Soviet Union, according to his biographer. Only Orwell noted that the Soviet Union didn't deserve the praise it received regarding its activities in Spain. Since he never went to Spain, Sinclair didn't have much to go by. All he did was continue to extend the admiration he had of the country as he assessed its role in fighting fascism. Now he didn't just praise Russia's revolution, agricultural collectivization, and industrial policy, he praised its foreign policy. As he watched the British appease Hitler and refuse to do anything for Spain, and his own country cling to the Neutrality Act to remain out of the conflict, Sinclair concluded that "the hopes of civilization rest upon the Soviet Union." Stalin's Russia was the "one nation and only one which can be counted on for whole-hearted and unstinted support" for fighting fascism. It was time for the left to unite around the Soviet Union, to cut the country some slack, since it was the only country willing to send aid to Spain and see fascism as the vicious threat it was.[29]

The slack was extended further than it needed to go. Sinclair's confusion about the Soviet Union drove him in dizzying directions. In 1936 he met with Earl Browder, leader of the Communist Party USA, and the two agreed that Spain was the most important issue to focus on and that it required sympathy for the USSR. Sinclair moved beyond sympathy, though, and became a sycophant. Like a schoolboy in love, he could write passages such as these: "Our philosopher, Ralph Waldo Emerson, advised us to hitch our wagon to a star, and just now the Soviet star seems to be the biggest and brightest star in the whole sky." He explained that the Eisenstein affair taught him to cut slack toward Stalin, and when he did, he seemed to justify the suppression of artistic expression in the Soviet Union. The Eisenstein affair showed him "the difficulties which the administrators of the Soviet Union have encountered in endeavoring to build order out of the chaos placed at their disposal." None of this had anything to do with the legitimate cause of Spain. Of course, his praise might have been due to the fact that "millions of copies of my books" sold in the USSR. If so, this only made sadder his inability to examine what was going on there.[30]

By 1938 Stalin had his fair share of critics in the United States, especially among left-wing intellectuals. Many had watched with disgust the infamous "Purge," or "Moscow Trials," where loyal Bolsheviks admitted to crimes against the state for daring to question Stalin's leadership; most were sent to their death. But the trials didn't worry Sinclair. "These old Bolsheviks had got used to imprisonment and torture under the czar," Sinclair explained in an apologetic manner that could only disturb sensitive readers, "and nobody ever made them confess." It seemed that Sinclair was stuck in the past—using the attacks on the Bolshevik Revolution in the wake of World War I to justify totalitarianism. To suggest that people would never admit to crimes that they didn't commit showed that Sinclair really didn't have a handle on the way Stalin's power worked. Leading lights of the anti-Stalinist left—James Rorty, Eugene Lyons, and Sidney Hook—tried to make this clear to him. Sinclair was right to point out that these intellectuals' hero, Leon Trotsky, didn't deserve the praise they gave him, seeing as Trotsky was complaining about a system that he himself helped to make. But this did not justify sloughing off the trials the way Sinclair did by stating, against all evidence, that the USSR had "made great advances toward democracy."[31]

Just as the Spanish republic was falling to the fascists, the Soviet Union decided to pull off a diplomatic move that should have given Sinclair pause. On August 23, 1939, Stalin signed a nonaggression pact with Hitler—pulling the Soviet Union out of the war against fascism. Learning of this move, Sinclair wrote a friend, "I am waiting with great suspense to understand what the Russian move means." Its meaning should have been very clear: Stalin could not be relied upon to fight fascism as Sinclair believed him to be. But instead of drawing this conclusion, Sinclair decided that Stalin had actually "achieved a masterpiece of diplomacy in getting his two deadliest enemies to fighting, while he sits on the sidelines and waits." Why not let England and Germany go at it? David, Sinclair's son, was writing him and telling him he was insane to think this way. Drawing on his own miserable visit to the Soviet Union earlier, David wrote, "From what I learned about the attitude of the Russian people, I should be very much surprised if the average Russian had the same naive faith in his government's propaganda that you have." That must have stung. What also stung was when the Soviet Union, building on the nonaggression pact with Germany, invaded Finland. Resistance broke out. The warnings Sinclair had been given about the Soviet Union became irrefutable. There was nothing defensive about the invasion of Finland. Sinclair had to face the cold reality that the Soviet Union, though it would become an ally again during World War II, was not the holy land he once made it. The "last hope of civilization" no longer inspired any hope.[32]

By 1940 Spain was in the hands of fascists and the Soviet Union had fallen in Sinclair's estimation. Hitler was running roughshod across Europe, and fascism seemed victorious. That year, Archibald MacLeish, who had worked on *The Spanish Earth* film with Hemingway and was now the Librarian of Congress, wrote a biting essay entitled "The Irresponsibles." He condemned those who had taken their experience in World War I—a disillusioning war that created the "lost generation" of expatriate writers during the 1920s—and turned it into a justification to remain pacifist in the face of fascism's rise in Europe. For MacLeish, these "irresponsibles" were denying that fascism was "a revolt against the common culture of the west" that needed to be resisted, with counterarguments and bigger weapons. Ironically, Sinclair might have fit the category of "irresponsible." He had claimed that World War I was the last capitalist war he would support. By the 1930s he had drifted back toward the antiwar sentiment that framed his political thinking prior to World War I. He would write a year before his governor's race in 1933, "Modern war and modern Capitalism are synonymous, and the life of Capitalism is the life of war." Still, Sinclair was never a pacifist, and fascism worried him immensely—the way MacLeish thought it should. By 1940 there seemed little he could do but stop glorifying the Soviet Union and throw in with whatever country would be willing to put an end to Hitler's menace. Already by 1938, he was "praying for war" that could come "before Spain is wrecked." After Spain fell, his prayers would only become stronger.[33]

It wasn't hard for Sinclair to justify his support for World War II. His Popular Front ideals solidified his antifascism. He hoped that any war against Hitler would be combined with a war to temper the inhumane side of capitalism at home. He believed that a war on fascism was also a war on the selfishness of wealth. "The privileged classes," he explained, "would rather see civilization perish than sacrifice their own power to exploit." It was now the democratic labor union movement, including the UAW and the Steelworkers, that could wage the most effective war against wealth at home. To wage it, they needed to draw on an inclusive Americanism—one that celebrated the nation's ethnic differences while also making economic solidarity the highest cause that bound together the nation's citizens—the way that the characters in *No Pasaran* did. They also had to look outside the confines of the United States to what was happening in the larger world. And so, armed with his novel-writing skills and his ability to spin stories that could entertain, Sinclair marched to war. This time history seemed more on his side.[34]

NINE

MR. MIDDLEBROW GOES TO WAR AGAIN, HOT AND COLD

1940–1960

How pleasant if life had been all literature;
if you could fight your enemies with a pen, and
annihilate them with a witty sequence of dialogue!

—UPTON SINCLAIR, 1946

We in America are busy selling the world our gadgets;
I urge that we work harder at selling them our
democratic ideas and ideals."

—UPTON SINCLAIR, 1952

B Y LATE 1938 SINCLAIR FELT HIS LIFE WAS IN A RUT. HE WAS
not satisfied with the writing he had been doing; works like *The Flivver King* and *Little Steel* had come quickly and easily, even more so *No Pasaran*. Much of what he wrote was rejected by publishers, and much of what he published didn't sell. *No Pasaran's* sales moved slowly, and *Our Lady* sold only five hundred copies, a pathetic number for the author of *The Jungle*. "For a long time I have been dissatisfied because I did not have a really good idea for a novel," he explained to a book editor. But then on December 6, 1938, a new idea flashed into his head. Ideas often flashed into Sinclair's mind, and he could do himself a disservice by leaping at them. But this time it was different. The flash portended big things. "I went all through an enormous long novel in the course of an afternoon and a night," he explained. This novel would take on Europe, "a theme" that he "shrank from" in the past. "There is so much pain and terror in it," he explained. He thought the idea might sustain a "trilogy" of books.[1]

In fact, it became the largest accomplishment of his later life. He had created a character, Lanny Budd, that would endure through eleven novels and thirteen years of writing. The first book was published in 1940 as *World's End*, and it told the story of a young boy born out of wedlock to a wealthy weapons manufacturer, Robbie Budd, and Robbie Budd's first love, Beauty. Lanny passes into adolescence as World War I strikes, and his mother takes up with an artist named Marcel, who had gone off to war while his father was making big money off the war. As Lanny becomes a young adult, he winds up traveling with Professor Alston, a U.S. diplomat preparing for the end of war. Lanny witnesses postwar negotiations, becoming a secretary for a meeting about the League of Nations. Lanny also meets George Herron—Sinclair's original sugar daddy, who worked for Woodrow Wilson during World War I. Herron worries openly about the war's punitive peace. And Lanny learns about America's intervention in Russia, while a friend of his, Kurt, becomes a German spy. Sinclair then describes Lanny's and others' disillusionment with the peace negotiations, while describing how Beauty falls in love with Kurt. Lanny then finds himself torn between the Bolshevism of his uncle and the conservatism of his father, traveling to the center of the international political spectrum toward some sort of socialism (much like Sinclair's, it would seem). *World's End* ends here.

The novel was the culmination of Sinclair's writing career. He had been striving for a number of years to write historical fiction, and this work successfully intertwined fictional and historical figures. Sinclair was also aiming to write for as wide an audience as possible. He explained the year before starting *World's End*, "I would rather be read by 100,000 workers than by five or ten thousand literary highbrows, even though the latter make a great deal more noise." Since being influenced by the "realism" of Jack London and Mark Twain in the early twentieth century, Sinclair had grown disenchanted with the increasing prominence "literary modernism" won among America's intelligentsia. He felt that writers like James Joyce and William Faulkner were so complex in their experimentation with literary form that they wound up alienating the average readers he wanted to write for. Telling a straightforward story about Western history through the eyes of a young man coming of age—this sort of task seemed left behind by those who preferred to jar their readers by breaking up their narrative structure and shifting perspective and voices during a story. He was proud to be thought of as a middlebrow writer.[2]

Sinclair was also writing more subtly, not creating propaganda but a novel with a plot line that developed along with the story of Western Europe's past. Sinclair explained to one editor who rejected the Lanny Budd book that he had been "scolded all" his "life for writing propaganda and thesis novels." With *World's End*, he had finally "attained a serener and more contemplative state of mind." Instead of being a propagandist, he was now a "historian of the world's blunders and calamities." He was now living up to his promise "seven or eight years ago" to retire "from politics" and "become a historian of the follies and blindness of my time." He wasn't trying to convert his readers to socialism or telling them to take up a gun and rush over to Spain; rather, he was telling a story. It might have been a fantastic story, with a character getting into situations that were slightly unbelievable, but it didn't sacrifice every other consideration to political argument.[3]

Sinclair had time to nurture this sort of storytelling, for he was now an official shut-in. Craig had completely abandoned the outside world, and Sinclair spent his days taking care of her when he wasn't writing. Their house deteriorated. Black widow spiders took over, and then came silverfish. In 1942, they escaped to the town of Monrovia "in the orange country to the east," using their Ford sedan to move bit by bit into an Italian villa–style house surrounded with fruit trees. Friends stopped visiting at this point, and Sinclair even refused to see his son David. All Sinclair had to worry about was his wife and his writing. The world of Lanny Budd became Sinclair's own. He wrote at least a thousand words each day. "I hammered on my little typewriter for three hours every morning," Sinclair explained, "revised the half dozen pages every afternoon, and walked in the garden every evening, composing the next day's installment." That was his life.[4]

Hello to Arms!

As much as Lanny Budd allowed Sinclair to tell a story, politics could never be entirely left behind, especially not now. Sinclair was on the warpath again. To tell a story about World War I and the botched postwar settlements was to send a political message: *We messed up last time and now we're paying for it as we watch Germany get revenge against its old enemies. This time, we have a responsibility to right our wrongs, fight a war, and make sure the peace is just.* Of course, Sinclair knew that many Americans were drawing a different conclusion from World War I by reconfirming their isolationism. World War I appeared to have been a mistake, so why take a risk on Europe again, many asked. That argument grew stronger in the wake of the famous hearings of Senator Gerald Nye. He was a progressive Republican from North Dakota. His committee met from 1934 to 1937 and interrogated some of America's wealthiest people, including J. P. Morgan and members of the DuPont family. Nye discovered what everyone had already known but no one had set out so boldly: bankers and arms manufacturers had struck it rich during World War I. Now looking at Hitler running roughshod over Europe, some concluded that all war did was make the wrong people wealthier. Fascism was clearly an ideology that had it in for the left, but the left in the United States was split on whether to go to war against fascism. There were those, like Sinclair, who moved smoothly from their earlier Popular Front antifascism to supporting the war. These included the playwright Robert Sherwood and, of course, Archibald MacLeish (whose "Irresponsibles" article served as a cri de coeur for this group). But there were others who remained steadfastly opposed to war. Norman Thomas, for instance, would protest American intervention in Europe, as would, following Nye's investigation, numerous progressives in the Midwest.

Consider Philip LaFollette, son of Robert. He had been a major organizer of the Progressive Party, the last third party that Sinclair would support in 1938. Three years later, showing just how divided the left was on the question of the European war, Sinclair and LaFollette faced each other in a debate. On March 13, 1941, thousands of people crammed into the John Marshall High School auditorium in Pasadena, California. Sinclair figured he knew the anti-interventionist mind-set well enough (having drifted back into it himself during the 1930s) to take it on. The audience was split. Socialists booed Sinclair as he spoke in favor of U.S. intervention, and Sinclair had to quiet down his supporters when LaFollette spoke. Sinclair explained that he had read Hitler's writing and knew just how diabolical this German leader was. He realized, as he had written to another isolationist, that the Nazi "badness is so completely unbelievable" because it was so awful and beyond the comprehension of those with good intentions. This posed a problem, for during World War I, much of the prowar propaganda had demonized Germans; there was still a mistrust of anti-German propaganda among some in America. But in this case, the stories about a demented leader with plans to take over the world and exterminate the Jews were real. For the sake of his audience, Sinclair traced Hitler's expansion; he was already in France by this time, so how could anyone doubt his ambitions? "You and I, as believers in democracy, can do just one thing today, if we want peace and that is to say that Britain shall not go down." This needed to be a war to save democracy, and it needed to be conducted better than the last war if it was to save democracy.[5]

Sinclair was once again allied with FDR. International politics now trumped Sinclair's doubts about the later stages of New Deal reform. The president, after all, was desperately seeking out ways to circumvent the Neutrality Act of 1935, which prevented shipments of arms to belligerent powers and which was consistently revised only to say the same thing over and over as the 1930s marched on. Now the leading belligerent was Winston Churchill, whom Sinclair had called his "new friend" in his debate with LaFollette. Roosevelt chafed at his country's neutrality, knowing that Britain needed support and that if it fell, all of Europe would be in fascist clutches. The president gave speeches about the threat of fascism and then tried to revise the Neutrality Act in 1939. He began to organize military research, taking the first steps in 1940 that would eventually produce the atomic bomb. And he most famously started to "lend" weaponry, especially submarines, to Sinclair's "new friend." He did this while saying that he wouldn't lead the country into war, knowing full well that to say the opposite was to risk a loss in the 1940 presidential election. To a large extent, FDR in 1940 followed Woodrow Wilson in 1916: he argued publicly against war, while knowing full well that the United States would eventually have to enter it. Needless to say, he had Sinclair's vote.[6]

Sinclair could debate Philip LaFollette and throw out quips about how America First, the leading anti-intervention organization increasingly dominated by conservatives, should be renamed "America First Aid to Nazism." But most of all he could write. The next installment of the Lanny Budd series came out in 1941 and was titled *Between Two Worlds*, a nice title for a book covering the time from the end of World War I to the Wall Street crash of 1929. In it, Lanny, who himself moves into his twenties during the novel, mixes it up with European historical events, unable to turn his back on Old World affairs. Sinclair spends some time on Lanny's love affairs, the first with an older French woman, Madame De Bruyne. The love affair is slightly controversial, since De Bruyne is older than Lanny and previously married. She will die of cancer during the course of the novel, and Lanny will then marry a younger woman from America's leisure class, Irma Barnes. Sandwiched in between these affairs, Lanny watches his British friend Rick turning socialist, while his father supports Harding and Hoover. Lanny also continues to hang out with George Herron, who bemoans the failure of the League of Nations and who writes a book about the issue that doesn't sell well in the United States, "where everybody was done with Europe, forever and ever, amen." Lanny winds up meeting Mussolini, while his journalist friend Rick goes off to Germany to witness the growing popularity of Hitler and Nazism. Becoming an art dealer, Lanny now has more excuses to travel through Europe, and Sinclair started to draw more inspiration from his friend Martin Birnbaum, a now-famous art dealer, who gave Sinclair loads of advice on the novel.[7]

Lanny travels to Rome. Italy starts moving to the center of the story as Mussolini's rise to power portends the future of Europe so evocatively. Lanny is abducted by fascist militia in Rome, asked about his affiliation with socialists, and then booted from the country. At the same time, Lanny reads *Mein Kampf* and starts growing depressed about Europe's future, including his friend Kurt (now Beauty's ex-lover), who drifts toward the right. Lanny meanwhile drifts further toward democratic socialism. *Between Two Worlds* ends with Lanny eloping with Irma Barnes, whose mother is ashamed that Lanny was born out of wedlock. The young couple moves to Long Island as America cruises through the jazz age (Long Island, it should be pointed out, was the setting for *The Great Gatsby*). Lanny winds up going into New York City, where he sees poverty and meets with Socialists and Communists. He warns his father, who has been growing richer as the decade proceeds, that he shouldn't trade on Wall Street. They both witness the crash of 1929, and there the novel ends, with Lanny and Irma married and leaving for Europe.

Sinclair felt he had a good thing going, and his new publisher, Viking Press, kept encouraging him, so he rushed ahead to write *Dragon's Teeth*, his third Budd novel. It would become a transformative work, at least for Sinclair and his relation to the outside world, which seemed increasingly distant, given his shut-in life. The book, dedicated to men and women fighting for "freedom and human decency" in Europe, picked up Lanny's story in the wake of the Great Crash. Lanny and Irma have a baby girl, Frances, but this happy moment doesn't capture the overall feel of their relationship. As the novel proceeds, Lanny will become frustrated by his wife's apolitical nature (indeed, it is hard for readers to understand just why the couple got married in the first place). Lanny's apparent attraction to the country of Germany makes more sense at this point. He travels there and witnesses Hitler speaking to a gathering of devoted Nazis; Lanny's only frame of reference for the fervor he sees is an evangelical tent meeting in the United States. Noticing that the left was divided between Communists and Socialists, Lanny fears there's an opening for Hitler to seize power. He meets Hitler, who tries to charm him, and he debates his uncle Jesse, who believes that Communists will prevail in Germany. Lanny, of course, wins the debate and watches as "National Socialism"—"power without conscience"—takes over Germany.[8]

At this point, the novel turns more fantastic. Lanny learns that Johannes

Robin, a Jewish businessman and friend, has been abducted. Lanny then embarks on his new career as a self-appointed spy and rescuer of Jews from the clutches of Nazis. To free Johannes, Lanny meets with Goebbels and then Goring, the latter promising to turn Johannes over if Lanny will provide money and a yacht to the Nazi cause. Lanny meets Johannes in jail and tells Irma, in a way that Sinclair clearly intends as foreshadowing, "Johannes was too trusting. He thought he could handle matters by diplomacy; but [the Nazis] have knocked over the conference table." Lanny's first attempt at his new career as double agent works, miraculously, and Johannes is freed. But soon thereafter, Lanny learns that Johannes's son, Freddi Robin, is in Dachau. Now Lanny rushes to Freddi's rescue, and once again, he uses his connection to Goring to arrange for Freddi's freedom. The story is, of course, hard to believe, but what is perhaps more fantastic is that Sinclair was writing about Dachau before most Americans had ever heard of Germany's death camps (Sinclair praised one of the few writers—Dorothy Thompson, who was also Sinclair Lewis's wife—who did write truthfully about Germany's policy toward the Jews). Sinclair, by having two Jewish characters almost fall into the grasp of Nazis, was making clear for his reading audience that a war against Nazis was a war against anti-Semitism and brutal dictatorship. At last, Sinclair's prescience finally pays off, as he foresees a world that will come to be, one that many others had missed.[9]

By the time bookstore clerks put *Dragon's Teeth* out on shelves, the European war had come home to the United States. Japan, allied with Germany, attacked Pearl Harbor on December 7, 1941, a date that would live in "infamy," as FDR told his fellow citizens. Sinclair took time away from writing his fourth Budd novel to telegram FDR. He suggested that the president give a fireside chat that would address the entire world and explain "the meaning of democracy as freedom, social justice, international order, and good faith." FDR did wind up linking the social justice of the New Deal to the struggle against fascism, but for now, Sinclair had to settle for something simpler—FDR's pledge to go to war. Sinclair rejoiced to hear that Churchill rushed to the United States to plot strategy, and he thrilled as FDR lined up the generals and troops now ready to take on fascist powers in every arena he could—Asia first, of course, and then Europe via North Africa. The march was on for Dachau.[10]

Things seemed to be going Sinclair's way now in another realm as well. His Lanny Budd novels were hitting the best-seller lists. Even the *New York Times* touted his developing skill as a historical novelist. "The artist in Sinclair gets the better of the old crusader," the newspaper reported. "He is ready to admit that human life is too complicated to fit any formula." The *New Yorker*, a magazine that typically looked down upon the simplicity of Sinclair's writing, admitted that *Between Two Worlds* had "remarkable skill, insight, and moral courage." And the *Times Literary Supplement* was "impressed" by the novel whose narrative was "vigorous, fecund, and closely studied." *Dragon's Teeth* won more than good reviews; it won the Pulitzer Prize in 1943. Sinclair was notified by the editor of a daily newspaper in Monrovia of the news. He explained that his "first remark to the editor was 'I couldn't be any more surprised if you should tell me that I had been named King of Siam.'"[11]

Better still, for Sinclair, the United States was mobilizing for war the way it had mobilized during World War I, that is, by building socialism bit by bit. The month *Dragon's Teeth* came out, the War Production Board started to convert industrial production to wartime production; private profit could not be allowed to persevere in the face of this calamity. Automakers started to make tanks, and FDR himself told businesses that the common good must trump profit. He also taxed the wealthiest ranks to fund the war, much more than Wilson did during World War I. Citizens faced rations; everywhere they turned, the home front seemed as engaged as the military fronts opening in Asia and North Africa. For Sinclair this meant that the economic depression was ending, something he had doubted could happen in the previous decade. Americans were now "moving toward socialism by the English-Fabian and not by the German-Marxist route," meaning via "a steady slide into collectivism, a movement as inexorable as the advance of a glacier." Now, so long as the United States also oversaw an intelligent transition toward international governance after the war, this peaceful socialism at home could be mirrored in a peaceful transition toward international governance and socialism. The United States would have to prevent another punitive peace, Sinclair warned, and convert Germany to a cooperative economy that would turn its industrial might toward higher ideals. If this was done, and Sinclair was hopeful it could be, then all would be well in the world.[12]

Sinclair was too old to fight in the war, and his ill wife kept him close to home. Nonetheless, he could occasionally make radio broadcasts to the world explaining the war's aims as he saw them. But for the most part, he continued to write. Now he was writing to the sounds of American tanks thundering through North Africa and battleships in the Pacific Ocean leapfrogging toward Japan. "The mood in which I am working on the

fourth volume of World's End series," Sinclair explained, "is quite different from the mood in which I began it." The storyline plodded ahead
nonetheless. *Wide Is the Gate* went back to the 1930s and opened with
Freddi's freedom and eventual death. Lanny gets busy in America preaching against Hitler and finds his relationship with his wife deteriorating
due to his increased political awareness. Irma had never been much of a
character, and suddenly Sinclair turns her into a symbol of the American
naiveté that needed education. "Irma has lived all her life in free countries,"
Sinclair observed and wrote, "and finds it hard to realize there are any
other sort. She has never witnessed an act of violence in her twenty-six
years on earth, and she has difficulty in making real to herself the idea that
such acts are frequently committed." As the novel proceeds, Lanny finds
himself falling in love with Trudi Schultz, a German woman he had met
four years earlier. She pledges herself to resisting Nazism, and he pledges
himself to continuing with his covert activity and raising money for her
resistance, ironically using money from artwork bought by Goring to fund
her cause.[13]

Trudi starts giving Lanny documents that expose German plans for
world domination, and Lanny feeds them to his friend Rick, who publishes them in newspapers. Suddenly, the Gestapo tracks Trudi down, and
so, once again, Lanny must rush to the rescue. He travels with Irma
through Germany and tells her of his plan to rescue Trudi. Irma is upset
that Lanny would help someone she perceives as a Communist, but this
won't stop him. He drives with Trudi and Irma in his car, heads to a meeting with the führer, and has Trudi hide in the car while he discusses art
with the führer and Irma falls for Hitler's prattling. After freeing Trudi in
Austria, Irma and Lanny part ways. "The parting between Irma Barnes
and Lanny Budd was like the parting between Germany and Czechoslovakia" and "between the New Dealers and the old-line Republicans in
Washington," Sinclair explained, promising to "split the whole world down
the middle." Lanny and Irma eventually divorce, and Lanny turns to his
new love, Spain, and considers fighting on the side of the Republicans
there. Moving up into the year 1936, Lanny grows angry at Leon Blum,
the Popular Front leader of France, who refuses to provide support to the
Spanish loyalists, and becomes sickened by pro-Hitler activists in the
Oxford movement of Britain. Lanny professes his love for Trudi, while
Irma marries a man who has ties to Mussolini. Lanny and Trudi become
a couple and move throughout Europe. But once again, Lanny must rush
into a new rescue, this time searching for Alfy, his friend Rick's son, who

is reported missing in action in Spain. After a bizarre turn of events, Lanny returns to Paris, having freed Alfy from a fascist prison and remaining in love with Trudi.[14]

Sinclair's material was starting to turn almost surreal. Lanny was freely floating through Europe as dictators took over, in a way difficult to fathom. Sinclair and his story were saved by Cornelius Vanderbilt Jr., a descendant of one of America's wealthiest families and a liberal newspaperman who had become a "presidential agent" for FDR during World War II. Vanderbilt and Sinclair became fast friends, and Sinclair picked his brains for new material. Sinclair's next entry became, following conversations with Vanderbilt, *Presidential Agent*. Here Sinclair gives Lanny something more of a purpose. Meeting with Professor Alston, who had introduced Lanny to diplomatic work in the wake of World War I, he gets a meeting with FDR at Hyde Park right after he has returned from Spain and just before that country falls to fascists. Lanny pleads with FDR to help Spain, and FDR, much as he told Sinclair during the governor's race, explains that he can only take the American people as far as they'll go. Lanny explains his relationship with Trudi, and FDR introduces the idea of becoming a "presidential agent" who will do "intelligence" work for him. In many ways, Lanny fits the persona of someone who would work at the Office of Strategic Services (OSS), which had been set up in 1941 to do intelligence research in Europe and was a forerunner to the Central Intelligence Agency (CIA). Most of the people who joined were from wealthy backgrounds and were willing to risk their lives, in one writer's words, "roving wartime Europe like latterday proconsuls."[15]

With his new role, Lanny travels to France in order to meet with Trudi, who left without leaving word of her whereabouts. Lanny begins his next rescue attempt, believing Trudi to be in the Chateau de Belcour in France. He has a meeting with leading Nazis, where he gets drunk, spouts fascist rhetoric, and then learns that prisoners are in fact held at the chateau. Using his status as an art dealer, Lanny gets into the chateau and cases out the security. He then makes it into a cell where he hypnotizes a prisoner, who tells him that Trudi has been taken to Germany. He heads to Germany with his father, who is now selling arms to the country, and meets Goring at his ostentatious palace. Lanny arranges a meeting with Hitler and preaches the power of telepathy to the German dictator, who winds up blabbing to Lanny about his plans to take over Austria. Lanny also learns that Trudi is dead in Dachau, revealing his first botched attempt to save a loved one from Nazism through his own personal effort, symbolizing that more than just one man's action is required. Lanny then has follow-up meetings with Hitler, trying to persuade him not to invade Austria, even having astrologers feed the Nazi leader nasty predictions about how things would go wrong there. All the while, Lanny writes down notes from his meetings, including one where Hitler pledges to invade Poland, and sends them back to FDR. *Presidential Agent* ends where it began, with a meeting between FDR and Lanny, the president admitting frustration with the American public's understanding of the European dilemma.

While Sinclair was writing *Presidential Agent* and his next installment, *Dragon Harvest*, American troops had broken through Italian control in North Africa and were heading into Italy from the south. By July 1943, Mussolini was sacked, and by mid-1944, Americans had taken Rome. At the same time, bombs were raining down on Germany, and Eisenhower was preparing for D-Day, ready to cross the English Channel and liberate France. Sinclair read newspapers and took close notes while pounding away in his backyard about Lanny, who was still five years behind the time line of contemporary history. As the war in Europe was coming close to an Allied victory, Lanny was just meeting with Hitler in 1939 to inquire about his plans to invade Poland. Returning to meet with FDR, Lanny debates the merits of England's Prime Minister Neville Chamberlain; FDR is hopeful, and Lanny is pessimistic about England's history of appeasement. Lanny also grows increasingly worried about homegrown fascists in the United States, having met Henry Ford and Father Coughlin, both of whom spouted anti-Semitism. Meanwhile, FDR is desperately trying to change the terms of the Neutrality Act, as Lanny goes off to Germany. This time, Lanny has his newest love, a left-leaning writer named Laurel Creston, pose as a fortune-teller and meet with Hitler. Laurel suggests that Hitler should slow down his ambitions for conquering the world and think twice about invading Poland. Of course, the idea that a fortune-teller could curb Hitler's ambitions was preposterous, and so in accord with historical reality, the invasion takes place. Lanny goes back to London for the "first days of war" as England stands up against Hitler. He then watches as France falls.[16]

War's End and More

Just a few months before *Dragon's Harvest* was released, FDR returned from the Yalta Conference, where he had met with Stalin and Churchill to discuss the now-imminent collapse of Nazi power and plans for Europe's future. Then on April 12, 1945, FDR died. The very next day, Sinclair telegrammed Eleanor Roosevelt, saying that "we have lost the greatest statesman of our time and it is a personal loss to every man and woman in this country whether they know it or not." Meanwhile, the war proceeded, and on May 8, victory was declared in Europe. This left only the Asian theater of the war. The battles, though, were growing worse there. The Japanese were being beaten, but the country still resisted with warships and kamikaze pilots. Harry Truman struggled with what to do as he pondered a long land war with Japan. He learned that the United States had developed a new sort of bomb, and he was ready to use it in order to cut the Asian war short.[17]

Sinclair was far behind in his own time line on the Lanny Budd novels, but he was still pushing forward on them, and he now considered a book that would draw in Asia—the missing dimension so far. In *A World to Win*, published in 1946, Sinclair goes back to 1940, describing England's entry into the war and FDR's tepid first steps toward providing aid. Lanny meets with FDR and expresses his concern about fascists in America's midst— including William Randolph Hearst (ironically, a man in whom Sinclair once had a great deal of faith)—and then suggests that the president use the term "arsenal of democracy" in a speech. He then meets his old friend Kurt in France and learns of Germany's plans to invade Russia. He meets with Hitler again, then members of the French underground, then Einstein, who briefs him on physics, all the while falling more deeply in love with Laurel Creston. Lanny takes a cruise to Japan with Laurel, allowing Sinclair to take up the Asian dimension of his story. In China, Lanny meets Sun Yat Sen, the nationalist leader, and witnesses one of many Japanese offensives against the country. He and Laurel drive ambulances for the Chinese, fall in love, get married, and decide to have a child. Before leaving the area, Lanny meets Mao Tse Tung and then travels to Russia, where he meets with Stalin. Lanny toasts Stalin, who promises to pledge himself to inter-national governance in the wake of the war.[18]

Sinclair was now eager to make the Lanny Budd series serve as something of a hagiography of FDR, whose death he still mourned. Continuing to hunt down secrets, Lanny is now pursuing how far the Germans have come in planning a hydrogen bomb and, in the process, meets with French underground leaders. He even shares some of his secrets with Churchill, who is present at the White House during one of Lanny's visits. Lanny is now chafing to get back to Germany and do more spying, but FDR considers it too dangerous, especially now that Laurel is about to have a baby. Lanny pokes around North Africa, arriving in Algiers before U.S. troops reach the area. He also focuses on France, trying to build relations with the resistance and General de Gaulle. On his way to meet with Stalin, his plane is shot down. He descends into the Sahara Desert, where he's captured and taken to a German camp. Flown to a meeting with Hitler, he just barely escapes Germany as the bombs rain down from Allied planes. Lanny gets to England and then meets again with FDR. The novel ends with Lanny stating the obvious, "I am putting my faith in Roosevelt."[19]

By 1948, with the country moving from World War II into the first phases of the cold war, Sinclair wasn't sure how to end the Budd series, but he was orienting more and more of it around FDR. In *One Clear Call* (1948), Lanny explains that he "considered Franklin Roosevelt the greatest man in the world." Lanny is now in his forties and is still having meetings with Hitler and sending reports back to the greatest man in the world. In Italy, he witnesses Mussolini's fall from power, and then returns to Germany to mislead Hitler about FDR's plans. But his cover is blown, and he has to escape Germany hiding in a truck. He returns to the United States to travel with Laurel and then is summoned by FDR to travel to Palestine and research the future of Judaism. Lanny seems sympathetic toward Zionism and has little good to say about Arabs, who have allied with Hitler. He realizes that the Arab-Jewish conflict will require the attention of international governance institutions once the war is over. Then Lanny rushes to England and is able to witness D-Day. He is happy to find that the French resistance he had reported on was strong enough to assist the Allied landing in France. He serves as an interpreter for the U.S. Army as it marches into France and then learns that Kurt, his old friend and now a Nazi, has been captured. He rushes to interrogate him. Then Lanny meets with FDR and tells him that he'll have to face down Stalin and, in a note that Sinclair must have felt compelled to slip in, endorse "production for use" in the United States.[20]

Finally, Sinclair ends the series. If a reader piled up the books in the series so far, they would already be a foot high. The whole thing seemed to have spun out of control, but now he knew where to end, for a stage of history had definitely passed with FDR's death and the end of World War II. Lanny is now in Europe and witnesses—fantastic as it seems—the Battle of the Bulge, Hitler's last desperate military push. Lanny comes back to the United States, meets with FDR, and is told to prepare for a meeting with Stalin. And so Lanny finds himself at the Yalta Conference, worrying about FDR's health. FDR, of course, dies, and Lanny travels to Europe to witness the liberation of Europe. He even discovers Beauty's old lover, Marcel, in a concentration camp. Then, Lanny is off to New Mexico, where he meets Robert Oppenheimer and learns about the bomb that will be dropped on Hiroshima to end the war in the Pacific. The war ends finally, and Lanny decides to create a newspaper entitled *Peace*, which will argue for international governance. He even does séances and hears FDR's ghost speak to him, exclaiming, "The shepherd speaks!" Lanny meets with Truman, then Stalin, and Sinclair ends the novel by having Lanny express his hopes for international governance, peace, and cooperation.[21]

Sinclair could now look back on his accomplishment, noting as he had already by 1946 that "millions of people all over the world are getting information as to how we and they are drawn into World War II" from his Budd novels. After "ten years' incessant labor," he was ready to put Lanny aside for a moment. He could soak in the praise bound to come with such an accomplishment. Most critics agreed that the novels were a fine source of history that helped Americans figure out why they had intervened in Europe. "The books are more like a course in current history than novels," Max Eastman explained. "It is good history, if mediocre fiction," George Orwell concurred. Sometimes, *Time* magazine pointed out, the books seemed like little more than a brisk read through the newspapers. The historian Perry Miller couldn't help liking the books, even though he thought the narrative was "clumsy" and the style "corny." Another reviewer believed the Budd novels were "unbelievable" and "absurd," with Lanny "omnipresent" and "like God." It was Howard Mumford Jones, a cultural historian and critic at Harvard, who developed this point more fully. For Jones, Budd was "a combination of the Count of Monte Cristo, Sherlock Holmes, Harry Hopkins" who is "always appearing at the right moment and at the right spot, always international yet always American, now a socialist, now a millionaire, now an art dealer, now a mystery man, the master of encyclopedic knowledge, irresistible to women, yet pure as Galahad." No person on earth could get "around with the speed of light like Lanny Budd." Endlessly fantastic, the Budd novels were also "endless monotony."[22]

Sinclair could not allow this criticism to go unanswered. In his defense, he explained his goal in writing the series; sure, he reasoned, the novels were unbelievable, but all a reader had to do was adopt a "naive frame of mind and enjoy the pleasure of seeing the world panorama." Sinclair believed Americans needed "adventure stories and dramas." And, besides, "somebody has to write for the masses and not just for the Harvard Professors." For Sinclair, the Budd books reached a general reader who "reads to be entertained and to widen his vision of the world in which he lives." Though there might be "critics who look down their noses at these stories," Sinclair glowed with satisfaction over them. He aimed to entertain the public while educating it about contemporary history. He wore the badge of middlebrow novelist and historian with pride.[23]

It should be no surprise that Sinclair hoped to make the Lanny Budd books into a movie or a radio show. They seemed written for that format, with their broad panoramas on the world's situation and their shifts from one locale to another. Sol Lesser was ready to help, having done what Sinclair still considered a good job on the Eisenstein fiasco, even if others didn't think so. Lesser spoke with Douglas Fairbanks Jr., who seemed interested in the project for a brief moment. Then Sinclair didn't hear from Lesser for a while, and there was some dispute over who had rights to movie production, author or publisher. When Lesser wrote to Sinclair in 1949, the year the Budd series was completed, he explained that he had grown occupied with making *Tarzan and the Slave Girl*. But Sinclair need not worry, Lesser explained, since he would turn his attention afterward to Lanny Budd. Unfortunately for Sinclair, when he did, Lesser found that no one was interested in a movie about Nazis. It seemed that by 1950, Americans were more concerned with a new enemy—Stalin, a man Lanny had both toasted and warned about.[24]

Hello to Arms Again: The Cold War

The year of the last Lanny Budd novel, 1949, was a wicked one. Communists had just taken China after a struggle with Nationalist forces backed by the United States. Later that year, the Soviet Union exploded an atomic bomb, signaling that the United States was not alone in its ability to destroy the world, and leading some Americans to worry that there were Soviet spies in their midst. These two events fell on the heels of the Berlin Blockade—an event that particularly bothered Sinclair. Germany had been divided after the war, east and west, and the Soviets prevented goods from traveling into the western portion of the country that was under the control of the United States. Truman considered military action and then decided on an airlift. Tensions mounted as U.S. planes broke

226 UPTON SINCLAIR AND THE OTHER AMERICAN CENTURY

through the blockade and flew goods into West Berlin. It was clear that the cold war had begun in earnest.

Sinclair had become more sympathetic toward the Soviet Union during World War II. He couldn't pretend that the country was the best promise to the world the way he had in 1936, but at least Stalin was sacrificing Soviet lives and resources in the fight against Hitler. *That* couldn't be doubted. Stalin had never appeared as a cuddly father figure in the Lanny Budd books, the way he did in sycophantic treatments like *Mission to Moscow*, but the Soviet dictator came off pretty well nonetheless. In 1945 Sinclair could write, in a short piece for the *New Leader*, "Beyond any doubt the Soviet system represents a social gain for the Russians," even though he didn't mean by this that he endorsed Stalin. Nonetheless, the editors at this anti-Stalinist publication believed the Lanny Budd books were too soft on the Soviet dictator. The fact that Sinclair stopped writing the Budd series in 1949 suggests he might have felt an era had passed, a period of antifascism changing to a period of anti-Communism. When Lesser told him that no one cared about the German Nazis by 1949, only the Soviet Communists, that brought the point home even further. Sinclair himself was very upset by the Soviet blockade of West Germany, which he described as "an act of war." He had made it clear by now that he never ducked his responsibility during wartime.[25]

So Sinclair declared war. Like many Americans, he began to see the Soviets differently from the way he had seen them during World War II. The USSR was becoming a "reactionary dictatorship." In sacking governments throughout Eastern Europe, especially in Czechoslovakia, Stalin renewed his country's long tradition of "nationalist imperialism." It had been the invasion of Finland, not the Moscow Trials, that had set Sinclair off against Stalin earlier, and he seemed more willing to scrutinize foreign expansionism than Stalin's domestic operations. Sinclair once hated how anti-Stalinist critics put Stalin and Hitler in the same category of totalitarian rulers; now he himself went a step further: Soviet Communism was *worse* than Nazism. He argued that "Soviet Communism" was "far more dangerous than German Nazism or Italian Fascism, for these movements were frankly nationalistic." This was a bizarre statement; after all, World War II had been fought over the fact that fascists were anything but "nationalistic." Sinclair made more sense when he pointed out that Stalin was more dangerous than Hitler because Communist ideology purported to liberate people from oppression while

National Socialism, or Nazism, was power politics, pure and simple. As the cold war proceeded, Sinclair believed it didn't matter what the Soviets' intentions were, since the country's leaders were "planning to impose their system upon the rest of the world by methods of force and terror." These were fighting words.[26]

The war turned personal quickly. As Sinclair would explain in 1954, "I have marked out all Communist names from my address book." He had actually started to do this earlier. In 1946, following Craig's wishes (she was always more paranoid about Communists than he was), Sinclair began to avoid Kate Crane-Gartz, the wealthy woman who had funded many of his prior initiatives and who had become a friend of Craig's. Crane-Gartz had grown enamored of Communists. She tried to convert Craig and Uppie to her cause, and grew insistent, dropping by the house even after they moved to Monrovia and sending them postcards inviting them to her house. Sinclair explained that Crane-Gartz "asked us [to] come [to] her home and answer the communists," but "Mary Craig had made up her mind to do no more" of this. She had "seen enough of their trickery." Besides, this was turning into a war. Craig and Uppie went "into hiding." They bought a trailer and traveled in the mountains outside of Monrovia. Craig bought numerous cottages, and once someone located them, they would move again. Sinclair would describe his meals to people as a "picnic affair." His secretary couldn't keep track of his whereabouts. He became like Lanny Budd, flitting about in clandestine form. Even that wasn't good enough, so they moved to Buckeye, Arizona, from 1951 to 1952. They had to move back to California after Craig had a heart attack in 1954, but they still kept the curtains to their Monrovia home drawn. The shut-in life helped shut out Communists.[27]

What really brought the war into focus for Sinclair wasn't Crane-Gartz but Korea. When North Korea crossed the infamous Thirty-Eighth Parallel, which divided it from South Korea, in June of 1950, President Truman still had China on his mind. Conservatives blamed him for letting China go Communist, and the president remembered warnings about the British appeasement of the Nazis. Truman was eager to draw a line against Communist expansion, and this seemed the perfect place to do so. The United Nations met and condemned North Korea's invasion, and Truman immediately sent in troops to protect South Korea. Sinclair gave out a war whoop. Though it wasn't entirely clear whether the Soviet Union had approved North Korea's decision to invade, Sinclair believed they had. This was a war to push back Soviet imperialism; when Communists accused him of standing on the other side and defending American imperialism, he pointed to the United Nations' support for the police action. Besides, he did not—as did General MacArthur and hawkish conservatives at home—want to unify Korea or push northward and invade China. That would be insanity. Sinclair endorsed, instead, containment. "I do not think that we are under any obligation to unify Korea," he explained once U.S. troops had pushed the North back to the Thirty-Eighth Parallel, "and I think we have done what we set out to do which was to teach the Reds that they cannot go on seizing territory and enslaving new peoples." Sinclair was all in favor of Truman sacking General MacArthur, who had wanted troops to cross over and take out North Korea. War was the right course of action, but MacArthur's plan would have been folly, in Sinclair's view.[28]

Besides, what made the cold war distinct from previous battles was that it could never be reduced to military action. This was a war of ideas. It required showing the world that American democracy was better than Soviet totalitarianism. And so, much more than World War I, this was a war made by intellectuals—those who could argue and articulate values and principles to as wide an audience as possible. Sinclair joined the ranks. He worked with Americans for Liberation from Bolshevism and broadcast his views on Voice of America and Radio Free Europe. He cajoled the State Department to carry his books overseas. He showed enormous respect for intellectuals who went over to Europe in order to promote American ideas, especially Melvin Lasky, who published the newspaper *Der Monat* in Germany in order to promote U.S. foreign policy and ideas about democracy. Sinclair threw in with the Congress for Cultural Freedom (CCF), an international organization that put on conferences and other events that touted American culture (Europeans often thought Americans lacked any culture) and democratic ideals. In 1952 Sinclair wrote a speech for a CCF conference for no money (if he had known the organization took money from the Central Intelligence Agency, he might have reconsidered) in which he denounced the "Soviet monster" whose "revolution" was "devouring its children." Sinclair believed that the CCF was doing the right thing. "We in America are busy selling the world our gadgets," he bemoaned. "I urge that we work harder at selling them our democratic ideas and ideals."[29]

Of course, he also wrote for the cause. He even retrieved Lanny Budd from his literary grave to become an anti-Communist fighter this go-round. The book he wrote was to be called *Lanny Budd Flies Again*, but that sounded too much like the popular radio show *The Lone Ranger Rides Again*, so instead it was called simply *The Return of Lanny Budd*, though Sinclair admitted to Sol Lesser that *Lanny Budd's Cold War* would have been more appropriate. The book opens with Lanny being summoned to the White House, where Truman tells him he is losing faith in the Soviet Union. Lanny himself was "coming to dislike Stalinism as he had formerly disliked Hitlerism." He continues to focus on the Robin family and finds that Hansi Robin's wife, Bess, is a Soviet spy. Lanny watches as this breaks up the couple's marriage. Swashbuckler that he still is, Lanny travels to Germany and meets up with Melvin Lasky, making anti-Communist speeches. In typical Budd fashion, he is captured by Soviets and thrown into jail. He is then rescued by a Japanese colonel and becomes a celebrity of cold-war America, returning to give broadcasts on the radio in support of a domestic policy favoring labor unions, civil rights, and the welfare state, and a foreign policy in line with Truman's policy of containment. Lanny Budd became a cold-war liberal.[30]

So too Sinclair. He was now a fierce opponent of the Soviet Union and had endorsed containment. But he never went as far as two of his friends, Max Eastman and John Dos Passos, both of whom drifted further to the right. Eastman, for instance, had turned his belief in personal liberation (once lived out in the streets and bedrooms of Greenwich Village's bohemian culture) into praise for the free market and was writing for conservative publications like *Reader's Digest*. Sinclair argued that Eastman was "for resistance to Soviet dictatorship, and I am with him completely, but I am not willing to shut my eyes to the defects of the economic system we have at home." Sinclair was willing to hunt down Communists in the U.S. government, the way Whittaker Chambers helped to do in the famous case of Alger Hiss, the State Department employee who had been spying for the Soviet Union. Chambers, who argued that anti-Communism had to sustain its energy from the absolute certitude only religion could provide, was right to finger Alger Hiss, Sinclair explained, but the man's "political and economic conclusions" were all wrong. For Sinclair, fighting Communism required the United States to ensure a certain level of equality for all of its citizens, building a welfare state that would protect civil liberties without allowing too many Americans to fall into poverty.[31]

Sinclair found a political home during the 1950s, and it would be his home until his death. His socialism bled into what historian Arthur Schlesinger Jr. called the "vital center" of postwar politics—a center between Communist ideology and right-wing libertarianism—that was squarely liberal. Sinclair would never vote for the Socialist Party candidate for president again; instead, he admired the two Democratic candidates of 1956 and 1960, Adlai Stevenson and John F. Kennedy. Sinclair was also happy to learn that the Intercollegiate Socialist Society, which he had started before World War I, had changed its name to the League for Industrial Democracy (LID), dumping the term *socialist*. He had eschewed his onetime New Deal ally Henry Wallace, whose Progressive Party of 1948 he considered a cover for the Communist Party. Sinclair, in fact, threw his support to Americans for Democratic Action (ADA), the leading anti-Communist liberal organization of the postwar years. His political views were now those of ADA. He stood for labor unions, the welfare state, civil rights for African Americans, and civil liberties for all. Though Sinclair was strangely silent in 1952 about his friend Charlie Chaplin being prevented from reentering the United States due to allegations that he was a Communist (all false), he was not silent about Senator Joe McCarthy, or what came to be called McCarthyism. Those who equated McCarthy with Stalin, like his old friend Waldo Frank, were wrong in Sinclair's eyes, given that McCarthy was not "able to jail anybody." Nonetheless, the senator from Wisconsin had "lied recklessly" and smeared far too many innocent people, and Sinclair was growing increasingly worried about McCarthy as well as the anti-Communist regulations like the McCarran Act and the Communist Control Act. He had always been for civil liberties, he pointed out, but now his support was stronger and more outspoken. "I believe in civil liberties of the true democratic sort," meaning that Communists supported civil rights only in order to get their political views across and to create the necessary conditions for a revolution that would abolish civil rights in the end. He now appreciated civil liberties for their own sake.[32]

His new perspective on liberalism was applied not just to politics but also to religion. Sinclair was bothered by a religious "revival" during the cold war, especially an increase in fundamentalism. His old friend Fulton Oursler, who had converted to Catholicism, wrote a book called *The Greatest Story Ever Told* about Jesus Christ, and its popularity disturbed Sinclair. He didn't like the book's literalism, which seemed to Sinclair to take the word of the Bible as the word of God, or the rigidity of Oursler's faith. Nor could he have liked the most famous of all religious figures at this time. Billy Graham, who broadcast on television every week starting in 1952 and who was a syndicated newspaper columnist, became

America's most prominent religious revivalist. Though Graham was a registered Democrat, his politics seemed increasingly Republican, as he lashed out at labor unions and celebrated free markets. For Graham, Communism was not just wrong but "master-minded by Satan." Graham also argued for a literal reading of the Bible—reviving the fundamentalism of the 1920s that Sinclair had recoiled against, even if he agreed with evangelicalism's stringent morality about drinking and smoking. While traveling around the mountains outside of Monrovia in his trailer, moving from cabin to cabin, Sinclair ran into numerous fundamentalist Baptists who held tent meetings. He decided there was something going on here that needed addressing.[33]

Sinclair wrote *A Personal Jesus* (1952) to provide an alternative to the Bible thumping he heard in those tent meetings near Monrovia. Sinclair's Jesus was to be "humanitarian," "not sectarian." Like Unitarians, Sinclair deemphasized the Jesus who performed miracles, and focused instead on the "historical" Jesus. "I want to make it possible for modern men and women to read about Jesus with understanding and sympathy, and without parting with their common sense." Walking on water and feeding the masses on just a few loaves of bread—these things had to be jettisoned. As far as Jesus curing people, well, maybe that was psychosomatic, much the way that Craig had cured him of hiccups, Sinclair reasoned. Here Sinclair sounded like another popular religious figure in postwar America, Norman Vincent Peale, whose "power of positive thinking" drew upon the tradition of mind cure. One difference between Peale and Sinclair was that Sinclair believed Jesus was a liberal who would have pushed aside America's cult of business success—the sort Peale catered to—and would have cherished America's welfare state.[34]

Sinclair seemed utterly mainstream by the 1950s: he was anti-Communist, liberal, and mainline Protestant (or at least in line with mainline Protestant churches). He had also become less strident in his faith, more relaxed, even more openly confused about the world. Lanny Budd seemed to teach Sinclair a lesson about complexity and nuance. In the beginning of *The Return of Lanny Budd*, Sinclair explained that it was "hard to think of anything more disconcerting to a husband and wife who were spending all their time talking and writing about peace" than to hear about the Soviet Union's increasing aggression throughout the world. Here was the rub: he wanted to be anti-Communist, but he feared nuclear war. In an open letter to Stalin, Sinclair counseled the Soviet dictator not to worry about American talk of "preventive war," suggesting that its advocates were out of touch with reality. But he would write to a friend a year later that the only thing that prevented the USSR from gobbling up the world was "the knowledge that our side has the heavier weapons and is ready and determined to use them." Lanny Budd had taught Sinclair that sometimes bad things had to be done in order to prevent something worse, but in this case, Sinclair realized, he was talking about the destruction of the earth. His fear was palpable, as he explained in a play he wrote entitled *Dr. Fist* (it was never published or performed). The play examined, as did others of Sinclair's, the ramifications of nuclear weapons. "All my life I have been writing plays and novels to prove this or that; I have done myself great harm by it. This time I face the most awful muddle in human history and I don't know what can be done about it." The bomb had foiled Sinclair, as he wrote two plays about families escaping nuclear holocaust yet still argued for nuclear armament to fight the cold war. The second play about the bomb, *The Enemy Had It Too*, told the story of a family moving from New York City after a nuclear attack, only to be rescued by Martians. "We created terrible means of destruction," one character explained, "but we did not have the moral force to control ourselves, and we were not fit to be trusted with such weapons." And yet, Sinclair continued to support building up nuclear arms. An intellectual quandary indeed.[35]

If the cold war confused Sinclair, it also led to a great deal of self-examination as he looked back at his past. No doubt the words that will long be remembered as emblematic of the cold war were those asked at meetings of the House Un-American Activities Committee (HUAC) as its members hunted Communists in the United States: "Are you now or have you ever been a member of the Communist Party?" Sinclair could answer this question with an unambiguous no. But for anti-Communists like Senator Joe McCarthy who were leading the inquisition, membership in the CP wasn't really the issue. "I'm not so much concerned about whether they have a card in their pocket saying, 'I am a member of the party.' I'm concerned about those men who are doing the job that the Communists want them to do," McCarthy explained. If Sinclair cared about this issue and looked back upon his life during the 1930s, he might have grown bothered. He never joined the Communist Party, for sure, but he also cut the Soviet Union a lot of slack and had worked with Popular Front organizations that were clearly Communist-inspired. And so the cold war pressed in on him, making his own sense of self, bound up with his personal history, seem less certain and more conflicted.[36]

Sometimes Sinclair tried to rewrite his personal history to fit the challenges of the cold war. He argued that he had been an anti-Communist earlier than was true. He told one person in 1952 that the purge trials of 1935–1936 and then the Stalin-Hitler pact of 1939 "put an end to my hopes" in the Soviet Union "forever." This was a classic case of misremembering: he had denounced the anti-Stalinist intellectuals who decried the purge trials, and he even thought the Stalin-Hitler pact was a brilliant coup on Stalin's part. But his reworking here was in private conversation. When it came to his public persona, things proved even more difficult. He knew that his own novels were being used to promote Communism abroad. No matter what he had written since, *The Jungle* remained his most popular novel, and some in Europe thought its description of meatpacking in the United States remained true into the 1950s. Sinclair explained: "America has changed a lot since then—thank God! It may be that the 'critical authors' had something to do with that change." He pointed out, "The truth of 1953 is not the truth of 1906." But still he worried that his books had been mistranslated into Russian in order to portray him as a Communist, since he was now being called a "miserable renegade," which implied that some believed he had once been a Communist. So he went on Voice of America radio and set the record straight:

My books have dealt for the most part with the evils existing in my country. I was what was called a muckraker. And now these books are being used in the Communist half of the world to tell their people that those conditions exist in America now. And it is utterly false, for there is not a book that I have written about evil conditions in America that has not helped to bring about remedies for those conditions. I'm not claiming all the credit, I'm just claiming a little.

The world had changed, and Sinclair tried to change with it. Sometimes he could bask in glory, but at other times he simply grew more confused about the world—a world that seemed bent on self-destruction, a world populated by scary dictators and one beyond his comprehension.[37]

Perhaps the most confusing aspect of the cold war for Sinclair was whether the United States could win it. That wasn't a question only of nuclear strategy; it was about a more pressing moral question: did the nation have the internal cultural resources that could win this war of ideology? Sinclair knew that as the cold war spread from Europe to Asia, as it already had by the Korean War, it would become more difficult to fight. After all, Asia saw the United States as rich and out of touch with its own poverty and economic underdevelopment. Poorer countries looked upon America's wealth with suspicion, and so did Sinclair. He hated the mass culture that the United States was coming to be known for in the postwar years. He refused, for instance, to buy a television. With his wife, he plugged his ears when bobby-soxers screamed for the next teen idol on the radio. The youth culture of the 1950s was starting to look remarkably like the youth culture of the 1920s, with its insipid immorality and escapism. "Drinking in college and high school is rampant, and juvenile delinquency has become a national problem," Sinclair complained. America's political leaders, especially Eisenhower, seemed too lazy and stupid to articulate the democratic ideals that the country needed to live up to in order to defeat Communism. Ike was too busy playing golf to care about anything else.[38]

Sinclair agreed that the United States was becoming a better country, due in some part to his own activism. But America's mass culture of television jingles, rock 'n' roll, and Hollywood escapism left Sinclair cold. He started to wonder how much his own country was catching up with him only to leave him behind in the end. After all, the culture being promoted by organizations like the Congress for Cultural Freedom and the State Department were not his novels (as much as he begged for them to be). It was the writing of modernists like Ezra Pound and William Faulkner in literature and the paintings of Jackson Pollock and abstract expressionists. Sinclair's middlebrow literary and artistic tastes, even if they were to the liking of Harry Truman (who claimed to have read the Lanny Budd series), didn't seem to project the necessary complexity and sophistication America's foreign policy elite wanted to show off around the world. Whether it was his middlebrow predilections, his lifelong tendency to write too much too fast, or his depressing domestic life and lack of stability as he moved from cabin to trailer, Sinclair found it harder and harder to get his work published. *A Personal Jesus* was turned down by eight publishers, and a book about alcoholism and writers took a year to find a publisher. When it did, it was the little-known Channel Press, and Sinclair was appalled to learn that its editor went door to door to try to sell his book. There were also a string of books that simply failed to find a publisher. In 1955 Sinclair would write to Carl Jung, the famous psychologist who had happened to review Sinclair's book about Jesus, that "in the past four years or so I have written six books, large or small, and found a publisher for only one." That this was written to a psychologist might suggest just how much frustration had crept into Sinclair's psyche.[39]

What Sinclair did publish during the cold war, once Lanny Budd had been put to rest, was inconsequential. There was *Another Pamela*, a rewrite of a sixteenth-century British story about class differences. Sinclair set his rewrite in Pasadena and told of a poor (yet virtuous) maid working for a wealthy family. Pamela recoils at the son of the family, who drinks too much, but she is eventually seduced by him. The story was flat, and one of his last to be published by a major publisher. There was *What Didymus Did*, which was turned down by U.S. publishers and then published in Britain. This was a scattered tale about a man seeing an angel, starting a new cult, and then falling in love with a woman who claimed to be a virgin mother. The leading character, Tom, realizes that his "ascetic discipline" contrasts with the way "young people of our time are behaving." This muddled criticism of postwar America is lost in a rambling and bizarre story.[40]

Sinclair continued to feel the paradoxes of the cold war. His politics swam in the mainstream, but he worried about being left behind by a mass culture that cherished hedonism. His last work of the 1950s captured this perfectly. After failing to get numerous works published, Sinclair finally finished up a play from 1959 to 1960 that was successfully performed in New York City. Titled *Cicero*, it told the story of the great Roman statesman and orator as he falls prey to Mark Antony's attack. There's little action in the play, and mostly it consists of Cicero's speeches, all of which seem directed more at postwar America than at the Roman Empire. In the first act, Sinclair has Cicero rail against the "decadence of our country! We rule the world but we cannot rule ourselves." The Romans have grown prosperous and thus lazy, Cicero reasons. "We no longer have to struggle, so we do not grow strong. The young find everything made easy for them, and all they need do is seek their pleasure." It was hard not to have visions of jitterbugging teenagers when hearing Cicero shout these words at the audience. Nor was it hard to think of historical analogies when Cicero, near the end of his life, provided this warning: "I would say to the future: Look for signs of decay in your people and warn them." Sinclair remained a critic and moralist even as he found himself more in agreement with his country's foreign and domestic policy. He seemed ready to retire, to put away the role of historian of human follies and simply recede.[41]

TEN

SOCIALIST EMERITUS

1960–1968

*I have been a rebel, but now I am accepted;
my cause is being accepted.*

—UPTON SINCLAIR, 1963

A S MUCH AS SINCLAIR SEEMED TO EMBRACE COMPLEXITY IN later life, he could never give up on the moral stridency that turned off so many of his friends throughout his life. Sinclair remained, into his older age, a Puritan who still liked to condemn people's drinking, smoking, and general hedonism. He was still the prize prude of the radical movement, as he called himself during the 1920s, even if he wasn't much of a radical by 1960. In fact, his last book, *Affectionately Eve* (1961), which was written in the form of fictionalized letters, would go back to the 1920s and tell the tale of a woman who falls in love with cultural radicals and commits adultery. It was another inconsequential work, all the more so because it fixated on a bygone era.[1]

That's what made a letter Sinclair sent to J. Edgar Hoover in 1958 so interesting. Sinclair wasn't known as a critic of the Federal Bureau of Investigation's chief. This might be surprising, since a civil libertarian like Sinclair would have been expected to have doubts about a man whose career began during World War I and from then on focused largely on hunting radicals. But Sinclair had asked Hoover for help in writing his Lanny Budd novels, as he had asked many others, and the two had a mildly pleasant correspondence. Sinclair even found himself on the same side as Hoover on juvenile delinquency, an issue that large numbers of Americans became concerned about in the late 1950s. Both Hoover and Sinclair worried about reports of young hoodlums running rampant in schools, smashing windows, and harassing teachers. But disagreement emerged. Sinclair accused Hoover of "overlooking the economic factor" in juvenile delinquency. "We can never expect children to be law-abiding when they are brought up in wretched slums and confronted all their lives, by newspapers, movies and TV, with the spectacle of other people spending enormous sums of money (which they have inherited and could never have earned) upon every imaginable kind of vanity and folly. That is the main cause of all crime, and our youngsters now see many times more of it than you and I did when we were of their age." Sinclair still saw social and environmental factors as important in determining social behavior. What was significant about the statement, though, was that Sinclair had given up on predicting the future by this time, but on this issue, he nailed it. He foresaw a major step that President Kennedy would take when he was elected just a year later. The president would start assembling a Committee on Juvenile Delinquency, out of which came many ideas that linked poverty and delinquency. That would get the ball rolling on a project to be completed by Lyndon Baines Johnson—the creation of the Great Society.[2]

Indeed, Sinclair would become a great supporter of Kennedy and then Johnson, especially with the birth of the Great Society. By 1964 Sinclair had stopped commenting on politics. He explained to his son, "I know definitely, I cannot write any more—I have said my say, and the public is tired of me." But Johnson's presidency warmed Sinclair's heart as he read newspaper reports. The president pushed through civil rights legislation that demolished segregation and disenfranchisement in the South. Sinclair had argued for such reform, if only to send a clear message to the world during the cold war that the United States stood for democracy and equality for all races. Johnson also created domestic programs to put inner-city youth back to work; Head Start, which helped fund preschools for impoverished kids; Medicaid, which provided assistance with medical costs for poor people; and Medicare, which helped the elderly on the same count. It was as if Sinclair's dreams had come true; the glacier of socialism moved ahead in the guise of American liberalism. Vietnam was also part of Sinclair's dreams. Communism needed to be contained, and that's what the president was doing in Vietnam, preventing its spread from North to South Vietnam. Sinclair gave his last war whoop when he learned about Johnson's decision to Americanize the Vietnam War. Asked by a reporter if he supported Johnson's policy in Vietnam, Sinclair replied: "Absolutely! I think the Chinese Communists want to take all Asia," and that the United States should prevent it. Sinclair was right in the mainstream of American politics—a supporter of both the Great Society and the Vietnam War.[3]

Johnson knew this, and he invited Sinclair to the White House to celebrate a bill that strengthened the federal government's role in meat inspection. Sinclair appeared in a wheelchair and shook the president's hand. There he met a young man who was doing a great deal to protect consumers' rights. His name was Ralph Nader, and he believed his life's cause had been prefigured in much of what Sinclair had done as a muckraker. Nader leaned down toward Sinclair sitting in his wheelchair and said, "We're continuing your work, Mr. Sinclair." Sinclair responded, "I see that you are. Keep watching them." For Sinclair, the whole event was deeply meaningful. He had been in the White House sixty years before to hear Roosevelt pound the table and promise to rein in corporate malfeasance. And now he was returning to a White House that was building on the reforms of the past to enact the Great Society and prevent the spread of Communism throughout the world. Less than a year after his visit to the White House, Sinclair passed away. His years of retirement had culminated in that visit to the White House. They were, for the most part, good ones, as he watched his radicalism melt into the country's mainstream. He seemed ready to go to his eternal rest, assured of victory.[4]

Late Retirement

It's easy to see an era passing when JFK assumed the presidency in 1960. The decade of the 1950s, both literally and symbolically, ended. An era had also passed in Sinclair's life. Toward the end of Eisenhower's presidency, Craig's health plummeted even further than it already had as a result of her heart attack in 1954. For a moment, a new diet worked. It consisted of "rice, fruit, celery, and pineapple juice, plus a little dried milk powder and vitamins." Upton also adopted it, since it cured his headaches while helping Craig's heart troubles. Nonetheless, Craig pushed herself to write her autobiography and pushed herself too hard. By the late 1950s, she suffered from "light strokes." Sinclair would find her lying facedown on the floor and have to haul her off to the hospital. She became "delirious" and difficult to care for. One doctor suggested that whiskey might help her heart problems. Sinclair, putting aside his lifelong status as a teetotaler, bought his wife booze. "Craig insisted that I should never buy it in Monrovia where I was known; I must drive out on one of the boulevards and stop in some strange place and pay for a bottle with some imbecile name that I forgot." The booze didn't help. Craig was going insane, and Sinclair wanted to put her out of her misery but instead had to wait through a long and tortuous decline. On April 26, 1961, Craig passed away.[5]

Sinclair was now left alone in an old house where he rattled around. It dawned on him just how much Craig had filled a void in his life. They had begun their lives together in search of the right diet and then marched side by side to protest Rockefeller's brutality at Ludlow. She had read so many of his writings over the years and had been a good check on his impulsive desire to throw himself into action. She had raised money and bought them nice houses, like the one he occupied now. Sinclair thought that he could return to the solitude of his early adult years when he lived on islands and wrote romantic poetry and novels. But he couldn't. The alone- ness was particularly harsh because he had led a shut-in life with Craig, so that now "I literally do not know one human being in the town where I live." Craig had warned Upton that he needed a wife to take care of him. But she also warned he must not take up with a "floozie."[6]

Friends introduced him around to women, and not long after Craig's death, Sinclair married Mary Elizabeth Willis, on October 14, 1961. The bride was seventy-nine years old, a southern belle herself (raised in South Carolina) and a retired schoolteacher whose brother happened to be pres- ident of Scripps College. It was clearly a marriage of convenience, though the two got along nicely. One thing for sure, Mary was spry. This allowed Sinclair to travel again, something he hadn't done for some time. It became the sort of travel that symbolized his retirement from politics and writing. He went east in 1962 with Mary to receive a Page One Award from the New York Newspaper Guild and a Social Justice Award from the United Auto Workers (UAW). Then in 1963, he went to the Lilly Library, now the repository of his papers, and spoke to four thousand people, while doing interviews with librarians and archivists. He went from Blooming- ton, Indiana, to Milwaukee, Chicago, and New York City. He spoke at his alma maters, City College of New York and Columbia, and he even did television interviews with Mike Wallace and other newsmen. From there it was on to Toronto, where he went on television to be asked questions by people to see if they could guess who he was (they couldn't). He was now a figure that some might not recognize, but that many believed should have been recognized.[7]

All of these activities pointed to the fact that Sinclair was moving into retirement. So too did his decision to edit a book of letters sent to him from famous people. As well, he decided to write what had been requested of him for some time now—a complete autobiography. Sinclair gave up on writing anything entirely original after *Affectionately Eve* came out in 1961, and many of the projects that had never found a publisher were slipped into file folders and sent off to the Lilly Library. Sinclair felt no need to do what he did in the past: press and press for the publication of things that were best left to collect dust. He did try to get his older books reissued, and he even set up a foundation to continue this project after his death. All of this portended that he was now finally leaving public life, as did the kind words offered by onetime enemies of Sinclair. Ed Ainsworth, who had worked for the *Los Angeles Times* and attacked Sinclair during the governor's race, befriended his new neighbor in Monrovia and wrote nice things about Sinclair in retirement. Sinclair was now no longer an angry rebel but rather a nice old man who deserved respect.[8]

When Sinclair saw his face on television screens after his interviews in New York City in 1963, he must have known something had changed. The media that once aggravated him so greatly and led him to write the screed *The Brass Check* was now treating him like an aged man of wisdom. He had already been surprised by a "notice" he saw in *TV Guide*, which announced a "new adventure series, Lanny Budd, Presidential Agent, based on the Upton Sinclair novels" that went into "production here in October for ABC syndication." The show never aired, but his novel *The Gnomobile* did make it onto screens in America's movie theaters. In 1965 Sinclair had been invited to the studios of Walt Disney to see the set for the movie made from his book, and he marveled at the big furniture built to make adults look small. In 1967 Walt Disney released the film. It veered from the novel by renaming the gnomes and, in typical fashion, replacing the sadder ending in Sinclair's novel with an upbeat one. It even introduced songs, the characters singing along happily, "In the Gnomemobile, the Gnomemobile, we're hunting for Gnomes in the Gnomemobile." This was typical for Disney films of the period. What was really remarkable was that Walt Disney, known for trying to squash labor-union organizing among his cartoonists back in the early 1940s, now placed Upton Sinclair's name in its credit lines. Things had changed since Hollywood had attacked Sinclair thirty years ago as a dangerous radical. He was now a kind old man who wrote children's stories with safe environmental messages, no more dangerous than Dr. Seuss.[9]

Sinclair also exulted in the changed reception he met when speaking on college campuses during the 1960s. He could recall being shut out of the

University of Wisconsin and the University of Chicago when he had gone there to speak and research *The Goose-Step*. When he spoke at the University of Buffalo in 1967, he watched as students in "tight-fitting blue denim pants and long hair" filed in. He was taken aback at receiving a standing ovation. He explained that colleges "keep inviting me to come and give lectures" and that the "students always rise and applaud." If these students knew his feelings about Vietnam, they might have hesitated before applauding. But to them, if the question of Vietnam wasn't broached, Sinclair appeared a hero, someone who had stood up to wrongs in the past and had righted them.[10]

Sinclair gave up on writing by 1964. By then, he was in awe of books written by others. He particularly enjoyed the work of Vance Packard, a best-selling author of books that exposed the advertising industry's use of subliminal psychology and derided the waste built into America's consumer society. Sinclair believed he could see the outlines of a revival of muckraking in the work of Packard and others (including Ralph Nader). The year he was awarded the Page One and Social Justice awards, a book of muckraking had taken the country by storm. It was entitled *The Other America*, and it showed in cold detail how poverty—the sort that Sinclair had dissected sixty years earlier in *The Jungle*—still existed in the United States. The book tore aside the curtain of prosperity that had settled on America's postwar economy and pointed to the society's darker side. This was certainly a work in a tradition established by Sinclair.[11]

Sinclair was aware of *The Other America*'s author, Michael Harrington. Harry Laidler, who was still organizing for the League for Industrial Democracy (LID), wrote to Sinclair in 1964, telling him that Harrington was coming to Los Angeles to drum up support for LID. Laidler hoped his old friend Sinclair would help this young socialist find contacts in the city. What Sinclair might not have known at this time was that Harrington had helped oversee the writing of the Port Huron Statement in 1962 by a scruffy bunch of college students organizing within Students for a Democratic Society (SDS). Harrington grew concerned that the statement was not sufficiently anti-Communist, a point that Sinclair would no doubt have supported him on. Nonetheless, Sinclair's excitement about his improved reception on college campuses and the rejuvenation of LID had something to do with the energy and activism that came to constitute the "New Left." A long-term historical perspective suggests that Sinclair had something to do with this renewal of left-wing activism, even if his sustained support of Vietnam suggested he was slightly out of touch with the students hearing him speak at the time.[12]

The speech he gave at the University of Buffalo would be his last. In 1967, he moved east with Mary to be closer to family, taking up residency in Rockville, Maryland. Mary's married daughter came by regularly to their apartment to make sure the old couple was eating properly. By the end of the year, Mary passed away, so Sinclair was left alone again. His son, David, was now on good terms with him and looked after him. But this couldn't prevent his health from deteriorating. He suffered a "major intestinal operation and a severe hip injury" in 1968. That year, he moved to New Jersey to be closer to David, and on September 21, 1968, he celebrated his ninetieth birthday at a Bound Brook nursing home. Just two months later, on November 26, 1968, he passed away.[13]

Postscript

That Sinclair struggled with illness and eventually passed away in 1968 seems symbolic, at least when we step back and get a wider perspective on U.S. history. That year witnessed protests mounting against the Vietnam War; the language of "peace and love" proliferated throughout the New Left's rhetoric, and it seemed as if hope might triumph. At the same time, a whirlwind of violence hit—not just in Vietnam but in the assassinations of Martin Luther King Jr. and Robert Kennedy, riots in the streets of Chicago at the Democratic Party convention, and mayhem in the ghettoes. The American right started to ride a "backlash" against this violence, calling for a return to "law and order," and smelling political victory. Before Sinclair passed away, Richard Nixon had won the presidency. Nixon was from California like Sinclair, and it was clear that the state that had produced EPIC, the Townsend plan, Ham and Eggs, and the Utopian Society during the 1930s could also produce right-wing reactionaries during the 1960s. In Orange County, not far from where Sinclair lived before moving east in 1967, networks of right-wing activists gelled, drawing energy from Barry Goldwater's run for president in 1964 and pushing onward to attack the welfare state, labor unions, and civil rights legislation. Though Nixon was more moderate than Goldwater, his rhetoric in favor of a "silent majority" struggling to be heard amidst riots and college protests took a page from Goldwater's earlier campaign and provided a glimpse of the right's winning advantage over the left. The right promised to restore the social order lost during the late 1960s. Consider as well that Ronald Reagan had become governor of California in 1966 and had thrown his hat into the ring to become the Republican Party candidate for president in 1968, which he would have to wait another twelve years to achieve. Both Reagan and Nixon had a strong read on the future of U.S. politics. In terms of the American century, 1968 would become not a year to honor Sinclair's death, but a year when Reagan's and Nixon's legacy began its long march.

Sinclair hated Nixon. In 1946 he had watched Nixon smear Jerry Voorhis, a congressman who had won office after working with EPIC, as a Communist. In considering Nixon's 1968 victory, Sinclair might have gone to his death a pessimist. But Sinclair also had reason for hope, if he could hang on to the faces of those University of Buffalo students and Ralph Nader. After all, the New Left was injecting idealism back into politics, talking of "participatory democracy" as well as racial and economic equality. But there was another side of the young student left that exhibited itself in August 1968 at the Chicago Democratic Party convention (just four months before Sinclair died). Then a Festival of Life was held to protest the Democratic Party's support for the Vietnam War. Sinclair would disagree with the substance of this cause (he supported the Vietnam War), but he had helped develop the tactics used in Chicago. Sinclair had been a master of left-wing political theater, marching with black armbands outside of Rockefeller's offices in Manhattan, then invading Rockefeller's church more than fifty years before the Chicago convention. In the wake of Sacco and Vanzetti's death sentence, Sinclair suggested that activists pose as judges and hold a mock trial to prosecute Boston's justice system; a gavel would go down at the end and offer a resounding verdict of guilty.

Sinclair would have understood why the Youth International Party (Yippies) had secured a stage in Chicago and planned to endorse their own candidate for president—a pig from a local farm that symbolized the dirtiness of political power. Theater as political protest—this Sinclair knew well. But could he have guessed that the protest in Chicago 1968 would turn so violent, with police clubbing young people in the streets? Could he imagine that when young people chanted "The Whole World Is Watching," while being beaten up in the streets of Chicago, many Americans would side with the police over the voices supposedly representing justice? Could he imagine what many political observers called the "backlash"? The Yippies helped play out the contradictions that had marked Sinclair's life—the contradiction between idealism and realism, between knowing what should be said and knowing how to say it, between the need to get a point across in a high-profile manner and the need to respect one's opposition. Sinclair struggled with this during his life and left that struggle for others to take up when he passed away.

Consider also Ralph Nader. He had drawn direct inspiration from Sinclair's life. One of his articles exposing the meat industry's abuses in 1967, the year he met Sinclair at the White House, was entitled "We're Still in the Jungle." A few years earlier, Nader had exposed the automobile industry for building dangerous cars, an industry Sinclair had targeted in the 1930s for labor abuses. Nader focused less on how corporations exploited workers and more on how they exploited consumers. He assembled idealistic lawyers and armies of researchers to expose corporate malfeasance while devising ways to hold Congress accountable, pressuring members to regulate corporations in the name of the public good. Nader had tactical genius; he didn't wear blue denim and long hair but rather suits and cropped hair. But there was a purist element lurking behind that appearance, and it came out thirty years after Nader met Sinclair at the White House. In 1996 Ralph Nader ran for president of the United States, knowing full well that he could never win and becoming, in the process, a "spoiler" who drew left-wing votes from the Democrats. Nader ran again in 2000 and 2004, each time his candidacy drawing more criticisms from those who should have been on his side. Sinclair might have chuckled at hearing talk about "vote swapping" in 1996 and 2000, but he probably rolled in his grave knowing that Nader ran in 2000 alongside a battle between Al Gore and George W. Bush. As Sinclair wrote in opposition to those considering a third party over FDR in 1936, "It is better to get a half loaf than nothing at all, and Roosevelt is much to be preferred over Hoover." By 2000, Nader mocked "half loaf" talk, and his career, from hard-nosed realist to cavalier purist, tells us something about the left that lived past Sinclair's death. It was fiercely committed to ideals, but often lacking in political judgment. It went for Sinclair's purism more than for the realism that marked his later life.[14]

As I have told it here, Sinclair's life can be understood as a set of contradictions but also as a story of increasing political maturity, moving from idealism toward realism. Go back to his childhood, and look at the picture of the child with the pursed lips and cocky idealism. Consider Sinclair's phase as Arthur Stirling, the artist recoiling emotionally from the business side of book publishing, his epic poem unable to find a publisher turning him angry and vengeful. Look at Sinclair breaking big with the publication of *The Jungle*, all the while dreaming of a little utopia far away from the world, in the small confines of Helicon Hall. Then Sinclair tempering his purist political judgments with an injection of reality—learning from World War I that he must stick to his principles but also admit when he is wrong. Sinclair realized that a lone intellectual publishing a small magazine had little influence over the course of events—the censorship, the jailings, the betrayal of the Fourteen Points. Sinclair would creep into political exile and self-imposed marginality during the 1920s and then creep back out of it toward the end of the decade by writing a historical novel about Sacco and Vanzetti and, in the process, learn how political ideology clouded people's judgment. The Communists wanted Sacco and Vanzetti to be guiltless martyrs; Sinclair wanted justice but, at the same time, to remain loyal to the truth.

Then there was EPIC—perhaps Sinclair's proudest political moment, when he learned to speak in terms that Americans could understand while also learning the limits of political idealism in a particularly harsh way. After EPIC, he watched as the United States rose to become a world power during World War II and the cold war, when military power was being used, very often, for good. But he also faced the destructive force of the atomic bomb and worried that technology might have raced ahead of humans' capacity for moral judgment. One thing for sure, he stopped making prophecies about the future, knowing the world was too imperfect to be predictable in any meaningful way. But he never left behind his idealism, his hope for a better world. Sometimes his obstinate nature was healthy. He would be given his just rewards for idealism in the Page One Award from the Newspaper Guild and the Social Justice Award from the UAW. His work was recognized for its inspirational power every time a group of young college idealists stood up and applauded his speeches.

Achieving recognition was another theme in Sinclair's life, and the most obvious route to recognition was publicity. The search for it started when Sinclair learned that it didn't matter how good a story was as long as it had good publicity. He made mental notes that stuck in his cranium when his publisher printed false notices about a young poet's death in New York's newspapers, right before *The Journal of Arthur Stirling* hit the shelves. Learning his lesson, Sinclair started his own publicity office after *The Jungle* came out. He wanted to control the explosion of publicity—to ensure that his point about what needed to be done about the problems he exposed could be heard above the din of controversy. This was a noble and necessary action. But he also witnessed the downside of becoming a celebrity. His painful divorce from Meta Fuller was made all the more painful by being broadcast in the newspapers. He fell victim to the new world of imagery and spin that constituted the bedrock of celebrity culture. Hollywood newsreels that looked very real but were entirely staged killed Sinclair in his run for governor in 1934, as did the billboards with his own words emblazoned on them. After the fateful year of 1934, Sinclair receded from publicity, living a shut-in life with his wife, who was all too happy to lock out the world. But then, after Mary Craig's death, came a brief flurry again in the 1960s, when Sinclair appeared on national television shows, albeit a bit more relaxed. When he was interviewed for "Personal Close-Up" in 1963, in his mid-eighties, Mike Wallace asked him about his sex life. Sinclair laughed and suggested that he and Mary were having a good time. Some might think this simply embarrassing or just cute, but it was also a sign of how celebrity had its own pressures, how it could marvel at gossip while forgetting the public accomplishments of a figure, how it whittled things down to the most personal detail. Throughout his life, Sinclair used his status as a celebrity to make his arguments, but it also used him.[15]

His celebrity status propelled Sinclair into the public eye. His life became a chronicle of history as he traveled through the American century. For contemporary readers, Sinclair was like Forrest Gump; or to be fairer, he was like Lanny Budd (though no one could achieve the heights of that socialist playboy). But Sinclair was first and foremost a writer, and he should be evaluated on those terms. On this count, his legacy is clear. *The Jungle* is still read by many Americans, long after its publication one hundred years ago. When found in college classrooms, it is often taught in a tradition of "protest literature," placed alongside *Uncle Tom's Cabin* and *Looking Backward*, two books that Sinclair admitted made an enormous impact on his life. Sinclair always thought of literature as a means to correct and condemn injustices. During his lifetime, he promoted novels that had something to say about what was wrong with American society, including Sinclair Lewis's *Babbitt*, Theodore Dreiser's *An American Tragedy*, and John Steinbeck's *The Grapes of Wrath*. If being read long after publication is any measure of a novel's standing in the eyes of history, as it was for the novels that Sinclair championed, then *The Jungle* is a great accomplishment.[16]

But the question remains, what is the right way to remember *The Jungle* (and, to a lesser extent, the other novels Sinclair wrote throughout his life)? Should we read *The Jungle* as literature, that is, give copies of the book to young writers who want to learn something about crafting a good story and mastering techniques of dialogue and language? Certainly not. *The Jungle*, written when Sinclair was suffering from poverty and a domestic life that bordered on hell, was overwrought and even outlandish at times. It piled on too many details and went for the emotional jugular in order to make its point. Its optimistic ending seemed out of place in light of the bleak narrative that preceded it. It is rightfully remembered today less as literature and more as protest and an historical event. What made the book succeed was that Sinclair took what I have called the other American century and made it speak to the American century. The novel took stories that were typically hidden from the eyes of American middle-class readers and made them cry out. Bubbly Creek, kids drowning in unpaved streets, prostitution, a lack of sanitary conditions, brutal and exhausting working conditions, the working class's lack of power—these social observations are the things that we remember the novel by, not its mastery of literary technique. We remember how it created the regulatory legislation that Theodore Roosevelt pioneered, not its story line or narrative structure.

Still, this is a remarkable legacy. Sinclair made the other American century speak as loudly as it could. All of his literary works tried to do this, some with more success than others. *King Coal* showed how a young idealist could come into a mining town, draw inspiration from its families, and then organize to resist the exploitation of company owners. *Oil!* exposed the greed embedded in the American industrial system, which needed energy more than it needed good working conditions for those doing the extracting of its energy. *Boston* laid out, in stark terms, the prejudices of New England's aristocracy against the immigrant labor force it exploited, and then recoiled at, when figures like Sacco and Vanzetti adopted radical ideologies, in part, out of frustration. The Lanny Budd series continued this tradition by showing Americans naively believing that they could ignore the problems of Europe without ever facing the wrath of Hitler.

Then there was Sinclair's political activism: organizing for civil liberties, after the U.S. government had made a mockery of the cause during World War I, and then conceptualizing and running EPIC as a way to combat the Great Depression. His political loss in 1934 didn't stop him from making the faces of poverty speak to Americans throughout the

Great Depression, as he embarked on numerous struggles for a Popular Front against recalcitrant business owners like Henry Ford and the managers of "Little Steel." Along with his good works, Sinclair also made some mistakes. He could suggest that the Soviet Union was leading the cause of social justice in the world during the 1930s. He could write bad novels because he put politics before aesthetic concerns. He could sound like a Puritan and turn people off who might otherwise support his cause.

Eventually it would all catch up to him. During the cold war, Sinclair found himself, shocking as it seemed, floating in the mainstream. In part due to Sinclair's efforts, the other American century knocked on the door of the American century and was let in. Labor unions were no longer smashed, the way they had been when tents were burned at Ludlow or when Packingtown workers were crushed in 1904. Government no longer looked the other way for the sake of business, the way it did prior to the Meat Inspection Act of 1906. Instead, it started to consider the views of labor and consumer groups who were demanding social justice. The United States no longer ran roughshod over the world—the way it did over Cuba during the Spanish-American War (a war Sinclair romanticized in his youthful stories)—but tried to listen to the demands of "undeveloped" societies in order to craft an alternative to the Communist vision of the Soviet Union. Sinclair said yes to all of these developments, and yes to the general idea that the other American century should inform the American century.

By banging on the door of the American century, Sinclair offered hope that a life of ideas could inform political reality. He showed how intellectuals could speak truth to power and, sometimes, even be heard. His life also makes clear how difficult this could be, how it's not as simple as having your say in the public square. When Floyd Dell suggested that Sinclair belonged to the "Voltairean tradition of the literary man as a fighter against wrong," he was precise in his description. But what he couldn't recognize was how the world would change and make this tradition so difficult. It's no longer so easy to get your voice heard; it involves great compromise in an age of spin and celebrity—an age that traces its origins, in some ways, back to Sinclair's run for governor of California in 1934, with its newsreels and outright lies parading as truths, and maybe even as far back as the mythmaking of Arthur Stirling. Against the odds, Sinclair used his celebrity status to allow the uglier side of American history remind us of America's promise, both to itself and to the world.

NOTES

Since I have cited every source that was quoted or closely referenced, I have not included a bibliography here. I should also note that I drew largely on the Upton Sinclair Manuscript Collection held at the Lilly Library in Bloomington, Indiana. It is a superb collection, even though all of Sinclair's papers prior to 1907 burned in the Helicon Hall fire. I also used the Intercollegiate Socialist Society (ISS) Papers at the Tamiment Library in New York City. Besides those two sources, I have relied mostly on the writings of Sinclair and secondary works of U.S. history. For anyone wanting to read more of Sinclair's work, the best source still remains Ronald Gottesman's *Upton Sinclair: An Annotated Checklist* (Kent, Ohio: Kent State University Press, 1973). Without that work, I do not know how I could have begun this project.

INTRODUCTION. THE PROBLEM OF BEING UPPIE

The epigraph to this chapter is drawn from Sinclair to Alfred Baker Lewis of the Rand School of Social Science, February 24, 1926, Sinclair Mss., Series I, Box 6.

1. Upton Sinclair, *The Industrial Republic* (New York: Doubleday, 1907), xiv.
2. Walt Whitman, *Complete Poetry and Selected Prose*, ed. James Miller (Boston: Houghton Mifflin, 1959), 68, 479. Sinclair would cite Whitman as a proto-socialist in his tract on socialism and literature, *Our Bourgeois Literature* (Chicago: Charles H. Kerr, 1904), 23.
3. *Time*, quoted in Leon Harris, *Upton Sinclair: American Rebel* (New York: Crowell, 1975), 313.

4. I should also note my debt to a marvelous biography of one of Sinclair's friends and enemies, Walter Lippmann. See Ronald Steel, *Walter Lippmann and the American Century* (Boston: Little Brown, 1980).

5. Sinclair, "Organizing the Sinclair Letters," *New Republic*, May 2, 1960, 24.

6. Floyd Dell, *Upton Sinclair: A Study in Social Protest* (New York: George H. Doran, 1927), 12.

7. Olivier Todd, *Malraux: A Life* (New York: Knopf, 2005), 323.

8. Todd, *Malraux*; for the recent debates surrounding Orwell, see Christopher Hitchens, *Why Orwell Matters* (New York: Basic Books, 2002); David Cesarani, *Arthur Koestler: The Homeless Mind* (London: Heinemann, 1998).

9. Sinclair to Betty Sinclair, August 25, 1941, Sinclair Mss., Series I, Box 47; Sinclair quoted in "The Story of Upton Sinclair: Upton Sinclair Explains . . . ," *Los Angeles Record*, September 19, 1929, 1; *Boston* (New York: Albert and Charles Boni, 1928), vol. 1, vii.

10. James Agee and Walker Evans, *Let Us Now Praise Famous Men* (1939; reprint, New York: Ballantine Books, 1960), 11.

CHAPTER ONE. "A VERY DEVOUT AND EARNEST LITTLE BOY": 1878–1892

The chapter title comes from an interview with Ronald Gottesman, Sinclair Manuscripts, Series III, Box 36.

The epigraphs to this chapter are drawn from, respectively, Henry Adams, *The Education of Henry Adams* (New York: Time Incorporated, 1964), vol. 1, 3; and "Laski on Sinclair," *The Living Age*, November 1934, 276.

1. Sinclair to A. Friedman, March 23, 1953, Sinclair Mss., Series I, Box 57.

2. Walter Lippmann, "Upton Sinclair," *Saturday Review of Literature*, March 3, 1928, 642; Upton Sinclair, "At Odds," *Saturday Review of Literature*, April 7, 1928, 744.

3. Matthew Josephson, *The Robber Barons* (New York: Harvest, 1962), 73.

4. Alan Trachtenberg, *The Incorporation of America: Culture and Society in the Gilded Age* (New York: Hill and Wang, 1982), 89.

5. "Populist Party Platform" (1892), in *Great Issues in American History*, ed. Richard Hofstadter (New York: Vintage, 1969), 148.

6. Upton Sinclair, "Every Man His Own Reviewer," *The Independent*, November 17, 1904, 1150.

7. Upton Sinclair, "What Life Means to Me," *Cosmopolitan*, October 1906, 591; Sinclair, *The Autobiography of Upton Sinclair* (New York: Harcourt, Brace and World, 1962), 4; Upton Sinclair, *Telling the World* (London: T. Werner Laurie, 1939), 193. See also Edward L. Ayers, *The Promise of the New South: Life after Reconstruction* (New York: Oxford University Press, 1992), 13.

8. Upton Sinclair in *Haldeman-Julius Weekly*, February 24, 1923, 3. See, for instance, Upton Sinclair, "In the Net of Visconti," serialized in *The Argosy* in 1899, and "In the Days of Decatur," *The Argosy*, January 1901, 185.

9. See Floyd Dell, *Upton Sinclair: A Study in Social Protest* (New York: George H. Doran, 1927), 23; Upton Sinclair, *The Cup of Fury* (Manhasset, N.Y.: Channel Press, 1956), 27.

10. Sinclair quoted in Leon Harris, *Upton Sinclair: American Rebel* (New York: Crowell, 1975), 8; Upton Sinclair to W. Wootton, September 23, 1946, Sinclair Mss., Series I, Box 52.

11. Casey Blake, *Beloved Community: The Cultural Criticism of Randolph Bourne, Van Wyck Brooks, Waldo Frank and Lewis Mumford* (Chapel Hill: University of North Carolina Press, 1990), 25.

12. Upton Sinclair in an interview found in Sinclair Mss., Series III, Box 36, no date given but probably late 1920s; Upton Sinclair recounted childhood illness in "Raw Food Table," *Physical Culture*, January/February 1910, 33; *The Story of the Bible* recounted in Upton Sinclair to Robert Oliver, June 23, 1932, Sinclair Mss., Series I, Box 19.

13. "Sinclair was 'Regular Boy,'" *End Poverty*, April 1934, 7.

14. Statement by Sinclair (untitled), found in Sinclair Mss., IV, Box 1; Sinclair to Lelia, June 15, 1939, Sinclair Mss., Series I, Box 44; Sinclair, *The Autobiography*, 10, 11.

15. Sinclair, *Telling the World* (1939), 193, 190; On ten-cent museum, Sinclair to Howard Bland, March 23, 1923, Sinclair Mss., Series I, Box 5.

16. Fred Hobson, *Mencken: A Life* (New York: Random House, 1994), 47.

17. Upton Sinclair, *What's the Use of Books* (New York: Vanguard Press, 1926), 10.

18. Sinclair, "Raw Food Table," 35; also Sinclair, *Telling the World*, 192.

19. William Dean Howells, *A Hazard of New Fortunes* (1889; New York: Signet, 1965), 54; Upton Sinclair, *The Toy and the Man* (Westwood, Mass.: Ariel Press, 1904), 12; Henry James, *The American Scene* (1907; Bloomington: Indiana University Press, 1968), 111. The snow story comes from an interview Richard Gottesman did with Sinclair in January 1963, transcribed and in Sinclair Mss., Series III, Box 36.

20. Sinclair, *The Autobiography*, 16.

21. This paragraph draws upon Edwin Burrows and Mike Wallace, *Gotham: A History of New York City to 1898* (New York: Oxford University Press, 1999); the Metropolitan Museum is also discussed in Russell Lynes, *The Lively Audience: A Social History of American Visual and Performing Arts, 1890–1950* (New York: Harper & Row, 1985), 317; Michael McGerr, *A Fierce Discontent: The Rise and Fall of the Progressive Movement in America, 1870–1920* (New York: Free Press, 2003), 13.

22. Kit and Frederica Konolige, *The Power of Their Glory: America's Ruling Class, the Episcopalians* (New York: Wyden Books, 1978), 8.

23. Sinclair to Haldeman-Julius, April 24, 1923, Sinclair Mss., Series I, Box 5; *The Autobiography*, 21. See also Ronald Gottesman interview, cited above.

24. Sinclair to Floyd Dell, June 7, 1926, Sinclair Mss., Series I, Box 7; Sinclair, *The Autobiography*, 16–19.

25. Sinclair, *The Autobiography*, 55.

26. Paul Schneider, *The Adirondacks: A History of America's First Wilderness* (New York: Henry Holt, 1997), 259; Upton Sinclair, *The Book of Life* (Girard, Kans.: Haldeman-Julius, 1921), vol. 1, 160; See Sinclair, "What Life Means to Me," 1906, 592, about Central Park.

27. Adams, *The Education of Henry Adams*, vol. 1, 35.

28. Sinclair to Frank Harris, May 28, 1917, Sinclair Mss., Series II.

29. "Jokes His Job, Bicycle Trips the Hobby of Young Sinclair," *End Poverty*, May 1934, 3; on Sunday school experience, see Upton Sinclair, *What God Means to Me: An Attempt at a Working Religion* (Pasadena, Calif.: privately published, 1935), 1; joke found in scrapbook of Sinclair's mother, accessible in the Lilly Library's book collection of Upton Sinclair's writings.

CHAPTER TWO. "WOULD-BE SINGER AND PENNILESS RAT": 1892–1904

The first epigraph to this chapter is drawn from *The Education of Henry Adams* (1918; reprint, New York: Time Incorporated, 1964), vol. 1, 91.

1. Joke found in Scrapbook in Lilly Library Collection.

2. "When I Was a Teener," in Sinclair Mss., Series III, Box 36; see also S. Willis Rudy, *The College of the City of New York: A History, 1847–1947* (New York: Arno Press, 1977), 171.

3. Sinclair in *Haldeman-Julius Weekly*, February 24, 1923, 4; Sinclair, "Confessions of a Non-Conformist," 1950, 4; Sinclair in *Haldeman-Julius Weekly*, February 24, 1923, 4; "Should Our Son Go to City College," *The City College Alumnus*, February 1953, 15.

4. Sinclair in *Haldeman-Julius Weekly*, March 3, 1923; February 24, 1924; for Columbia's history I rely upon Thomas Bender, *New York Intellect: A History of Intellectual Life in New York City, From 1750 to the Beginnings of Our Own Time* (New York: Knopf, 1987), 284.

5. Jane Addams, *Twenty Years at Hull-House* (New York: New American Library, 1961), 63; Frederic Howe, *Confessions of a Reformer* (New York: C. Scribner's Sons, 1925), 8.

6. Floyd Dell, *Upton Sinclair: A Study in Social Protest* (New York: George H. Doran, 1927), 41; Christopher P. Wilson, *The Labor of Words: Literary Professionalism in the Progressive Era* (Athens: University of Georgia Press, 1985), 18.

7. "Smash the Stranglehold of Finance!" *Common Sense*, March 1933, 14.

8. "Battle with Misfortune," *The Argosy*, January 1900, 448.

9. Sinclair, *The Autobiography of Upton Sinclair* (New York: Harcourt, Brace and World, 1962), 36; "Confessions of a Young Author," *The Independent*, November 20, 1902, 2749; James Quentin Reynolds, *The Fiction Factory, or, From Pulp Row to Quality Street: The Story of 100 Years of Publishing at Smith & Street* (New York: Random House, 1955), 29, 72; the Street and Smith description of its stories comes from the back page of Ensign Clarke Fitch (Upton Sinclair's pen name), *The Naval Cadet* (New York: Street and Smith, 1903), no page number.

10. *The Naval Cadet*, 36.

11. Stephen Crane, *The Red Badge of Courage and Four Great Stories* (New York: Dell, 1960), 29; William Cotkin, *William James, Public Philosopher* (Baltimore: Johns Hopkins University Press, 1990), 136; on Stephen Crane, I rely upon Linda Davis, *Badge of Courage* (Boston: Houghton Mifflin, 1998).

12. "Clif Faraday on the New York or a Naval Cadet Under Fire," *True Blue*, vol. 1: May 14, 1898, 14; "Smash the Stranglehold of Finance!" 14; Douglas Churchill, "Upton Sinclair, 60, Looks Back on His Crusades," the *New York Times Magazine*, September 18, 1938, 22; "Confessions of a Young Author," 2751.

13. Sinclair, *Autobiography*, 68–69.

14. Upton Sinclair, "The Battle with Misfortune," 441; *Upton Sinclair: Biographical and Critical Opinions* (Pasadena, Calif.: privately printed, 1923), 24; Upton Sinclair to Stedman, April 12, 1899, Sinclair Mss., II, Box 1; "Love's Progress," in Sinclair Mss., IV, Box 1, 18.

15. "Sinclair's Youthful Poetry Fails to Fill Family Larder," *End Poverty*, May 1934, 3; "Review of Reviews," *The Independent*, February 6, 1902, 328; *Springtime and Harvest: A Romance* (New York: The Sinclair Press, 1901), v.

16. Sinclair, *Autobiography*, 42; Meta Fuller, "Thyrsis and Corydon," III, found in Meta Fuller Stone Mss., 5; Sinclair quoted in Leon Harris, *Upton Sinclair: American Rebel* (New York: Crowell, 1975), 41.

17. Fuller, "Thyrsis and Corydon," III, 30.

18. Upton Sinclair, *King Midas* (New York: Funk and Wagnalls, 1901), 15.

19. Sinclair, *Springtime and Harvest*, vii; "Review of Reviews," 329; "Confessions of a Young Author," 2750.

20. Sinclair, "What Life Means to Me," *Cosmopolitan*, October 1906, 592; *Autobiography*, 80.

21. Upton Sinclair, *Prince Hagen* (Boston: L. C. Page and Co., 1903), 176.

22. "Confessions of a Young Author," 2750; "My Cause," *The Independent*, May 14, 1903, 1125; *The Journal of Arthur Stirling* (London: William Heinemann, 1903), 232; "What Life Means," 592; "Postscript to the Journal of Arthur

Stirling," *The Journal of Arthur Stirling: The Valley of the Shadow* (Pasadena, Calif.: privately printed, 1906), 205.

23. "My Cause," 1903, 1122; "Postscript to the Journal of Arthur Stirling," 205.

24. *The Journal of Arthur Stirling*, 120, 159, 207, 210–212, 328.

25. "My Cause," 1122.

26. "What Life Means to Me," 592; Kemp to Sinclair, May 1907, Sinclair Mss., Series I, Box 1.

27. Nick Salvatore, *Eugene V. Debs* (Urbana: University of Illinois Press, 1982), 152.

28. Michael E. McGerr, *A Fierce Discontent: The Rise and Fall of the Progressive Movement in America* (New York: Free Press, 2003), 64–65. Sinclair, "The Cost of Competition," *The International Socialist Review*, October 2, 1906, 199, on the native sources for socialism in America. See Daniel Borus's Introduction to Edward Bellamy, *Looking Backward* (Boston: Bedford Books, 1995).

29. Christopher Lasch, *The Agony of the American Left* (New York: Knopf, 1969), 36; David Shannon, *The Socialist Party of America* (New York: Macmillan, 1955), 16; James Weinstein, *The Decline of Socialism in America, 1912–1925* (New York: Vintage, 1969); on compensation versus confiscation, see Upton Sinclair, "Socialism's Triumph in 1913," *Saturday Evening Post*, May 8, 1909, 8.

30. "You Have Lost the Strike! And Now What Are You Going to Do About It?" *Appeal to Reason*, September 17, 1904, 1.

31. Quoted in Howard Quint, "Upton Sinclair's Quest for Artistic Independence—1909," *American Literature* 29 (1957): 195.

32. "Manassas," *Times Literary Supplement*, April 20, 1933, 274.

33. "My Cause," 1122.

34. Sinclair quoted in Harry Laidlaw, "Intercollegiate Socialist Society," in *The Intercollegiate* (1911 scrawled on top of this document found in Intercollegiate Socialist Society Records, Tamiment Library); Upton Sinclair, "The Message of Socialism to Collegians," *The Independent*, August 8, 1910, 355; William English Walling to Upton Sinclair, January 31, 1905, Intercollegiate Socialist Society Records, Tamiment Library, I: Correspondence.

35. Jack London, "Revolution," in *Essays of Revolt* (New York: Vanguard Press, 1926), 112 (though it was never recorded, it's been suggested that this speech was the one that London gave at Carnegie); *Money Writes!* (New York: A. & C. Boni, 1927), 49.

36. Upton Sinclair, "The Interesting Career of Jack London," *The World*, December 1, 1916, 3; Jack London, *Martin Eden* (1908; New York: Modern Library, 2002), 119, 186; Upton Sinclair, "Russia Studies Jack London; Memorial Suggested by Sinclair," *The Daily News*, April 3, 1925, 17.

37. *Autobiography*, p. 248; Upton Sinclair, "'Spirits' in American Literature," *Listen*, October–December 1954, 11; "Jack London," *The New Age*, March 1, 1917, 421; Charmian London to Sinclair, September 20, 1918, Sinclair Mss., Series I, Box 2.

38. Frank Norris, *The Octopus* (1901; reprint: New York: Airmont, 1969), p. 15; Theodore Dreiser, "The Epic Sinclair," *Esquire*, December 1934, 33; Jack London, *Martin Eden*, p. 228. See also Frank Norris, *The Responsibilities of the Novelist, and Other Literary Essays* (New York: Doubleday, Page and Company, 1903), 11–12, and David E. Shi, *Facing Facts: Realism in American Thought and Culture, 1850–1920* (New York: Oxford University Press, 1995).

39. Howells quoted in Alan Trachtenberg, *The Incorporation of America: Culture and Society in the Gilded Age* (New York: Hill and Wang, 1982), 196; Daniel H. Borus, *Writing Realism: Howells, James, and Norris in the Mass Market* (Chapel Hill: University of North Carolina Press, 1989), 36–37.

40. Upton Sinclair, *Our Bourgeois Literature: The Reason and the Remedy* (Chicago: Charles H. Kerr & Company, 1904), 12; "Farmers of America Unite!" *Appeal to Reason*, October 15, 1904, 2; "The Socialist Party: Its Aims in the Present Campaign," *Collier's*, October 29, 1904, 10; Jack London, *Martin Eden*, 386–387.

41. Upton Sinclair, "Postscript to the Journal of Arthur Stirling," 207; "Sinclair's Youthful Poetry Fails to Fill Family Larder," 3.

CHAPTER THREE. SOCIALIST "CELEBRITY": 1905–1914

The epigraphs to this chapter are drawn from, respectively, Upton Sinclair, *The Jungle* (New York: New American Library, 1960), 40; and Upton Sinclair, "What Life Means to Me," *Cosmopolitan*, October 1906, 594–595.

1. Roosevelt's self-characterization quoted in Otis A. Pease, ed., *The Progressive Years: The Spirit and Achievement of American Reform* (New York: G. Braziller, 1962), 318; and John Milton Cooper, *The Warrior and the Priest: Woodrow Wilson and Theodore Roosevelt* (Cambridge, Mass.: Belknap Press, 1983), 318; the conversation with Morgan comes from H. W. Brands, *T. R.: The Last Romantic* (New York: Basic Books, 1997), 437.

2. Roosevelt on muckrakers, quoted in John Chamberlain, *Farewell to Reform: The Rise, Life and Decay of the Progressive Mind in America* (Chicago: Quadrangle Books, 1965), 140. For more on this period, see Michael McGerr, *A Fierce Discontent: The Rise and Fall of the Progressive Movement in America* (New York: Free Press, 2003).

3. Upton Sinclair, "Is the Jungle True?" *The Independent*, May 17, 1906, 1129; "What Life Means to Me," 593.

4. Ray Ginger, *Altgeld's America* (Chicago: Quadrangle Books, 1965), chapter 1.

5. Sinclair, "Is the Jungle True?" 1130; "Introduction to the Viking Press Edition," *The Jungle* (New York: Viking Press, 1946), vii; "The Children of

Packingtown," *Success Magazine*, November 1906, 756, 797; the quote about Bubbly Creek being coated with grease and filth comes from Ernest Poole, "The Meat Strike," *Independent*, July 28, 1904, 179.

6. Glenn Porter, *The Rise of Big Business* (New York: Crowell, 1973), 49; A. M. Simons, *Packingtown* (Chicago: C. H. Kerr, 1899), 3, 23; James Harvey Young, *Pure Food: Securing the Federal Food and Drugs Act of 1906* (Princeton: Princeton University Press, 1989), 130; William Cronon, *Nature's Metropolis: Chicago and the Great West* (New York: W. W. Norton, 1991), 229.

7. Upton Sinclair, "Farmers of America Unite!" *Appeal to Reason*, October 15, 1904, 2; Charles Edward Russell, *The Greatest Trust in the World* (New York: Ridgeway-Thayer Company, 1905), 123.

8. Sinclair, "Introduction to the Jungle," viii; Upton Sinclair to Jim Fuchs, June 7, 1926, Sinclair Mss, Series I, Box 7.

9. Sinclair, "What Life Means to Me," 594; "The Jungle: A Story of Chicago," *Appeal to Reason*, February 11, 1905, 1.

10. Sinclair, *The Jungle*, 4; Sinclair, in Preface written for *The Jungle*, found in Box 63 of the Sinclair Mss, Series III.

11. *The Jungle*, 136; Upton Sinclair, "Is Chicago Meat Clean," *Collier's*, April 22, 1905, 13.

12. Upton Sinclair, "With Mother Bloor in the Jungle," *Time*, September 3, 1951, 8; "The Jungle's Aftermath," *Physical Culture*, April 1910, 355, 356.

13. Upton Sinclair, "The Meat Inspection Situation," *Collier's*, June 16, 1906, 24; "The Jungle's Aftermath II," *Physical Culture*, May 1910, 503.

14. Young, *Pure Food*, 132; Beveridge quoted in James Harvey Young, "Two Hoosiers and Two Food Laws of 1906," *Indiana Magazine of History* 88 (1992): 315. See also James Wharton, "Eating to Win," in *Fitness in American Culture*, ed. Kathryn Grover (Amherst: University of Massachusetts Press, 1989), 87.

15. Sinclair, "The Meat Inspection Situation," 26.

16. Isaac F. Marcosson, *Adventures in Interviewing* (New York: Dodd Mead and Company, 1919), 286; *Book of Life*, vol. 2, 24; "The Jungle Vindicated," *The Bookman*, July 1906, 482.

17. Upton Sinclair, *The Autobiography of Upton Sinclair* (New York: Harcourt, Brace and World, 1962), 92; Sinclair, *The Overman* (New York: Doubleday, Page and Company, 1907); Sinclair, *A Captain of Industry* (Girard, Kans.: Appeal to Reason, 1906).

18. Upton Sinclair, *The Industrial Republic: A Study of the America of Ten Years Hence* (New York: Doubleday, Page and Company, 1907), 190, 200, 206, xiv; "The Warren Defenders," *Appeal to Reason*, June 19, 1909, 1; Sinclair to Louis Filler, June 1, 1938, Sinclair Mss., Series I, Box 41.

19. Upton Sinclair, "A Physical Culture School for Boys," *Physical Culture*, October 1909, 357.

20. Upton Sinclair, "A Home Colony," *The Independent*, June 14, 1906, 1402.

21. Upton Sinclair, "Home Colony: Six Months After," *The Independent*, February 7, 1907, 306; "A Home Colony," 1404; "Upton Sinclair's Colony to Live at Helicon Hall," *New York Times*, October 7, 1906, 2; Jo Davidson, *Between Sittings: An Informal Autobiography* (New York: Dial Press, 1951), 30; "Home Colony: Six Months Later," 307; The Helicon Hall statement that I quote from here is reprinted in *A Catalogue of Books, Manuscripts, and Other Materials from the Upton Sinclair Archives* (Bloomington, Ind.: Lilly Library, 1963), 53.

22. Paul F. Boller, *American Transcendentalism, 1830–1860: An Intellectual Inquiry* (New York: Putnam, 1974), 123.

23. Sinclair, *Autobiography*, 129. For Gilman's plans, see George Cotkin, *Reluctant Modernism: American Thought and Culture, 1880–1900* (New York: Twayne Publishers, 1992), 99, and for Gilman's influence on Sinclair, see his "A Home Colony," 1404.

24. Sinclair, "Home Colony," 1403, 1404.

25. Sinclair, "A Home Colony," 1405; "New Helicon Hall," 580; "Helicon Hall Cold to Visiting Trio," *New York Times*, February 17, 1907, section 5, p. 1; Upton Sinclair, *The Brass Check* (Pasadena, Calif.: privately printed, 1919), 63, 65.

26. Upton Sinclair, *The Metropolis* (New York: Moffat, Yard and Company, 1908), 65, 274.

27. Sinclair, *Autobiography*, 137. For a typical charge that Sinclair failed to understand the wealthy classes, see "A Recent Fairy Story," *The Outlook*, April 25, 1908.

28. Sinclair quoted in Howard Quint, "Upton Sinclair's Quest for Artistic Independence—1909," *American Literature* 29 (1957): 198; Sinclair to Mary and Gay Wilshire, June 20, 1909, Sinclair Mss., Series IV, Box 1. See also "Upton Sinclair Defends Himself," *New York Times Saturday Review of Books*, April 22, 1908, 240.

29. Upton Sinclair, "My Friend George Sterling," *The Bookman*, September 1927, 31, 30.

30. Sinclair to "Dearest," 1909, Sinclair Mss., VI, Box 1.

31. Sinclair to Journal of Medical Association, May 10, 1922, Sinclair Mss., Series I, Box 3; Sinclair, "Ideal Diet," 578; "Experiments with the Exclusive Meat Diet," *Physical Culture*, October 1910, 364, 365.

32. Sinclair, "A Physical Culture School for Boys," 357; "A New Helicon Hall," *The Independent*, September 1909, 581; "Wheat: The King of Foods," *Physical Culture*, September 1910, 237; "Living on Raw Foods," *Collier's*, April 16, 1910, 37.

33. Sinclair to J. H. Kellogg, July 20, 1910, Sinclair Mss., Series I, Box 1.

34. Robert Ernst, *Weakness Is a Crime: The Life of Bernarr Macfadden* (Syracuse,

N.Y.: Syracuse University Press, 1991), 55, 27; "Truth about Fasting," *Physical Culture*, August 1910, 139.

35. Sinclair, *The Fasting Cure* (New York: Mitchell Kennerly, 1911), 110.

36. Upton Sinclair and Michael Williams, *Good Health and How We Won It, With an Account of New Hygiene* (New York: F. A. Stokes Company, 1909), 10; Sinclair, "My Golden Rule of Health," *Physical Culture*, December 1910, 613; "Wheat," 233.

37. Sinclair, "The Raw Food Table," *Physical Culture*, January/February 1910, 36; "Returning to Nature," *Physical Culture*, June 1911, 626–627; "Wheat," 238.

38. "A Physical Culture School for Boys," 1909, 359; "A New Helicon," 583; "Mothers: Old and New," *Physical Culture*, July 1910.

39. Brochure quoted in Mark Taylor, "Utopia By Taxation: Frank Stephens and the Single Tax Community of Arden, Delaware," *Pennsylvania Magazine of History and Biography* 126 (2002): 315. Sinclair complained that no one explained the ideas behind the single-tax communities he joined: "Living in the Single Tax Colony," incomplete manuscript, Sinclair Mss., IV, Box 4.

40. Sinclair, "The Raw Food Table," *Physical Culture*, February 1910, 138; Gottesman interview, Series II, Box 1, 161.

41. Annie Laurie, "Sinclair Sorry He Is Married to Wife," *San Francisco Examiner*, January 30, 1909, 1; Leon Harris, *Upton Sinclair*, 116; *Love's Pilgrimage: A Novel* (New York: Mitchell Kennerly, 1911), 468; Jack London to Sinclair, February 1, 1910, Sinclair Mss., Series I, Box 1.

42. "Mrs. Sinclair Calls Women Jellyfish," *New York American*, August 29, 1911; this and other stories about the Sinclairs' marriage ending were found in the Stone Mss., Folder titled "Printed Materials."

43. Sinclair, "Happy Marriage: How Can It Be Assured?," *Physical Culture*, April 1913, 297–302; "Some Light on the Race Suicide Question," *Physical Culture*, May 1913, 430; "Marriage Used to Be a Sacrament," *New York American*, January 13, 1924, 2; Mrs. Champ Clark, Upton Sinclair and Frank Harris, "All About Love," *Pearson's Magazine*, November 1918, 42; "To Marry or Not to Marry," *Physical Culture*, March 1914, 228.

44. Upton Sinclair to David Howatt, August 10, 1913, found in Howatt Mss., Lilly Library; Mary Craig Sinclair, *Southern Belle* (Jackson: University of Mississippi Press, 1957; reprint, 1999), 116, 145, 228–229.

45. Sinclair, "Paris and Paris-ites," *Physical Culture*, January 1913; *Sylvia's Marriage: A Novel* (Pasadena, Calif: privately printed, 1914), 290; see also "Her Two Ventures," *Physical Culture*, February 1914.

46. *The Sinclair-Astor Letters* (Girard, Kans.: Appeal to Reason, 1914), 17.

47. Louis Adamic, *Dynamite: The Story of Class Violence in America* (New York: Chelsea House Publishers, 1958), 257–258, 124–125; George S. McGovern and Leonard F. Guttridge, *The Great Coalfield War* (Boston: Houghton Mifflin, 1972), 34; Sinclair to John D. Rockefeller, June 17, 1914, Sinclair Mss., Series I, Box 1.

48. Adamic, *Dynamite*, 259; See also David Montgomery, *The Fall of the House of Labor: The Workplace, the State, and American Labor Activism, 1865–1925* (Cambridge: Cambridge University Press, 1987), 346; "Pickets to Haunt J. D. Rockefeller Jr.," *New York Times*, April 29, 1914, 5.

49. "Sinclair Appeals to Wilson," *New York Times*, December 30, 1913, 3; "Pickets to Besiege Oil Company's Branches," *New York Times*, May 5, 1914, 3; Sinclair to John D. Rockefeller, June 17, 1914, Sinclair Mss., Series I, Box 1; see also "IWW Pickets Rockefellers," *New York Times*, May 4, 1914, 1, 3.

50. "Court Deals a Blow to 'Silence' Pickets," *New York Times*, July 8, 1914, 20; "Rockefeller Balks," *New York Times*, April 30, 1914, 5; "Mother" to Mary Craig, April 29, 1914, found in Sinclair Mss., IV, Box 1.

51. "Attack in Church on Rockefeller," *New York Times*, May 2, 1914, 1, 3; Mary Elizabeth Kenton, "Soul on the Open Road: Bouck White, the Life of an American Social Agitator" (Master's thesis, Wright State University, 1974), 41.

52. Sinclair quoted in Alfred Albrecht, "Upton Sinclair—The Miners' Champion," paper found in Box 62 of Sinclair Mss, Series I; "John D and Governor of Colorado Lied to President Wilson, and Associated Press Suppressed the Facts," *Appeal to Reason*, May 30, 1914, 2; "Resolution Adopted at a Meeting of the Citizens of Denver, May 15, 1914," found in Sinclair Mss., Series I, Box 1; "Speech of Upton Sinclair Before the Mass Meeting Held at the State Capitol, Denver, Colorado, May 15, 1914," found in Series III, Box 36 of Sinclair Mss.

CHAPTER FOUR. WAR!

The epigraphs to this chapter are drawn from, respectively, Randolph Bourne, "The War and the Intellectuals," in *The Radical Will: Selected Writings, 1911–1918* (New York: Urizen Books, 1977), 307; and Sinclair in *The Appeal to Reason*, March 18, 1922, 1.

1. *The Cry for Justice: An Anthology of the Literature of Social Protest* (Philadelphia: John C. Winston Company, 1915), 18; Sinclair, "A Letter to My Friends," (1915), Sinclair Mss., VI, Box 1.

2. Sinclair to Kate Crane-Gartz, July 18, 1927, Sinclair Mss., Series I, Box 8.

3. Sinclair to Irving Stone, April 10, 1951, Sinclair Mss., Series I, Box 56; Sinclair in *Appeal to Reason*, June 14, 1919, 4.

4. Upton Sinclair, "War: A Manifesto Against It," *The Clarion*, August 27, 1909, 1.

5. Upton Sinclair, "None So Blind," *Harper's Weekly*, March 27, 1915, 294; Sinclair to Committee of the Anti-Enlistment League, September 27, 1915, Sinclair Mss., Series I, Box 1; "After the War: A Forecast," *The American Socialist*, October 30, 1915, 2; "What Terms of Peace Shall Close Them?" *The Clarion*, May 7, 1915, 3.

6. David M. Kennedy, *Over Here: The First World War and American Society* (New York: Oxford University Press, 1980), 26; Sinclair, "Letter of Resignation," *Chicago Sunday Tribune*, July 22, 1917, 5.

7. London quoted in Alex Kershaw, *Jack London: A Life* (New York: St. Martin's, 1997), 272.

8. "Socialists Enunciate New Principles," *New Republic*, March 31, 1917, 263, 262; "A Socialist and Sinclair," *Pearson's Magazine*, November 1917, 221; *Upton Sinclair's Magazine*, August 1918, 7.

9. Dewey, quoted in Michael E. McGerr, *A Fierce Discontent: The Rise and Fall of the Progressive Movement in America, 1870–1920* (New York: Free Press, 2003), 282; William E. Leuchtenberg, *The Perils of Prosperity, 1914–1932* (Chicago: University of Chicago Press, 1993), 40; *Upton Sinclair's Magazine*, October 1918, 5. See also Robert B. Westbrook, *John Dewey and American Democracy* (Ithaca: Cornell University Press, 1991), 224; for figures on deaths during the war, see Leuchtenberg, *Perils of Prosperity*, 37.

10. Bourne, *Radical Will*, 312.

11. Sinclair to J. G. Phelps Stokes, February 8, 1916, Sinclair Mss., Series I, Box 1; *Upton Sinclair's Magazine*, July 1918, 16; *Upton Sinclair's Magazine*, November 1918, Supplement, 1; Upton Sinclair to George Bernard Shaw, May 19, 1917, Sinclair Mss., Series I, Box 2. On Wilson's doubts about the war, see John Milton Cooper, *The Warrior and the Priest: Woodrow Wilson and Theodore Roosevelt* (Cambridge: Belknap Press, 1983), 318.

12. Wilson quoted in Stephen Vaughn, *Holding Fast the Inner Lines: Democracy, Nationalism, and the Committee on Public Information* (Chapel Hill: University of North Carolina Press, 1980), 4; Sinclair to Ames Brown of CPI, August 18, 1917, Sinclair Mss., Series I, Box 2.

13. George Creel, *How We Advertised America: The First Telling of the Amazing Story of the Committee on Public Information That Carried the Gospel of Americanism to Every Corner of the Globe* (New York: Harper and Brothers, 1920), 5; Kennedy, *Over Here*, 26, 80.

14. *Upton Sinclair's Magazine*, October 1918, 7; "Speech of Upton Sinclair at Mass Meeting in Celebration of Russian Revolution, Los Angeles, March 10, 1918," found in Sinclair Mss., Series III, Box 36; "Lincoln Libelled," *Pearson's Magazine*, September 1919, 523; Stokes and Russell, quoted in John Patrick Diggins, *The Rise and Fall of the American Left* (New York: Norton, 1992), 102; *Upton Sinclair's Magazine*, September 1918, 5.

15. *Upton Sinclair's Magazine*, April 1918, 1; *The Lie Factory Starts* (Los Angeles: End Poverty League, Inc., 1934), 7; *Upton Sinclair's Magazine*, December 1918, 2; *Upton Sinclair's Magazine*, August 1918; Upton Sinclair to Rudolph Spreckle, October 28, 1918, Sinclair Mss., Series I, Box 2; *New Appeal*, February 15, 1919, 4; *Upton Sinclair's Magazine*, April 1918, 1.

16. *Upton Sinclair's Magazine*, November 1918, 3, 4; "Lincoln and Freedom," *Pearson's Magazine*, December 1919, 659.
17. Sinclair to James Oppenheim, September 29, 1917, Sinclair Mss., Series I, Box 2; Harris quoted in Robert Pearsall, *Frank Harris* (New York: Twayne, 1970), 126; Sinclair, "Censorship and Secret Treaties," *American Monthly*, May 1919, 69.
18. Quoted in Diggins, *Rise and Fall*, 100; Sinclair to Max Eastman, Sinclair Mss., Series I, Box 2; "Vers Liberninism," *The Masses*, November 1916, 19; Sinclair to Frank Harris, Sinclair Mss., Series I, Box 2.
19. The correspondence described here can be found in Sinclair Mss., Series I, Box 2.
20. Leslie Fishbein, *Rebels in Bohemia: The Radicals of the Masses, 1911–1917* (Chapel Hill: University of North Carolina Press, 1982), 25, 26.
21. *Upton Sinclair's Magazine*, December 1918, 3; Robert Rosenstone, *Romantic Revolutionary: A Biography of John Reed* (New York: Vintage, 1975), 333. Sinclair pleaded with Wilson in November 1918, as the war came to an end: see the November 1918 issue of *Upton Sinclair's Magazine*.
22. Frank Harris to Upton Sinclair, August 20, 1918, Sinclair Mss., Series I, Box 2; Harris to Sinclair, November 25, 1917, Sinclair Mss., Series I, Box 2; Kennedy, *Over Here*, 77; Sinclair to Wilson, October 22, 1917, Sinclair Mss., Series I, Box 2.
23. *Upton Sinclair's Magazine*, September 1918, 5; *Appeal to Reason*, August 23, 1919, 4; *Upton Sinclair's Magazine*, October 1918, 6; Nick Salvatore, *Eugene V. Debs: Citizen and Socialist* (Urbana: University of Illinois Press, 1982), 288.
24. "Lincoln and Freedom," 661.
25. "A Socialist Peace," *Pearson's Magazine*, August 1917, 81, 83; *Upton Sinclair's Magazine*, November 1918, 2; *Upton Sinclair's Magazine*, February 1919, 3; *Appeal to Reason*, June 14, 1919, 4.
26. Sinclair to Wilson, February 3, 1917, Sinclair Mss., Series I, Box 2; "Peace and Its Meaning," *Western Comrade*, March/April 1918, 37; *Appeal to Reason*, June 7, 1919, 4; "Peace and Its Meaning," 37.
27. "A Socialist Peace," 83; *Appeal to Reason*, September 4, 1920, 2.
28. *Appeal to Reason*, March 29, 1919, 4; *Appeal to Reason*, October 18, 1919, 3; *Upton Sinclair's Magazine*, July 1918, 16; *Appeal to Reason*, April 10, 1920, 3; *Appeal to Reason*, May 19, 1920, 2; *Appeal to Reason*, August 28, 1920, 2; *Appeal to Reason*, September 14, 1920, 2.
29. *Upton Sinclair's Magazine*, October 1918, 3; *Upton Sinclair's Magazine*, November 1918, 6.
30. *Appeal to Reason*, April 5, 1919; *New Appeal*, February 8, 1919; *Appeal to Reason*, September 20, 1919, 4.
31. *Appeal to Reason*, November 15, 1919, 4; *Appeal to Reason*, November 13, 1920, 2; *Appeal to Reason*, November 29, 1919, 4; *Appeal to Reason*, December 13,

1919, 3; "The Centralia Horror," *Nation*, March 27, 1929, 373; *Appeal to Reason*, January 24, 1920, 3–4; Leuchtenberg, *Perils of Prosperity*, 79; *Appeal to Reason*, May 15, 1920, 3. On the Palmer Raids, see James Weinstein, *The Decline of Socialism in America, 1912–1925* (New York: Vintage, 1969), 249.

32. Sinclair to Frank Harris, October 29, 1918, Sinclair Mss., Series I, Box 2; *Appeal to Reason*, September 13, 1919, 4; Robert Murray, *Red Scare: A Study of National Hysteria* (New York: McGraw-Hill, 1955), 114–116; *Appeal to Reason*, June 19, 1920, 3; January 15, 1921, 3. Carey McWilliams, *Southern California Country: An Island on the Land* (New York: Duell, Sloan & Pearce, 1946), 280; *Upton Sinclair's Magazine*, February 1919, 7.

33. Upton Sinclair, "Good News," *New Republic*, February 1919, 13.

34. *100%: The Story of a Patriot* (Pasadena, Calif.: privately printed, 1920), 143.

35. Frank Harris to Upton Sinclair, October 31, 1920, Sinclair Mss., Series I, Box 3.

36. *Upton Sinclair's Magazine*, August 1918; *Upton Sinclair's Magazine*, August 1918; Jack Reed to Upton Sinclair, November 6, 1918, Sinclair Mss., Series I, Box 2; Sinclair to Albert Shiels, April 18, 1919, Sinclair Mss., Series I, Box 2.

37. *New Appeal*, February 8, 1919, 4; *Appeal to Reason*, September 4, 1920, 2.

CHAPTER FIVE. "PRIZE PRUDE OF THE RADICAL MOVEMENT": 1920–1930

The epigraph to this chapter is drawn from Upton Sinclair to Harry Laidler, December 14, 1925, Sinclair Mss., Series I, Box 6.

1. Mencken quoted in Fred Hobson, *Mencken: A Life* (New York: Random House, 1994), 216; Croly, quoted in William Leuchtenberg, *Perils of Prosperity, 1914–1932* (Chicago: University of Chicago Press, 1958), 124.

2. Frederic Howe, *Confessions of a Reformer* (New York: C. Scribner's Sons, 1925), 196; Lynn Dumenil, *The Modern Temper: American Culture and Society in the 1920s* (New York: Hill and Wang, 1995), 68, 69; *Appeal to Reason*, July 5, 1919, 3.

3. "Critics Disagree," *Open Forum*, January 29, 1927, 3; see, for more on socialism, James Weinstein, *The Decline of Socialism in America, 1912–1925* (New York: Vintage, 1969).

4. *Appeal to Reason*, July 17, 1920, 3; *Appeal to Reason*, May 7, 1921, 1; *Appeal to Reason*, July 29, 1922, 2; *Appeal to Reason*, August 21, 1920, 3; "Upton Sinclair Writes to LaFollette," *Justice*, October 17, 1924, 5.

5. Sinclair to John Beardsley, February 9, 1929, Sinclair Mss., Series I, Box 10; Sinclair to Roger Baldwin, June 4, 1923, Box 5; "The Story of Upton Sinclair," *Los Angeles Record*, 1929, 11. See also "Jim Tully: A Study in Ingratitude," *Haldeman-Julius Monthly*, August 1928, 7; Sinclair to George Moyle,

January 8, 1927, Series I, Box 7; Sinclair to Doerschlag, September 28, 1926, Series I, Box 7; "The Sabbath Taboo," *Haldeman-Julius Monthly*, May 1925, 336; and on Abrams: Sinclair, "The House of Wonder," *Pearson's Magazine*, June 1922, 9–13.

6. For the decade's names, see Frederick John Hoffman, *The Twenties: American Writing in the Postwar Decade* (New York: Free Press, 1962), 418; Sinclair, "The Best Thing for America," *Open Forum*, February 26, 1927, 2.

7. Michael McGerr, *A Fierce Discontent: The Rise and Fall of the Progressive Movement in America* (New York: Free Press, 2003), 315.

8. Dumenil, *The Modern Temper*, 135; Sinclair, "The Flapper," *Open Forum*, September 26, 1925, 3; "The Story of Sinclair: Urges Exercise in Form of Play" (Chapter 10 in a Series)," *Los Angeles Examiner*, September 1929, 1; "Revolution—Not Sex," *New Masses*, March 1927, 11.

9. "Parents Do Not Want to Know the Truth about Young People," *New York American*, November 11, 1923, 5; "Why Are Our College Students Young Barbarians and Their Professors Tired and Discouraged?" *New York American*, August 5, 1923, 2; *Appeal to Reason*, April 30, 1921, 3; *Appeal to Reason*, May 7, 1921, 3; "Farmers Who Made the World Safe for Democracy Have Forgotten to Make It Safe for Themselves," *New York American*, October 21, 1923, 2; "Poor Me and Pure Boston," *Nation*, June 29, 1927, 713.

10. Broun quoted by Sinclair, *Appeal to Reason*, October 28, 1922, 2.

11. Joseph Wood Krutch, *The Modern Temper: A Study and a Confession* (New York: Harcourt, Brace and Company, 1929), 168; T. S. Eliot, "The Wasteland," *The Norton Anthology of Poetry*, ed. Alexander Allison et al., 3rd ed. (New York: Norton, 1983), 1012.

12. Ernest Hemingway, *The Sun Also Rises* (New York: Scribner's, 1926), 115, 247.

13. "Review of Steel Chops," *New Masses*, August 1929, 17; *Haldeman-Julius Weekly*, March 31, 1923, 4; Sinclair to Louis Adamic, July 31, 1926, Sinclair Mss., Series I, Box 7.

14. Hemingway, *The Sun Also Rises*, 42; Mencken, quoted in Hobson, *Mencken: A Life*, 215.

15. Sinclair, *The Autobiography of Upton Sinclair* (New York: Harcourt, Brace and World, 1962), 227; Mencken to Sinclair, June 1, 1925, Sinclair Mss., Series I, Box 6; Roderick Nash, *The Nervous Generation: American Thought, 1917–1930* (Chicago: Elephant Paperbacks, 1990), 152; Sinclair to Mencken, August 23, 1926, Sinclair Mss., Series I, Box 7; "Mr. Mencken Calls on Me," *The Bookman*, November 1927, 255; Hobson, *Mencken: A Life*, 271; Upton Sinclair, *The Cup of Fury* (Manhasset, N.Y.: Channel Press, 1956), 98.

16. Sinclair to Adamic, July 31, 1926, Sinclair Mss., Series I, Box 7; "A Letter," 281.

17. *Appeal to Reason*, December 13, 1919, 3.

18. Upton Sinclair, *The Profits of Religion: An Essay in Economic Interpretation* (Pasadena, Calif.: privately printed, 1918), 16, 47, 161.
19. Sinclair, *Profits of Religion*, 107, 127–132, 209, 218; "Holy Rollers," *Haldeman-Julius Monthly*, July 1925, 142; "Mother Eddy's 'Science and Wealth,'" *Haldeman-Julius Monthly*, March 1925, 225; *Profits of Religion*, 266.
20. Sinclair, *Profits of Religion*, 192.
21. Upton Sinclair, *The Brass Check: A Study of American Journalism* (Pasadena, Calif.: privately printed, 1919), 42; "The Author's Adventures as Publisher," *The Authors' League Bulletin*, February 1925, 8; *Brass Check*, 241, 276; *Appeal to Reason*, May 8, 1920, 3.
22. Upton Sinclair, *The Goose-Step: A Study of American Education* (Pasadena, Calif.: privately printed, 1923), 239–241; *Appeal to Reason*, May 20, 1922; *Appeal to Reason*, June 10, 1922, 3.
23. *Goose-Step*, 55–56, 104–106, 308, Sinclair to Julius, August 18, 1922, Sinclair Mss., Series I, Box 4.
24. *Goose-Step*, 370, 372; "Killers of Thought," *Forum*, December 1926, 843.
25. *Goose-Step*, 455, 457.
26. James Harvey Robinson to Sinclair, November 24, 1922, Sinclair Mss., Series I, Box 4.
27. Lawrence Cremin, *The Transformation of the School: Progressivism in American Education, 1876–1957* (New York: Vintage Books, 1964), 37, 52; Upton Sinclair, *The Goslings: A Study of the American Schools* (Pasadena, Calif.: privately printed, 1924), 315.
28. *The Goslings*, 186, 240–242
29. "Upton Sinclair Defends the Law," *Nation*, June 6, 1923, 647.
30. Oaks quoted in Upton Sinclair, *Autobiography*, 229; *Haldeman-Julius Weekly*, May 26, 1923, 1; *Haldeman-Julius Weekly*, June 2, 1923, 2; "We Get Arrested a Little," *The Liberator*, July 1923, 22.
31. "Civil Liberties in Los Angeles," *Industrial Pioneer*, August 1923, 28–29; Robert Cottrell, *Roger Nash Baldwin and the American Civil Liberties Union* (New York: Columbia University Press, 2000).
32. Sinclair to King Gillette, September 4, 1923, Sinclair Mss., Series I, Box 5; Sinclair to Roger Baldwin, November 26, 1923, Sinclair Mss., Series I, Box 5; Sinclair to Taft, August 22, 1923, Sinclair Mss., Series I, Box 5; Sinclair to Governor Richardson, November 20, 1925, Sinclair Mss., Series I, Box 6; "Send Mrs. Whitney to Jail," *Open Forum*, June 4, 1927; "For Free Speech," *World Wide*, November 7, 1931, 1.
33. "Let in the Light," *Open Forum*, December 6, 1924, 1; "For Freedom of Speech," *Open Forum*, March 19, 1930, 2.
34. Upton Sinclair, *Mammonart: An Essay in Economic Interpretation* (Pasadena, Calif.: privately printed, 1925), 7, 9; Sinclair to Mrs. Lu Maerten, June 25, 1926, Sinclair Mss., Series, I, Box 7.

35. *Mammonart*, 95, 348, 334–336.
36. *Mammonart*, 112, 243–244.
37. Sinclair to Haldeman-Julius, May 8, 1924, Sinclair Mss., Series I, Box 6; *Money Writes!* (New York: Albert and Charles Boni, 1927), 194, 134, 171.
38. Floyd Dell quoted in Leon Harris, *Upton Sinclair: American Rebel* (New York: Crowell, 1975), 221; H. L. Mencken, "The Library," *American Mercury*, February 1928, 253; "Reading and Writing," *New Yorker*, December 10, 1927, 122; Heywood Broun, "It Seems to Heywood Broun," *The Nation*, December 7, 1927, 622.
39. Upton Sinclair in Circular Letter regarding *Love's Pilgrimage*, dated October 20, 1926, Sinclair Mss., Individual Items; "Author's Adventures as Publishers," 1925, 9; "From Upton Sinclair," *Open Forum*, May 30, 1925, 3; Sinclair to Norman Baker, January 18, 19, and 20, 1928, Sinclair Mss., Series I, Box 8.
40. Warbasse to Upton Sinclair, June 5, 1925, Sinclair Mss., Series I, Box 6; Sinclair to Roger Baldwin, May 13, 1924, Sinclair Mss., Series I, Box 6; Upton Sinclair Circular Letter, July 28, 1925, found in Sinclair, Individual Items Collection.
41. *What's the Use of Books* (New York: Vanguard Press, 1926), 2; "Pocket Series Has Solved Problem of Culture," *Life and Letters*, January 1924, 8.
42. Sinclair to Mr. Dakers, June 22, 1925, Sinclair Mss., Series I, Box 6.
43. Quoted in Henry May, *The End of American Innocence: A Study of the First Years of Our Own Time, 1912–1917* (New York: Knopf, 1959), 256.
44. Floyd Dell, *Upton Sinclair: A Study in Social Protest* (New York: George H. Doran, 1927), 13, 187.
45. Walter Lippmann, "Upton Sinclair," *Saturday Review of Literature*, March 3, 1928, 642; "Sinclair, At Odds," *Saturday Review of Literature*, April 7, 1928, 744.
46. Lawrence Morris, "Upton Sinclair: The Way of the Reformer," *New Republic*, March 7, 1928, 91, 93.
47. *Upton Sinclair's Magazine*, January 1919, 4; Sinclair to Sir Arthur Conan Doyle, July 27, 1927, Sinclair Mss., Series I, Box 8; *Appeal to Reason*, June 21, 1919, 4; *Appeal to Reason*, July 19, 1919, 4; "Upton Sinclair vs. George Viereck," *American Monthly*, July 1919, 149; "If This Be Authoritarianism," *Open Forum*, December 27, 1930, 3; Sinclair to H. Dunlop, January 17, 1929, Sinclair Mss., Series I, Box 10.
48. William Leuchtenberg, *Perils of Prosperity*, 93.
49. Sinclair to Horace Liveright, November 6, 1926, Sinclair Mss., Series I, Box 7.
50. "Censor: Fool or Knave," *New Masses*, August 1927, 16; "Poor Me and Pure Boston," 714; Sinclair to Joseph Bearek, August 10, 1927, Sinclair Mss., Series I, Box 8.
51. Thayer quoted in William Leuchtenberg, *The Perils of Prosperity*, 82.

52. *Appeal to Reason*, June 17, 1922, 1; "Now, as in the Days of Henry D. Thoreau, Massachusetts Has Its Greatest Soul in Jail," *New York American*, September 16, 1923, 3; "The Story of a Proletarian Life," *Open Forum*, July 3, 1926, 3; Sinclair to Governor Alvan T. Fuller, April 11, 1927, Sinclair Mss., Series I, Box 7; Sinclair to Alfred Baker Lewis, August 10, 1927, Box 8; "Upton Sinclair Suggests," *Nation*, June 12, 1929, 700; Sinclair to Mrs. Elizabeth Glendower Evans, August 24, 1927, Box 8.

53. Upton Sinclair to Robert Minor, February 8, 1928, Sinclair Mss., Series I, Box 9; Upton Sinclair to Mike Gold, April 4, 1928, Box 9.

54. Sinclair to Beaumont Wadsworth, April 10, 1928, Sinclair Mss., Series I, Box 9; Sinclair to Arthur Hill, July 23, 1928, Box 9; Sinclair to Boni, June 26, 1928, Box 9; Sinclair to Roscoe Gaige, October 18, 1928, Box 10; "Singing Jailbirds," *New Republic*, March 13, 1929, 100.

55. Upton Sinclair, *Boston: A Novel* (New York: A. and C. Boni, 1928), 262, 552, 320.

56. Quoted in Richard Pells, *Radical Visions and American Dreams: Culture and Social Thought in the Depression Years* (New York: Harper and Row, 1973), 42.

CHAPTER SIX. A BRIEF INTERMISSION—UPPIE GOES TO THE MOVIES: 1930–1934

The epigraph to this chapter is drawn from Lincoln Steffens to Upton Sinclair, January 22, 1933, Sinclair Mss., Series I, Box 21.

1. Hoover quoted in Arthur Schlesinger Jr., *The Crisis of the Old Order* (Boston: Houghton Mifflin, 1957), 158.

2. Upton Sinclair, *Mental Radio* (New York: A. and C. Boni, 1930), 4.

3. Sinclair to editor of *New Republic*, February 11, 1929, Sinclair Mss., Series I, Box 10; Sinclair, "Is This Jack London?" *Occult Review*, December 1930, 395; Sinclair, "Einstein and Spiritualism," *New Republic*, April 27, 1932, 301–302.

4. Sinclair to Mencken, February 17, 1931, Sinclair Mss., Series I, Box 15; Mencken to Sinclair, February 12, 1931, Sinclair Mss., Series I, Box 14; E. Haldeman-Julius, *My First 25 Years* (privately printed, 1949), 25.

5. Sinclair to Heinrich Schubert, November 20, 1931, Sinclair Mss., Series I, Box 17.

6. Sinclair to Betty, September 30, 1929, Sinclair Mss., Series I, Box 11; Sinclair to *Time Magazine*, September 28, 1931, Sinclair Mss., Series I, Box 16; Sinclair to Betty, April 10, 1930, Sinclair Mss., Series I, Box 12 (on the radio project).

7. Mary Craig Kimbrough Sinclair, *Southern Belle* (New York: Crown Publishers, 1957), 171; Sinclair, "The Movies and Political Propaganda," in *The Movies on Trial: The Views and Opinions of Outstanding Personalities Anent Screen Entertainment Past and Present*, William Perlman, ed. (New York: Macmillan, 1936), 189.

8. Sinclair to G. S. Williams, July 26, 1918, in which Sinclair outlines his railroad film, Sinclair Mss., Series I, Box 2; Sinclair to Haldeman-Julius, April 15, 1919, Sinclair Mss., Series I, Box 2.
9. Sinclair, "Truth," *The New Age*, December 7, 1916, 128; Hampton to Sinclair, August 24, 1920, Sinclair Mss., Series I, Box 3; Sinclair to Hampton, October 23, 1920, Box 3; Sinclair, "Labor and Motion Pictures," *Soviet Russia Pictorial*, June 1923, 124.
10. "This Is Rob!" (unpublished manuscript), Sinclair Mss., Series III, Box 35.
11. Sinclair, *Appeal to Reason*, April 1, 1922, 2; Sinclair, "Book Urchins," *The Forum*, November 1927, 741; Sinclair to Chaplin, August 18, 1918, Series I, Box 2; Sinclair to Chaplin, December 29, 1925, Box 6.
12. Fairbanks to Sinclair, December 13, 1924, Sinclair Mss., Series I, Box 6; Sinclair, "Socialism and Culture," *American Freemen*, June 13, 1931, 2.
13. Sinclair to Mencken, August 30, 1930; Sinclair to David, September 17, 1930; Sinclair to Darrow, September 25, 1930, all in Sinclair Mss., Series I, Box 13; Darrow to Sinclair, November 24, 1930, Box 14.
14. Sinclair, *The Wet Parade* (Pasadena, Calif.: privately printed, 1931), 27, 110, 260.
15. H. L. Mencken, "A Moral Tale," *The Nation*, September 23, 1931, 310.
16. Sinclair to MGM, March 10, 1932, Sinclair Mss., Series I, Box 18.
17. Thalberg, quoted in Richard Fine, *West of Eden: Writers in Hollywood, 1928–1940* (Washington, D.C.: Smithsonian Press, 1993), 105; Sinclair to Helen Woodward, November 9, 1932; Sinclair to Betty, November 21, 1932, both in Sinclair Mss., Series I, Box 20.
18. Sinclair to Betty, April 15, 1932, Sinclair Mss., Series I, Box 18.
19. Upton Sinclair, *Upton Sinclair Presents William Fox* (Los Angeles: privately printed, 1933), 46; Neal Gabler, *An Empire of Their Own: How the Jews Invented Hollywood* (New York: Doubleday, 1989), 71, 313.
20. Sinclair to Mrs. Fox, September 24, 1932, Sinclair Mss., Series I, Box 20.
21. Sinclair, *Upton Sinclair Presents William Fox*, 69–70, 80–81.
22. Sinclair, *Upton Sinclair Presents William Fox*, 61.
23. Mary Craig Sinclair, *Southern Belle*, 331; the details about Eisenstein are taken from Ronald Bergan, *Eisenstein: A Life in Conflict* (London: Little, Brown and Company, 1997).
24. Sinclair to Hunter, December 5, 1930, Sinclair Mss., Series I, Box 14.
25. Hunter to Sinclair, February 19, 1931, Sinclair Mss., Series I, Box 15.
26. Sinclair to Eisenstein, August 28, 1931, Sinclair Mss., Series I, Box 16; Hunter to Sinclair, October 9, 1931, Sinclair Mss., Series I, Box 17.
27. Sinclair to Woodward, February 28, 1932, Sinclair Mss., Series I, Box 18; Sinclair to Bernie Ernst, June 5, 1933, Box 22.
28. Stephen Lesser, "Sol Lesser and Upton Sinclair: A Record of Their Friendship," *Western States Jewish Historical Quarterly* 12 (1980): 138; Sinclair to

General P. E. Calles of Mexico, September 25, 1933, Sinclair Mss., Series I, Box 24; Sinclair, "In the Mail Box," *New York Post*, August 26, 1933, 13.

29. Seymour Stern, "The Greatest Thing Done on This Side of the Atlantic: Eisenstein's Original Vision of Mexico," *Modern Monthly*, October 1933, 532; Sinclair to Isador Lerner, May 11, 1933, Sinclair Mss., Series I, Box 22.

30. Sinclair to Lincoln Kirstein, August 3, 1935, Sinclair Mss, Series I, Box 33.

CHAPTER SEVEN. I, GOVERNOR OF CALIFORNIA: 1934

The epigraphs to this chapter are drawn from Sinclair to *Daily Worker*, July 23, 1934, Sinclair Mss., Series I, Box 27; Sinclair speech to EPIC workers, August 27, 1934, Sinclair Mss., Series III, Box 36; Sinclair speech, October 28, 1934, over KHJ Radio, Sinclair Mss., Series III, Box 36.

1. Quoted in John Patrick Diggins, *The Rise and Fall of the American Left* (New York: W. W. Norton, 1992), 165; Quoted in Arthur Schlesinger, *The Crisis of the Old Order, 1919–1933* (Boston: Houghton Mifflin, 1957), 214; Richard Pells, *Radical Visions and American Dreams: Culture and Social Thought in the Depression Years* (New York: Harper and Row, 1973), 77.

2. Sinclair, "What I Am Really Going to Do," *Liberty*, October 20, 1934, 6.

3. "Upton Sinclair Speaks on Campaign Issues at Statewide Picnic," *The Labor World*, October 10, 1930, 4; "Sinclair Congratulates Rolph," *Open Forum*, November 15, 1930, 1; Sinclair, "Not Without Laughter," *Open Forum*, October 4, 1930, 3; Sinclair, *The Lie Factory Starts* (Los Angeles: End Poverty League, 1934), 58; Sinclair to Broun, May 6, 1931, Sinclair Mss., Series I, Box 15.

4. Sinclair, "Converting the Rich to Socialism," *Call of Youth*, October 1933, 3; Sinclair to David, November 13, 1933, Sinclair Mss., Series I, Box 24; on his change of party affiliation, see Sinclair, *I, Governor of California, and How I Ended Poverty: A True Story of the Future* (Los Angeles: privately printed, 1933), 20.

5. Sinclair to David, July 21, 1934, Sinclair Mss., Series I, Box 27; Michael Kazin, *The Populist Persuasion: An American History* (New York: Basic Books, 1995), 113.

6. Robert McElvaine, *The Great Depression: America, 1929–1941* (New York: Times Books, 1984), 232.

7. Schlesinger, *The Politics of Upheaval* (Boston: Houghton Mifflin, 1960), 42; Long quoted in T. H. Watkins, *The Great Depression: America in the 1930s* (Boston: Little, Brown, 1993), 228–229; see also Alan Brinkley, *Voices of Protest: Huey Long, Father Coughlin, and the Great Depression* (New York: Knopf, 1982), 60, 71.

8. Sinclair, "Sinclair on Upton Sinclair," *The World Tomorrow*, May 10, 1934, 260; Sinclair, *The Way Out: What Lies Ahead for America* (Los Angeles: pri-

vately printed, 1933), 65; Leon Harris, *Upton Sinclair: American Rebel* (New York: Crowell, 1975), 299.

9. Sinclair, "The Socialist Party: Its Aims in the Present Campaign," *Collier's*, October 29, 1904, 12; *Appeal to Reason*, January 10, 1920, 4.

10. Nick Salvatore, *Eugene V. Debs: Citizen and Socialist* (Urbana: University of Illinois Press, 1982), 25, 148; on the Populists, see Lawrence Goodwyn, *Democratic Promise: The Populist Movement in America* (New York: Oxford University Press, 1976), and Steven Hahn, *The Roots of Southern Populism: Yeoman Farmers and the Transformation of the Georgia Upcountry, 1850–1890* (New York: Oxford University Press, 1983).

11. Sinclair, "The EPIC Plan: Can Poverty Be Ended?" *Common Sense*, May 1934, 8; on the Oakland cooperative, see Fay M. Blake and H. Morton Newman, "Upton Sinclair's EPIC Campaign," *California History*, Fall 1984, 309; on the Los Angeles co-ops, see Luther Whiteman and Samuel L. Lewis, *Glory Roads: The Psychological State of California* (New York: Thomas Y. Crowell Company, 1936), 146.

12. Sinclair to Warner Marsh, April 12, 1934, Sinclair Mss., Series I, Box 26; Sinclair, "An Open Letter to the American People," *Liberty*, June 10, 1933, 37; Sinclair, *Immediate EPIC: The Final Statement of the Plan* (Los Angeles: End Poverty League, 1933), 14; Sinclair, "Meet Mr. Heckler," *Upton Sinclair's End Poverty Paper*, March 1934, 12; Sinclair, *I, Governor*, 15.

13. Carey McWilliams, *Southern California Country: An Island on the Land* (New York: Duell, Sloan and Pearce, 1946), 273; "Sinclair as a Democrat," *New York Times*, August 30, 1934, 18; Blake and Newman, "Upton Sinclair's EPIC Campaign," 308; Upton Sinclair to Frank Winch, August 1, 1934, Sinclair Mss., Series I, Box 27; Sinclair, "If We Could Only Reorganize Our Industries Sanely," *New York American*, November 18, 1923, 2.

14. Sinclair, *The Way Out* (Los Angeles: privately printed, 1933), 74, 104.

15. Sinclair, *Immediate EPIC*, 10; Sinclair, *We, People of America, and How We Ended Poverty: A True Story of the Future* (Pasadena, Calif.: National EPIC League, 1934), 14.

16. Sinclair to Ernest Untermann, April 30, 1934, Sinclair Mss., Series I, Box 26; Sinclair to Editor of *Star-News Pasadena*, August 11, 1934, Box 27; Sinclair, "The EPIC Plan," 1934, 7; "What I Am Really Going to Do," 1934, 6; Sinclair to *Literary Digest*, June 27, 1935, Sinclair Mss., Series I, Box 33; *Time* quoted in Leon Harris, *Upton Sinclair*, 313.

17. "Upton's Winged Words Soar Across Atlantic," *EPIC News*, July 30, 1934, 5; "Candidates List Costs," *Los Angeles Times*, September 12, 1934, II 1, 2.

18 "Merriam's Work Told," *Los Angeles Times*, October 28, 1934, 10; "Merriam for Governor," *Los Angeles Times*, August 3, 1934, II 4.

19. "Epic Chief in Parley," *Los Angeles Times*, September 5, 1934, 1, 5; "Roosevelt Asks All to Join New Deal as Hopkins Backs EPIC," *EPIC News*,

September 3, 1934, 1; "Political Notes"; "Predict a Revolt Against Sinclair," *New York Times*, September 2, 1934, 12.

20. Sinclair, "What I Am Really Going to Do," 7; Sinclair, "What I Shall Do," *Liberty*, November 17, 1934, 34; "Platform Adopted," *Los Angeles Times*, September 21, 1934, 1, 5; "Latest EPIC Plan Upsets California," *New York Times*, September 30, 1934, E-1. For Sinclair's eating habits, see Sinclair to Robert Brownell, September 11, 1946, Sinclair Mss., Series I, Box 52.

21. Sinclair, *We, People*, 7; "Ending of Poverty Is the Only Issue," *End Poverty*, May 1934, 38; Frank Scully, *This Gay Knight: An Autobiography of a Modern Chevalier* (Philadelphia: Chilton Company, 1962), 59.

22. Sinclair, "What I Am Really Going to Do," 7. On the clubs' climbing numbers: Sinclair to Betty Sinclair, January 24, 1934, Sinclair Mss., Series I, Box 25; Sinclair to Edward Filene, March 5, 1934, Box 25; Sinclair to Louis Horchitz, June 11, 1934, Box 26; Reuben W. Borough, "Upton Sinclair's Epic, 1934," *The Occidental Review*, Summer 1965, 35; Greg Mitchell, *The Campaign of the Century: Upton Sinclair's Race for Governor of California and the Birth of Media Politics* (New York: Random House, 1992), 193.

23. "Honey and the Bee," *Upton Sinclair's End Poverty Paper*, April 1934, 9; songs found in File on EPIC Campaign, Sinclair Mss., Series I, Box 31; Sinclair, *Depression Island* (Pasadena, Calif.: privately printed, 1935), 48; Joyce Milton, *Tramp: The Life of Charlie Chaplin* (New York: HarperCollins, 1996), 340; Donald Singer, "Upton Sinclair and the California Gubernatorial Campaign of 1934," *Southern California Quarterly* 56 (1974): 381; see also in the same issue Judson Grenier, "Upton Sinclair: The Road to California."

24. "Realty Men in Warning," *Los Angeles Times*, September 28, 1934, 7; advertisement, *Los Angeles Times*, October 20 1934, ii2; "Churchmen Aid Merriam," *Los Angeles Times*, November 2, 1934, 4; "The Future of EPIC," *Nation*, November 28, 1934, 617.

25. "Hordes of Jobless Swooping on State," *Los Angeles Times*, October 24, 1934, ii2; "California Talks Only of Campaign," *New York Times*, October 21, 1934, E7; "Sinclair Charges Straw Vote Fraud," *New York Times*, October 25, 1934, 3; "Vote Fraud Gets Under Way," *Los Angeles Times*, October 21, 1934, 1, 5.

26. Greg Mitchell, *The Campaign of the Century*, 200; "Nine Tenths of State's Papers Oppose Sinclair," *Los Angeles Times*, September 22, 1934, 4; "Sinclair Taking Vacation: Candidate for Governor Retires Temporarily to Luxurious Mansion of Crane Plumbing Heiress," *Los Angeles Times*, October 9, 1934, ii5; "A Picture of Sinclairism," *Los Angeles Times*, October 29, 1934, ii4.

27. "Sinclair Hit By Hatfield," *Los Angeles Times*, October 21, 1934, 18; Sinclair, "What I Shall Do," 3; "Types of Attack on Sinclair Vary from 'Free Lover' to 'Bum,'" *EPIC News*, July 2, 1934, 5; Frank Scully, *Rogues' Gallery: Profiles of*

My Eminent Contemporaries (Hollywood: Murray and Gee, 1943), 197, 202; "End Poverty in Civilization," *Nation*, September 26, 1934, 351; Donald Singer, "Upton Sinclair and the California Gubernatorial Campaign of 1934," *Southern California Quarterly* 56 (1974): 375–399; Judson Grenier, "Upton Sinclair: The Road to California," *Southern California Quarterly* 56 (1974): 325–336; Pamphlet found in August 31 Folder of Sinclair Mss., Series I, Box 28; items found in Sinclair Mss., Book Items, Box VI: SEPTIC Plan and "Upton Sinclair Active Official of Communist Organizations."

28. Mitchell, *The Campaign of the Century*, 28; "Mayer Will Aid Merriam," *Los Angeles Times*, October 8, 1934, ii1, 2; "Schenck Says Movies Must Flee Sinclair," *New York Times*, October 6, 1934, 20; Mitchell, *The Campaign of the Century*, 499; Quote from Ian Hamilton, *Writers in Hollywood: 1915–1951* (New York: Harper and Row, 1990), 89.

29. "Storm on the Pacific," *New York Times*, October 28, 1934, X5; Scully, *Rogues' Gallery*, 195; "Sinclair Moves to Prove Coercion," *New York Times*, November 1, 1934, 15; *Variety* quoted in Mitchell, *The Campaign of the Century*, 185; *Hollywood Reporter*, as quoted in Donald Singer, "Upton Sinclair and the Gubernatorial Campaign," 394: See also Judson Grenier, "Upton Sinclair: The Road to California."

30. Greg Mitchell, *The Campaign of the Century*, 246.

31. "Sinclair's Enemies Go 'Progressive,'" *New York Times*, October 28, 1934, E7; "Radicalism Dealt Blow by Merriam," *Los Angeles Times*, September 30, 1934, 1, 3; "Merriam on Cooperatives," *Los Angeles Times*, October 22, 1934, 13.

32. "Creel Repudiates Sinclair Candidacy," *New York Times*, October 27, 1934, 1; "Won't Back Merriam," *New York Times*, October 27, 1934, 3.

33. "Haight Sees Struggle if Rivals Win," *Los Angeles Times*, November 3, 1934, 2; "Merriam Guarded in Campaign Talk," *New York Times*, November 4, 1934, 31; "Both Sides Guard California Polls," *New York Times*, November 6, 1934, 22; "Army Being Mobilized to Guard Polls," *Los Angeles Times*, October 18, 1934, 1, 2; "Topics of the Times," *New York Times*, November 10, 1934, 14; "Upton Sinclair's Address Before EPIC Convention," *EPIC News*, March 2, 1936, 5.

34. Sinclair to Adlai Stevenson, November 12, 1952, Sinclair Mss., Series I, Box 57; "Future of EPIC," *Nation*, November 28, 1934, 617.

35. Sinclair, "What I Shall Do," 1934, 35; "Unseat Senator Olson as State Chairman," *EPIC News*, December 17, 1934, 2; Sinclair to Olson, April 4, 1935, Sinclair Mss., Series I, Box 32; Reuben Borough, "Upton Sinclair's EPIC," 48; Sinclair to EPIC Club Members, April 7, 1935, Sinclair Mss. IV, Box 1; "Sinclair Defies Reds in Stormy EPIC Meeting Here," *Los Angeles Examiner*, May 19, 1935, 1.

36. Sinclair to DeKay, September 9, 1935, Sinclair Mss., Series I, Box 33; on the newspaper, Sinclair to Charlie Oursler, January 22, 1936, Sinclair Mss., Series

I, Box 35; Sinclair to Herbert Sullivan, January 25, 1936, Box 35; Sinclair to Max Knepper, December 8, 1936, Box 37; "A Statement to the Epics," *Upton Sinclair's National EPIC News*, January 13, 1936, 2.

37. Craig to Sarah, December 31, 1934, Sinclair Mss., Series I, Box 30; Sinclair to Saul Klein, April 18, 1935, Box 32; Sinclair to John Packard, February 1, 1935, Box 31.

38. "California Climax," *Time*, October 22, 1934, 13; Sinclair to Walter McNeil, December 27, 1934, Sinclair Mss., Series I, Box 30; Sinclair to Villard, August 22, 1935, Box 33; about the movie: Sinclair to J. M. Rich, January 5, 1935, Box 31; Sinclair to DeKay, January 15, 1935, Box 31.

39. Sinclair quoted in "Gov. Merriam's Vote Count Climbs Above Million Mark," *Los Angeles Times*, November 8, 1934, 4.

CHAPTER EIGHT. BEYOND CALIFORNIA, TOWARD A POPULAR FRONT: 1935–1939

The epigraphs to this chapter are drawn from, respectively, "EPIC in the Northwest," *Upton Sinclair's National EPIC News*, July 15, 1935, 2; "Spain," in *The Collected Poetry of W. H. Auden* (New York: Random House, 1967), 183.

1. Sinclair to George Goebel, August 24, 1935, Sinclair Mss., Series I, Box 33; Sinclair to Leila Barnett, August 16, 1937, Box 39.

2. "End Poverty in Civilization," *Nation*, September 26, 1934, 351; Sinclair to Irving Stone, January 26, 1939, Sinclair Mss., Series I, Box 43. For the details here, I rely upon Sinclair to George Hormel, May 7, 1934, Box 26; "EPIC Is Spreading," *Upton Sinclair's National EPIC News*, July 29, 1935, 1; "Still More Travel," *Upton Sinclair's National EPIC News*, November 11, 1935, 1, 2; Leon Harris, *Upton Sinclair: American Rebel* (New York: Crowell, 1975), 322; "News and Comment," *Upton Sinclair's National EPIC News*, December 23, 1935, 1.

3. "Report on a Tour," *Upton Sinclair's National EPIC News*, August 5, 1935, 1.

4. John Dos Passos, *The Big Money* (1936; New York: New American Library, 1979), xix. The information in this chapter and the next is indebted to Michael Denning, *The Cultural Front: The Laboring of American Culture in the Twentieth Century* (New York: Verso, 1998).

5. Sinclair, *What God Means to Me: An Attempt at a Working Religion* (Pasadena, Calif.: privately printed, 1935), 127, 28.

6. Sinclair to Van Wyck Brooks, October 14, 1938, Sinclair Mss., Series I, Box 42.

7. Sinclair, *Co-op: A Novel of Living Together* (Pasadena, Calif.: privately printed, 1936), 163; on Rutzebeck, see Sinclair to John Rust, May 11, 1937, Sinclair Mss., Series I, Box 38; "God for Capitalism," *EPIC News*, May 25, 1936, 2 (regarding film based on *Co-op*).

8. Sinclair, Letter to Friends, about writing children's book, dated September

1936, Sinclair Mss., Series I, Box 36; Sinclair, *The Gnomobile* (New York: Farrar and Rinehart, 1936).

9. Sinclair to K. P. P. Tampy, July 27, 1936, Sinclair Mss., Series I, Box 36; see also "A Democratic King versus Hypocrisy," *Los Angeles Examiner*, December 10, 1936, 3, 4, and *Wally for Queen!: The Private Life of Royalty* (Pasadena, Calif.: privately printed, 1936).

10. Sinclair, General Statement, January 21, 1937, Sinclair Mss., Series I, Box 37.

11. "Earl Browder Calls," *EPIC News*, August 24, 1936, 12; Sinclair to FDR, May 29, 1935, Sinclair Mss., Series I, Box 32.

12. Max Knepper, "My Plans for 1936," *Real America*, October 1935, 27; about Townsend, Sinclair to Conliffe, June 3, 1936, Sinclair Mss., Series I, Box 36; about vote swapping, Sinclair to the *Nation*, September 23, 1936, Box 36.

13. "Poverty the Issue," *EPIC News*, September 6, 1937, 1; "The Supreme Court," *EPIC News*, February 22, 1937, 1–2.

14. "The New Depression," *EPIC News*, November 29, 1937, 1; "An Open Letter to President Roosevelt," *EPIC News*, August 9, 1937, 2; "The Future of EPIC," *EPIC News*, November 9, 1936, 1; "This Brave New Party," *The Progressive*, July 16, 1938, 1.

15. "Hand or brain" quote: Sinclair, "To My Readers," *New Masses*, July 19, 1938, 11; "Communists and EPIC," *Upton Sinclair's National EPIC News*, August 12, 1935, 1, 2; on Jefferson, see Sinclair, "To My Readers," 1938, 11; "Stand by Democracy," *EPIC News*, August 10, 1936, 2; on Corey, see Richard Pells, *Radical Visions and American Dreams: Culture and Social Thought in the Depression Years* (New York: Harper and Row, 1973), 91; the "communism" as "Americanism" quote is quoted in many places, but see Arthur Schlesinger Jr., *The Politics of Upheaval* (Boston: Houghton Mifflin, 1960), 568.

16. Sinclair to Charles Holmburg, September 15, 1938, Sinclair Mss., Series I, Box 42; Sinclair, *Your Million Dollars* (Pasadena, Calif.: privately printed, 1939), 14, 18; on Ham and Eggs, see Carey McWilliams, *The Education of Carey McWilliams* (New York: Simon and Schuster, 1979), 71.

17. "The New Deal Sleeps," *EPIC News*, March 21, 1938, "History Repeats Itself," *EPIC News*, April 11, 1938, 2; "Another Victory for Production for Use," *EPIC News*, February 14, 1938, 1; Sinclair, *Telling the World* (London: T. Werner Laurie, 1939), 53.

18. William Leuchtenberg, *Franklin D. Roosevelt and the New Deal* (New York: Harper, 1963), 240; Sinclair, "A Telegram: The Answer," *EPIC News*, February 15, 1937, 8; see also Robert McElvaine, *The Great Depression: America, 1929–1941* (New York: Times Books, 1984), 292.

19. Sinclair, *The Flivver King* (Pasadena, Calif.: privately printed, 1937), 159.

20. About the UAW relationship, see Sinclair to John Farrar, August 14, 1937, Sinclair Mss., Series I, Box 39, and Sinclair, "My EPIC Idea Spreads," *The*

Progressive, October 23, 1937, 3; on the failed movie plan, see Sinclair to William Dodd, March 23, 1938, Box 40.

21. Sinclair to John Farrar, June 29, 1938, Sinclair Mss., Series I, Box 41; Sinclair to Orville Park, June 11, 1938, Box 41.

22. Sinclair to Philip Murray, May 4, 1938, Sinclair Mss., Series I, Box 41; Sinclair about *Daily Worker*, to John Farrar, July 22, 1938, Box 41; Sinclair to Irita Van Doren, December 10, 1937, Box 40.

23. Sinclair, "The Writer in a Changing World," *EPIC News*, January 4, 1937, 1; "Address of Upton Sinclair at the Western Writers Conference," *EPIC News*, December 7, 1936, 4.

24. Sinclair to Charlie Oursler, September 6, 1933, Sinclair Mss., Series I, Box 24; Sinclair to Julius Levenson, March 14, 1935, Box 32; Sinclair, *Telling the World*, 42. The rest of the information here draws from Sinclair to Stanley Anderson, March 19, 1935, Box 32; "Concerning Race Prejudice," *EPIC News*, June 1, 1936, 1–2; Sinclair, "An Open Letter to W. A. White," *New Republic*, December 7, 1938, 132; "Explaining Our Politics," *EPIC News*, August 17, 1936, 1.

25. Sinclair, "I'm Out of Politics!" *The Progressive*, October 16, 1937, 3: "Sinclair on the Ethiopian War," *Upton Sinclair's National EPIC News*, September 23, 1935, 2; Sinclair, "Capitalism Has Made It Plain," *New Masses*, December 15, 1936, 26; "A Problem with Tactics," *EPIC News*, August 3, 1936, 1.

26. Ernest Hemingway, *For Whom the Bell Tolls* (New York: Scribner, 1940), 467; George Orwell, *Homage to Catalonia* (Boston: Beacon Press, 1955), 4; Cowley quoted in Pells, *Radical Visions*, 309; Sinclair, "The People at Bay," *EPIC News*, March 29, 1937, 1; "Neutrality for Fascism," *EPIC News*, January 25, 1937, 1; "Help for Spain," *EPIC News*, July 19, 1937, 1.

27. Sinclair to Nancy Bedford-Jones, April 16, 1937, Sinclair Mss., Series I, Box 38; for the standard recruit into the International Brigades, see Robert A. Rosenstone, "The Men of the Abraham Lincoln Brigade," *The Journal of American History*, September 1967, 327–329.

28. Sinclair to Varian Fry, March 22, 1937, Sinclair Mss., Series I, Box 38; Sinclair to Francis Henson, March 1, 1937, Box 38; Sinclair to Don Fernando de los Rios, April 19, 1937, Box 38; Sinclair to Varian Fry, April 23, 1937, Box 38; Sinclair to J. K. Heim, July 21, 1937, Box 39; about new debt: Sinclair to O. L. Kimbrough, March 26, 1937, Box 38.

29. Kenneth S. Lynn, *Hemingway* (New York: Simon and Schuster, 1987), 452; Sinclair, "The Soviet Union and the Fascist Menace to the World," *International Literature*, December 1938, 52; Sinclair, "American-Soviet Friendship," *Soviet Russia Today*, May 1938, 24; Sinclair, "Russia in Controversy," *EPIC News*, February 28, 1938, 1; Olivier Todd, *Malraux: A Life* (New York: Knopf, 2005), 220–222.

30. Sinclair, "Greetings to USSR," *EPIC News*, November 1, 1937, 5; Sinclair, "Russia in Controversy," 1; Sinclair, "Earl Browder Calls," 1.

31. Sinclair to Sidney Hook, March 30, 1938, Sinclair Mss., Series I, Box 40; Sinclair to W. L. Blair, March 26, 1938, Box 40; *Terror*, 1938, 60–61; Sinclair to James Rorty, March 9, 1938, Box 40.

32. Sinclair to W. E. Woodward, September 2, 1939, Sinclair Mss., Series I, Box 44; Sinclair to W. E. Woodward, September 25, 1939, Box 44; David Sinclair to Upton Sinclair, December 5, 1939, D. Sinclair Mss., VI, Box 1.

33. MacLeish, *A Time to Speak: The Selected Prose of Archibald MacLeish* (Boston: Houghton Mifflin, 1941), 109; Sinclair, "Upton Sinclair on War and How It's Made," *New Clarion*, March 11, 1933, 268; Sinclair to W. E. Woodward, September 16, 1938, Sinclair Mss., Series I, Box 42.

34. Sinclair, "To My Readers," *New Masses*, July 19, 1938, 10.

CHAPTER NINE. MR. MIDDLEBROW GOES TO WAR AGAIN, HOT AND COLD: 1940–1960

The epigraphs to this chapter are drawn from, respectively, Sinclair, *A World to Win* (New York: Viking Press, 1946), 326; Sinclair "Upton Sinclair Exposes Soviet Fake Democracy," *Oakland Tribune*, July 20, 1952, A9.

1. Sinclair to James Henle (Vanguard Press), December 8, 1938, Sinclair Mss., Series I, Box 42; Sinclair to Albert Einstein, December 24, 1938, Box 42.

2. Sinclair to Francis Henson, August 9, 1937, Sinclair Mss., Series I, Box 39.

3. Sinclair to John Farrar, August 25, 1939, Sinclair Mss., Series I, Box 44; Sinclair to Commonwealth Club of California, June 2, 1944, Box 50; Sinclair to Aline Law, March 30, 1946, Box 51.

4. Sinclair to William Seabrook, October 22, 1943, Sinclair Mss., Series I, Box 49; Sinclair to David Sinclair, January 17, 1944, D. Sinclair Mss., Box 1; Sinclair, "My Ten Years' Hard," *John O'London's Weekly*, September 30, 1949, 1.

5. Sinclair, "Letter to Isolationist," *New Republic*, October 13, 1941, 479; Sinclair, *Peace or War in America: A Debate Between Upton Sinclair and the Hon. Philip F. LaFollette* (Girard, Kans.: Haldeman-Julius Publications, 1941), 12.

6. Sinclair, *Peace or War*, 27.

7. Sinclair, "First Aid to Nazism," *Nation*, January 11, 1941, 56; Sinclair, *Between Two Worlds* (New York: Viking Press, 1941), 189.

8. Sinclair, *The Dragon's Teeth* (New York: Viking Press, 1942), 270.

9. Sinclair, *Dragon's Teeth*, 390.

10. Sinclair to Adolf Berle (suggesting he talk to FDR), December 15, 1941, Sinclair Mss., Series I, Box 47.

11. R. L. Duffus, "A New Novel by Upton Sinclair," *New York Times*, June 16, 1940, 1; "Briefly Noted," *New Yorker*, March 22, 1941, 69; "Crowded Epoch," *Times Literary Supplement*, October 18, 1941, 517; Sinclair to Joseph North, May 7, 1943, Sinclair Mss., Series I, Box 49.

12. Sinclair, "Is Socialism Coming?" *World Review*, March 1942, 52; Sinclair, "To Solve the German Problem—A Free State?" *New York Times Magazine*, August 15, 1943, 36. For a classic Sinclair statement during the 1930s that the Depression could not be solved, see "'Soak-the-Rich' Taxes No Aid to Production," *Upton Sinclair's National EPIC News*, July 8, 1935, 10.

13. Sinclair to Editor of *Pasadena News*, March 23, 1942, Sinclair Mss., Series I, Box 48; Sinclair, *Wide Is the Gate* (New York: Viking Press, 1943), 85.

14. Sinclair, *Wide Is the Gate*, 271.

15. Sinclair, *Presidential Agent* (New York: Viking Press, 1944), 21, 29; Frances Stonor Saunders, *The Cultural Cold War: The CIA and the World of Arts and Letters* (New York: New Press, 1999), 34.

16. Sinclair, *Dragon Harvest* (New York: Viking Press, 1945), 495.

17. Sinclair to Eleanor Roosevelt, April 13, 1945, Sinclair Mss., Series I, Box 51.

18. Sinclair, *World to Win*, 169.

19. Sinclair, *World to Win*, 640.

20. Sinclair, *One Clear Call* (New York: Viking Press, 1948), 9, 622.

21. Sinclair, *O Shepherd, Speak!* (New York: Viking Press, 1949), 537.

22. Sinclair, "Concerning Lanny Budd," *The Book Find News*, August 1946, 5; Sinclair, "Farewell to Lanny Budd," *Saturday Review*, August 13, 1949, 18; "Worlds End to Fag-End," *Time*, June 3, 1946, 106; Max Eastman, "The Library: Proletarian Novelists, Old and New," *American Mercury*, April 1942, 496; George Orwell, "Propaganda in Novels," *The Tribune*, September 13, 1940, 14; Perry Miller, "Lanny Budd Rides Again," *New York Times Book Review*, August 29, 1948, 5; Frances Downing, "More Books of the Week," *Commonweal*, June 30, 1944, 258; Howard Mumford Jones, "The Confused Case of Upton Sinclair," *The Atlantic Monthly*, August 1946, 150.

23. Sinclair to Richard Watts, July 3, 1946, Sinclair Mss., Series I, Box 52; Sinclair, "Farewell to Lanny Budd," *Saturday Review of Literature*, August 13, 1949, 38; Sinclair, "Author to Critic," *The Atlantic Monthly*, October 1946, 29; Sinclair, "Book Readers versus Critics," *Time*, July 1, 1946, 8; Sinclair, "Farewell LB," 38.

24. Sol Lesser to Sinclair, August 1, 1949, Sinclair Mss., Series I, Box 54; Sinclair to Huebsch, June 12, 1950, Box 55.

25. Sinclair, "Let Us Have Democracy Whole," *New Leader*, February 10, 1945, 8; Sinclair to Irving Flam, August 1, 1951, Sinclair Mss., Series I, Box 56; on his dispute with the *New Leader*, I rely upon Sinclair to *New Leader*, July 26, 1946, Box 52.

26. Sinclair to George Shoaf, May 3, 1949, Sinclair Mss., Series I, Box 54; Sinclair, "Sinclair Hits Red Slavery," *Los Angeles Examiner*, April 11, 1949, 6; Sinclair, "We Must Win Asia to Win the Cold War," *Boston Daily Globe*, April 17, 1953, 22; Sinclair to Richard Fisher, November 15, 1952, Box 57;

Sinclair, *What Didymus Did* (London: Allan Wingate, 1954), 13.

27. Sinclair, "Life Without Liberty," *Institute of Social Studies Bulletin*, Winter 1954, 86; Sinclair, *The Autobiography of Upton Sinclair* (New York: Harcourt, Brace and World, 1962), 300; Sinclair to Phyllis Bottome, September 16, 1946, Sinclair Mss., Series I, Box 52.

28. Sinclair, to Editor of *La Revolution Proletarienne*, February 19, 1951, Sinclair Mss., Series I, Box 55; Sinclair, "US Can Claim Korea Victory Without Awaiting Unification," *The Battle Creek Enquirer and News*, January 18, 1954, 6; Sinclair to David, May 17, 1951, D. Sinclair Mss., Box 1.

29. Sinclair, "A New Unity," *New Republic*, July 14, 1952, 4; Sinclair, Statement to CCF, October 27, 1952, Sinclair Mss., IV, Box 1; Sinclair, "Upton Sinclair Exposes Soviet Fake Democracy," A9.

30. Sinclair to S. K. Ratcliffe, October 4, 1952, Sinclair Mss., Series I, Box 56; Sinclair to Sol Lesser, December 20, 1952, Box 57; Sinclair, *The Return of Lanny Budd* (New York: Viking Press, 1953), 148.

31. Sinclair, "Does Capitalism Mean Freedom? That's What Eastman Says Now," *The New Leader*, May 2, 1955, 18; Sinclair to Whittaker Chambers, July 10, 1952, Sinclair Mss., Series I, Box 56.

32. Sinclair, "On Waldo Frank," *Nation*, July 3, 1954, 2; Sinclair, "Phony Friends of Liberty," *Evening Outlook*, June 8, 1954, 4. On Henry Wallace, see Sinclair to Clinton Taft, October 18, 1949, Sinclair Mss., Series I, Box 54; on ADA, see Sinclair to Lillian Muniz, December 7, 1949, Box 55; for his interest in opposing the Communist Control Act, see Folder: December 14–31, 1963 in Sinclair Mss., Series I, Box 62, where there's a statement Sinclair signed against the Smith Act, the McCarran Internal Security Act, and the Communist Control Act.

33. Graham, quoted in Stephen Whitfield, *The Culture of the Cold War* (Baltimore: Johns Hopkins University Press, 1991), 81; Sinclair to Jung, November 15, 1952, Sinclair Mss., Series I, Box 57; Sinclair to Eric Gutkind, February 18, 1952, Box 56.

34. Sinclair to Jacob Sonderling, April 21, 1950, Sinclair Mss., Series I, Box 54; Sinclair, *A Personal Jesus: Portrait and Interpretation* (New York: Evans Publishing Company, 1952), 83.

35. Sinclair, *Return of Lanny Budd*, 6; Sinclair, "An Open Letter to Stalin," *The New Leader*, June 30, 1952, 2; Sinclair to Naomi Mitchison, April 1, 1953, Sinclair Mss., Series I, Box 57; Sinclair to S. Beryl Lush, October 28, 1955, Box 58; Sinclair, *The Enemy Had It Too: A Play in Three Acts* (New York: Viking Press, 1950), 79.

36. McCarthy quoted in Whitfield, *The Culture of the Cold War*, 38.

37. Sinclair to Deming Brown, March 10, 1952, Sinclair Mss., Series I, Box 56; Sinclair, "Letter to Editor," *The New Leader*, October 22, 1951, 27; Sinclair, "Reds Use His Books for Propaganda," *Denver Post*, June 7, 1953, 6; Sinclair

to Deming Brown, March 10, 1952; Sinclair talk with Central Program Services Division of Voice of America, September 19, 1958, Sinclair Mss., Series III, Box 36.

38. Sinclair, "Enemy in the Mouth," *Friends Intelligencer*, April 16, 1955, 222. I rely in this paragraph on: Sinclair, "We Must Win Asia to Win the Cold War," 22; Sinclair to Congressman Oren Harris (about never owning a television), January 11, 1958, Sinclair Mss., Series I, Box 59; Craig to Lewis, May 10, 1945, about bobbysoxers, Sinclair Mss., IV, Box 1; Sinclair, "Hillbilly Ike," *California Liberal*, January 1960, 3.

39. Sinclair to Jung, August 3, 1955, Sinclair Mss., Series I, Box 58; Sinclair to Claire Hutchet Bishop, August 23, 1951, Box 56; Sinclair to Leonard Harris, February 1, 1957, Box 59; see also Sinclair expressing anger about how the *Saturday Review of Literature* included only modernists and not himself in a story about American literature: Sinclair to Allan Mordell, October 18, 1949, Box 54.

40. Sinclair, *What Didymus Did*, 42; Sinclair, *Another Pamela, or, Virtue Still Rewarded: A Story* (New York: Viking Press, 1950).

41. The quotes are from "Cicero" file in Sinclair Mss., Series III, Box 30. The play is broken up, rewritten, and at times pageless. The first two quotes come from 12A and 3, and the last does not have a page number.

CHAPTER TEN. SOCIALIST EMERITUS: 1960–1968

The epigraph to this chapter is drawn from Sinclair to M. Spectorsky, September 5, 1963, Sinclair Mss., Series I, Box 62.

1. Sinclair to William Bohn, February 15, 1961, Sinclair Mss., Series I, Box 60.

2. Sinclair to J. Edgar Hoover, November 2, 1958, Sinclair Mss., IV, Box 1.

3. Sinclair to David, January 1, 1966, Sinclair Mss., Series I, Box 63; Sinclair quoted in "Sinclairs Live Here," *The Evening Star*, August 17, 1966, Section D, 1 (found in clippings in Box 2 of D. Sinclair Mss.); see also Sinclair, "Mr. Sinclair Inquires," *Nation*, January 4, 1965, back cover.

4. Sinclair and Nader conversation recounted in Justin Martin, *Nader: Crusader, Spoiler, Icon* (Cambridge, Mass.: Perseus Books, 2002), 70.

5. Sinclair, "A Tip from Upton Sinclair," *Modern Maturity*, December–January 1961–1962, 43; Sinclair, *The Autobiography of Upton Sinclair* (New York: Harcourt, Brace and World, 1962), 315, 316.

6. Sinclair to Mrs. Giffen, September 14, 1961, Sinclair Mss., Series I, Box 61.

7. "Upton Sinclair, Author, Takes Bride at 83," *Los Angeles Times*, October 15, 1961, 16A; Sinclair to Allatt, November 11, 1963, Sinclair Mss., Series I, Box 62.

8. Ed Ainsworth, "Remembering 'Uppie,'" *Saturday Review*, September 30, 1967, 32.

9. Sinclair to Bertha Klausner, August 31, 1961, Sinclair Mss., Series I, Box 61; Sinclair to David, December 19, 1965, D. Sinclair Mss., Box 2.

10. Article about Buffalo speech found in clippings that are in D. Sinclair Mss., Box 2; Sinclair to Friends of LID, May 18, 1963, Sinclair Mss., Series I, Box 62.

11. Leon Harris, *Upton Sinclair: American Rebel* (New York: Crowell, 1975), 351 (regarding Vance Packard).

12. Laidler to Upton Sinclair, October 13, 1964, Sinclair Mss., Series I, Box 63.

13. Abraham Blinderman, "Upton Sinclair at 90," *Christian Century*, September 25, 1968, 1200.

14. I rely here on Justin Martin, *Nader*.

15. Interview dated November 25, 1963, found in Sinclair Mss., Series I, Box 62.

16. Upton Sinclair, "Ex Libris," *Christian Century*, August 8, 1962, 962; Upton Sinclair, "The Voice Is the Voice of Evil," *New York Times Book Review*, March 18, 1951, 1.

INDEX

Page numbers in *italics* refer to illustrations.

Davidson, Jo, 70, 73
"Dead Hand" book series (Sinclair)
  sales of, 137
  self-published by Sinclair, 136
  titles of, 125–131, 137, 145
Debs, Eugene, 45, 46, 65, 86, 114, 118,
  133
  on "citizen producers," 172, 173
  EPIC inspired by, 171–172
  imprisonment of, 107
  on World War I, 98
Deep South, 19, 196
DeKay, John, 189
Dell, Floyd, 6, 25, 135–136, 138–139,
  140, 158, 251
Democratic Party, 168–170, 175, 176
Depression Island (Sinclair), 179
Dewey, John, 80, 100, 140, 170
Disney, Walt, 194, 243
Dos Passos, John, 167, 191, 203, 229
Doubleday Publishing Company, 65–66
Doyle, Arthur Conan, 140
Dr. Fist (Sinclair), 232
Dragon Harvest (Sinclair), 221
Dragon's Teeth (Sinclair), 216–218
Dreiser, Theodore, 53, 150, 159
Dumenil, Lynn, 120–121
Durkheim, Emile, 79

Eastman, Max, 104–106, 108, 112, 224,
  229
Eddy, Mary Baker, 126
education, Sinclair on, 80, 85, 128–131
Einstein, Albert, 150
Eisenhower, Dwight, 234
Eisenstein, Sergei, 159–163, 205
Eliot, T. S., 122
Emerson, Ralph Waldo, 39, 71, 114
End Poverty in California/Civilization.
  See EPIC
Enemy Had It Too, The (Sinclair), 232
England, 108, 205. *See also* World War I;
  World War II
EPIC, 184–186, 248, 250–251
  End Poverty in California, 170–175,
  177, 178
  End Poverty in Civilization, 190
  EPIC News, 194
Espionage Act, 102–103, 107

Evans, Walker, 190

Fairbanks, Douglas, Jr., 225
Fairbanks, Douglas, Sr., 154, 161
Fairhope, Alabama, 81
Fairy Glen (Quebec cabin), 39–40
Fall, Albert, 141
Farewell to Arms, A (Hemingway), 122
Farley, James, 176, 183
Farmer-Labor Party, 170
Farrar, John, 151
fascism, 202–208, 214. *See also* World
  War II
Fasting Cure, The (Sinclair), 79
Federal Emergency Relief Act, 169–170
Federal Theater Project, 191
Fels, Joseph, 82
feminism, 71–72
Filler, Louis, 69
Finland, 207, 226
First Methodist Church of Pasadena, 156
Fish, Hamilton, 185
Fitzhugh, George, 61
flappers, 120–121
Fletcher, Horace, 77
Flivver King, The (Sinclair), *187,*
  199–201, 211
Flowers, Sydney, 111–112
Ford, Arthur, 150
Ford, Henry, 62, 118, 199–201, 221
Ford Motor Company, 199–201
For Whom the Bell Tolls (Hemingway), 203
Fourierism, 71
Fox, William, 156–159
Fox Corporation, 156–159
France, 108, 109. *See also* World War II
Frank, Waldo, 167, 230
free-love doctrine, 85
Fuller, Alvan T., 143
Fuller, Meta. *See* Sinclair, Meta Fuller
  (first wife)
fundamentalism, religious, 230–231

George, Henry, 46
Germany
  World War I, 96–99, 108
  World War II, 202–203, 206–208
Ghent, W. J., 99
Gillette, King, 118